Thomas W. Cowger

THE NATIONAL CONGRESS OF AMERICAN INDIANS

The Founding Years

University of Nebraska Press

LINCOLN & LONDON

Chapter 5 appeared as "The Crossroads of Destiny: The NCAI's Landmark Campaign to Thwart Coercive Termination," *American Indian Culture and Research Journal* 20, no. 4 (Dec. 1996): 121–44. Reprinted by permission of the American Indian Studies Center, UCLA. © Regents of the University of California.

∞

First Bison Books printing: 2001
Most recent printing indicated by the last digit below:
10   9   8   7   6   5   4   3   2   1
Library of Congress Cataloging-in-Publication Data
Cowger, Thomas W., 1955–
The National Congress of American Indians : the founding years / Thomas W. Cowger.
    p.   cm.
Includes bibliographical references and index.
ISBN 0-8032-1502-9 (cl: alk. paper)
ISBN 0-8032-6414-3 (pa: alk. paper)
1. National Congress of American Indians—History. 2. Indians of North America—Politics and government. 3. Indians of North America—Government relations—1934–   4. Indians of North America—History—20th century—Sources. I. Title.
E98.T77C68   1999
323.1′197′006073—dc21
99-17940
CIP

*For Vicki, Cameron, Katelen,
and our families*

Contents

Photographs

Acknowledgments

This book has been a "collaborative effort" in which numerous people and institutions have had a hand. Chief among these has been Donald J. Berthrong and Donald L. Parman. Several years ago at his office door, Donald Berthrong graciously agreed to shepherd me, a raw and unproven student, through the graduate school process. He inspired and nurtured my interest in the field of Indian history and taught me how to sharpen my skills as a historian as well. He did it with great care and wisdom, goodwill, humor, and considerable patience. He has taught me more about the profession than he will ever fully realize. Donald Parman has generously shared his time and talents with me, even at the expense of his own projects. Like Donald Berthrong, he has often provided sound professional advice and spent countless hours reading and correcting draft copies of this book. His sensitive and constructive criticism not only improved this book but also my scholarship in general. I am proud to call both "Donalds" my mentors, colleagues, and friends.

The Smithsonian Institution awarded me a yearlong fellowship that provided both financial and intellectual support as I began the research for the project at the National Anthropological Archives (NAA) in Washington DC. Mary Elizabeth Ruwell, former director of NAA, Jake Homiak, current director, and their staffs, particularly Kathleen Baxter, Gail Yotis, and Paula Fleming, were helpful in countless ways: they were instructive, patient, generous with their time, and most important, a pleasure to be around. Special thanks go to James Glenn, senior archivist of NAA, who served as my adviser while I was in residence at the Smithsonian. Janet Kennelly, formerly of NAA, continues to share her time, knowledge, and interest in NCAI. She and Paula Fleming were indispensable in accessing, selecting, and acquiring the photos for this book. I am also grateful to JoAllyn Archambaut, director of the American Indian program at the Smithsonian, who supported an oral history documentary project in New Mexico that featured founding members of the NCAI. I would also like to extend special gratitude to the Purdue Research Foundation (PRF), which provided a grant that allowed me to complete the initial phase of this project as a dissertation. The Harry S. Truman and John F. Kennedy Libraries both generously provided travel stipends to visit their archives and manuscript collections. A research grant from the Oklahoma Foundation for the Humanities helped fund interviews. Grants from the East Central University Research Committee and from the National Endowment for the Humanities relieved me from classroom duties and greatly hastened the completion of the book. James Harris, head of the history department at East Central University, was supportive in working out the details of my release time.

In collecting material for this work, I received invaluable assistance from many people. Special recognition, aside from the Smithsonian staff, is extended to Dennis Bilger and Elizabeth Safly of the Truman Library; William Johnson, chief archivist of the Kennedy Library; and Robert Kvasnicka of the National Archives. I have conducted several interviews at different intervals over the past several years. I want to especially thank the following interviewees: Frances L. Horn, Charles Hobbs, Helen L. Peterson, Erma Hicks Walz, Art Manning, Robert L. Bennett, John Rainer, and Rose Robinson.

Thomas L. Pearcy, a long-time friend and colleague at Slippery Rock University, provided more help than he understands. It was reassuring to have frequent access to someone with his knowledge and solid insights and his mutual interest in ethnic, social, and political movements. Warren Metcalf, friend and colleague at Oklahoma University, shared his ideas on the "termination period" and twentieth-century Indian identity. Donald L. Fixico, Western Michigan University, made invaluable suggestions in the review process for the book. I am also grateful for the thoughtful contributions of the anonymous second reader, who reviewed the book for publication and significantly improved the final product.

Finally, and with all my heart, I thank Vicki, Cameron, Katelen, and my family, who took part every step of the way and helped me remember what is important in life. I am eternally grateful for their patience, love, and support. I proudly dedicate this book to them.

*The National Congress
of American Indians*

INTRODUCTION

I feel that the charters of the NCAI were very important in the history of the Indian people; they were like your Washington, your Jefferson and Adams. They were farsighted enough to organize themselves in order to hang on to what is left of this whole country. Those of us who succeeded these people are of the mind to continue holding on to what's left of our country.

JOHN RAINER, former executive director of the NCAI, 1993

Delivering the keynote address at the 1959 National Congress of American Indians (NCAI) convention in Phoenix, Arizona, D'Arcy McNickle, noted Indian political activist and a man of letters, reflected on the first fifteen years of the NCAI. Fully aware of the successes and failures of the Indian organization, McNickle cautioned his listeners not to judge harshly the founding years of the NCAI. In his address McNickle related an analogy between the NCAI and the well-intentioned fly:

It is told that a lowly fly once wanted to improve its station in life. It seems that while it had wings and could fly, it could not command the respect of other winged creatures, such as the eagle, admired for its bravery, or the song birds, whose warbling gave happiness. The fly was not brave, and of course it had no voice worth mentioning. So it gave this some thought. How could it, a mere nothing, win the respect it desired so greatly? It happened that in flying about thinking about this problem, it landed on the nose of the king. The queen who was playing croquet with the king cried out, "Oh, that horrid fly!" This did not improve the fly's self-esteem, but little did it realize that things were about to change. The queen quite forgot that she had a croquet mallet in her hand. She swung it, and hit the king with such a clout that he fell into a deep swoon. Thus it happened that the fly overthrew the king, and among all the animals thereafter it was called the "Mighty Fly." The conclusion is: Don't despise your ancestors. They may have done better by you than you realize.[1]

Speaking modestly and underestimating the political savvy of the Indian community, McNickle, nevertheless, identified important but little recognized contributions of the NCAI in its infant years.

The unnoticed efforts of most twentieth-century Native Americans are largely the result of the military defeat and economic dispossession of their predecessors centuries earlier. Modern Americans often view contemporary Native Americans as noble vestiges of a once proud but now lost romantic heritage. In this view, Native American histories end with placement on the reservations and fail to connect contemporary Indians with the past. Most modern Indian concerns, however, are rooted in age-old Indian struggles. Bringing Indian actors onto the twentieth-century stage allows us finally to drop the Indian headdresses and coup sticks and to see contemporary Native Americans as Lawrence Hauptman so aptly described, "warriors with attaché cases."[2]

The historiography on American Indians in the twentieth century remains sketchy and uneven, largely focusing on federal policy and relying principally on government documents. Consequently, these studies view federal policy as a reflection of changes in white society and as a slight to the influence of Native Americans. Scholars paint a misleading and unbalanced picture of twentieth-century Indians as nonresilient, passive recipients of change. Preeminent Indian historians Donald L. Parman, Francis Paul Prucha, and Robert F. Berkhofer Jr. have all called attention to the great need for additional research in twentieth-century Indian history, particularly during the post–World War II era, as well as for new approaches to the topic. As these scholars have noted, researchers have almost wholly ignored important topics such as post–World War II pan-Indian movements and intertribal organizations.[3] The absence of such studies limits our understanding of how native groups have reacted imaginatively and resourcefully to recent developments and changes in the larger society. More importantly, Native Americans have increasingly become prime movers in deciding their own fate.

The principal focus of the present study is the activities of the NCAI from 1944 to the mid-1960s. These years were one of the most crucial periods in the history of federal-Indian relations. Despite continual federal efforts to assimilate Indians forcibly into American society since the 1880s, approximately 250 reservations remained in the United States at the end of World War II. In the 1950s the United States government embarked on a controversial and ill-fated effort to terminate the federal trust status of Indian reservations. Between 1945 and the mid-1960s the government's termination policy affected an estimated 13,263 Indians and 1,365,801 acres of Indian land.[4] Termination, in actuality, affected only a relatively small number of Indians, but it aroused tremendous fear and hostility throughout Indian country. In its broadest sense, termination signified a final drive to assimilate the Indians once and for all into the dominant society. In its narrowest sense, termination represented a legal means to abrogate the federal government's trust obligations to tribes.

The National Congress of American Indians first arose in 1944 as a national pan-Indian organization that campaigned fervently and, on the whole, successfully against the termination policy. Indian delegates from twenty-seven states and representing more than fifty tribes and associations attended the first convention in 1944. One year later the NCAI claimed members from nearly all the tribes of the United States. Although men largely comprised the organization at the outset, by 1955 women made up at least half of the delegates. The NCAI always included important tribal leaders who sought to promote common Indian interests and identities on a national level. Recognizing the threat posed by termination, they fought to maintain Indians' legal rights and cultural identity.

The years 1944 to the mid-1960s represent the important founding years of the NCAI. Events in 1964 signaled a transition period. By 1964 the immediate threat of new termination legislation had all but passed from the Indian landscape. When President John F. Kennedy died unexpectedly in Dallas in November 1963, NCAI leaders' hopes for an "Indian Camelot" perished as well. Deep factionalism in 1962-63 also had almost destroyed the organization. After 1964 the NCAI sought new leadership and fresh directions, and the torch passed from the old guard to the new. The appointment of Vine Deloria Jr. as executive director in 1964 ushered in a modern and different era for the NCAI. Deloria successfully returned the organization back to financial and organizational stability. Deloria's administration ably guided the NCAI through serious conflicts of interest between reservation and urban Indians. Termination stirred major controversies, often pitting the more moderate reservation constituency against more militant urban-based forces.

I decided to stop my study of the NCAI at the mid-1960s for several reasons. By 1964 there were no major legislative battles, such as the first termination laws, for which NCAI could rally its members. While termination did not officially end as a policy until 1972, by the late 1950s and early 1960s it had come under heavy criticism, and support had faded. Then, with the founding of new national intertribal organizations such as the National Indian Youth Council and others in the early 1960s, the NCAI lost its unique position as the sole voice of the Indian people in Washington. Finally, from a practical perspective, at the time I was conducting my research at the Smithsonian, the National Anthropological Archives had only processed the NCAI papers through the year 1964.

The general outline of the termination era is well known, and the details of the Klamath and Menominee termination experiences are available in several monographs. Historical scholarship on the termination period, however, has tended to focus on the federal government and its formulation and implementation of the policy. Francis Paul Prucha's *The Great Father,* Larry W. Burt's *Tribalism in Crisis,* Donald L. Fixico's *Termination and Relocation,* and Larry Hasse's dissertation, "Termination and Assimilation," ably detail the origins, implementation, and ultimate abandonment of Indian termination.[5] But except for Fixico, these historians provide little information on the Indians' response to the changes in federal policy. Fixico, however, did not have access to the NCAI manuscript collection. Principally concerned with the processes of government paternalism, all these scholarly accounts on termination treat Indians as ancillary members of American society, as people acted upon by legislators and bureaucrats, rather than as actors in their own rights. None of the studies provides a systematic, comprehensive account of the influential role of the NCAI in the struggle against an eventual defeat of termination legislation.

Existing studies of intertribal political Indian activity and Indian nationalism are limited in number and scope. Hazel Hertzberg, for example, provides a valuable introduction in her study of the Society of American Indians found in *Search for an American Indian Identity,* but she deals primarily with the first three decades of the twentieth century and affords little insight into the more recent period.[6] A study of the activity of the NCAI during the critical termination years, therefore, fills an important void in Indian historiography. Perhaps most importantly, it demonstrates that contemporary Native Americans are members of vibrant societies not frozen in space or time.

I pursue several objectives in this book. Most of the book examines the ways in which federal-Indian relations and political events shaped Indian collective action. Because the records of the NCAI largely focus on policymaking and provide little insight into the social dynamics of the organization, I found it easiest to concentrate on political concerns. The object here is to understand the evolution of Native American political activism in the two decades following World War II. Tracing changes in public policy and examining the Native American response as seen through the eyes of the NCAI are my method. My focus in this study then becomes understanding historical relationships and ways in which the NCAI between 1944 and the mid-1960s shaped political actions, opportunities, and abilities to respond to outside pressures. It is a story of Indian successes and failures in trying to develop control over their own political, economic, and cultural agenda in constant struggles before federal and state courts and legislatures.

Demonstrating that NCAI members did not respond passively to the threat of termination and other political events, I show that the organization was an innovative vehicle of resistance to changes in federal Indian policy and that it served as an important instrument for the preservation of Indian culture and identity. The key role the NCAI played in the emergence of a new pan-Indian identity after World War II, I argue, indicates that culture and identity may survive because of, not only in spite of, new conditions. To provide context, the study also examines the relationship of the NCAI to other Indian reform groups. Finally, I place Indian affairs in the context of the postwar period by analyzing the relationship of the NCAI to the civil rights movement, McCarthyism, intolerance of cultural diversity, and the Cold War. In these ways this study of the NCAI stands at the intersection of Native American history, the history of American reform, and the history of the United States since 1940.

Where possible, I have tried to take this study beyond simply political history and intertwine social and ethnohistorical threads into the story. In this instance, "ethnohistorical" refers to the process of critically examining and evaluating the evidence provided by written documents in light of oral history. A problem that emerged in my research from the start was how to trace and define concepts of Indian identity. Recent theories on ethnic identity and political mobilization, for example, became especially useful in gaining insight into contemporary Native American culture and society and the dynamics of change. Through skillful manipulation of the political process, I maintain, the NCAI converted ethnicity into a pan-Indian or intertribal organization that became a permanent force in national politics. Redefinition and reaffirmation of ethnic identity were at the center of most native social and political movements in the twentieth century. Indians developed organizations to promote positive ethnic identity and expressions. They also sought to preserve ethnic identity by creating vehicles they could control.[7] The NCAI was and still is an institutional expression of identity. The existence and maintenance of the NCAI both expresses and perpetuates the national collective identity of participating Native Americans. These identities are both ethnic and political. Individual members of the NCAI, for example, do not always fully identify with all the political objectives of the organization, but virtually all feel a strong association with the larger Indian community. In this way, participants of the NCAI construct their ethnic identities and relations with one another through a shared national organization.

Ethnicity theory proves useful for understanding the manner in which individuals form interest groups to create and sustain identity.[8] In this instance, ethnicity theory provides a valuable alternative to acculturation and assimilation theories. Assimilation theory focuses more on the end or erosion of previously distinct groups. Studies of ethnic formation frequently view the creation of ethnic groups as the consequence of incorporation into larger societies.[9] Recent theories of ethnicity also show that people often mobilize into distinct groups following external pressures. In these models, changing economic, social, and political conditions define ethnic group membership.[10] Collective mobilization takes place when marginalized groups act to pursue common interests.[11] These refurbished ethnic groups then devise and use symbols to sustain the movement and to mobilize membership. The symbols that ethnic organizations employ are usually based on common traits such as history, culture, and language to encourage group identification.[12] Selected symbols must be agreed upon by all the participants.[13]

Some degree of political mobilization and organization characterizes almost all ethnic movements. Ethnic identification advances group consciousness to foster greater cohesion and political power. Ethnic groups mobilize to pressure empowered officials to allocate a larger share of available resources.[14] By generating awareness and discussion, ethnic groups formulate strategies of political action. Thus, ethnic identities, through collective action, enable participants to interact more fully within the larger political economy.[15]

Most scholars of ethnicity agree that people mobilize into collective interest groups based on relationships of dependency and domination.[16] Interactions between groups and the dominant society produce distinct ethnic group boundaries. The creation of ethnic identities thus serves as the nucleus for rallying symbols and boundary markers.[17] Some social scientists maintain that opposition creates ethnic identity. In this view, ethnic identities are not created in isolation but from resistance.[18] In other words, ethnic identities are developed, preserved, redefined, and manipulated by the demands of external forces. Thus, ethnicity is only realizable in the context of an in-group/out-group context or struggle, where relationships are asymmetric.[19]

With contemporary Native Americans, it appears certain that a shared ethnic identity persists and is maintained despite opposition from the dominant white society. Complex federal-Indian relations often produce conflict. Questions between white lawmakers and tribal councils over native sovereignty and rights create tensions among native peoples. Indians, moreover, since contact have successfully battled repeated attempts by Euro-Americans to destroy their culture and land base. Seen in this light, the ethnic identity of Indians in the twentieth century is largely the product of years of Indian-white interaction. In this century Indians have often coopted white political institutions with culturally acceptable Indian innovations. Thus, it is through the creation of such organizations as the NCAI that Indian ethnic identity is frequently fed and maintained.

Participants construct political identities like any other identities, through previous experience. During the four hundred years following European contact, Indians wielded little political power in the political mainstream. By the first half of the twentieth century, however, Indian groups such as the Society of American Indians (SAI), the American Indian Federation (AIF), and the NCAI had learned to set their own agendas and pursue their own interests in larger regional and national political arenas. Years of federal-Indian interaction evolved into an Indian posture in American pressure politics.

Scholars have searched for a vocabulary to express Indian ethnic identity movements that transcend tribal identities. Investigators into this phenomenon have labeled these movements pan-Indian, intertribal, supratribal, and pan-ethnic. With few exceptions, these labels generally describe the same tendencies and support a shared sense of ethnicity with community. Most investigations of intertribal activity center on cultural and religious manifestations.[20]

Pan-Indianism has received the most attention from social scientists. Many Native Americans, however, dislike the term. Several forces promote and shape pan-Indianism. Some scholars see pan-Indianism as a defensive response to white dominance.[21] Anthropologist Joan Ablon, on the other hand, argues that this new ethnic identity, with elements of pan-Indianism and tribal orientation, might be the result of increased interactions between tribes. In *Search for an American Indian Identity,* Hazel Hertzberg views pan-Indian movements as either reform, fraternal, or religious.[22] Political pan-Indianism in the United States has received little attention.

Several recent social scientists prefer the term supratribal to pan-Indian. Anthropologist Nancy Lurie first coined the expression in reference to distinctive Indian organizations that strove for political change. Stephen Cornell in *The Return of the Native* later adopted the label to describe the emergence of organizations such as the NCAI. Supratribalism, according to Cornell, is rooted in the dualism of national Indian policy. Federal officials, he believes, have vacillated between treating Indians as domestic dependent nations and as individual citizens. Supratribalism developed in direct response to the ambiguous and contradictory nature of the federal handling of Indians.[23]

Pan-ethnicity, much like pan-Indianism and supratribalism nomenclature, is the bridging of organizations and the creation of solidarities among subgroups of ethnic collectivities.[24] Scholars, however, seldom use the term. The multiplicity of interpretations and definitions used to describe Indian ethnic revitalization movements confirms the complex nature of the dynamics involved.

Speaking at the fifteenth annual convention, D'Arcy McNickle correctly recognized the accomplishments of the founding fathers of the NCAI. The efforts of the NCAI during its founding years to construct a modern Indian, intertribal national identity reflect the pride and strength in McNickle's statement. In its first twenty years the NCAI battled to protect the rights of Alaskan natives, to end voting discrimination, to create the Indian Claims Commission, to promote unrestricted legal counsel, to stop termination legislation, and to push greater Indian participation in decision-making processes. By passing broad resolutions, the founders mapped a political strategy that would appeal to many Indians. Through steering a moderate course, the NCAI leadership decreased the risk of distancing the reservation Indians from the urban, the more assimilated from the less, the older Native Americans from the younger, and individuals from tribal groups. The broad appeal of the NCAI successfully included a variety of interests and viewpoints. When the constitutional convention concluded in 1944, Native Americans had successfully created a new political voice that reverberated throughout the nation's capital and beyond. In sum, they created a legacy which proved that contemporary Indian actors continued to adapt, adopt, resist, and survive. This narrative, then, is the story of their efforts to create a shared identity to promote sovereignty and to push for civil rights for all Native Americans in the two decades following World War II.

1. RIVER OF EXPERIENCE

It would be pointless to argue whether Indian culture should or should not survive. If it had not survived, we would not be meeting here these days. Having survived thus far, it will doubtless continue into the future whether we deny it, or denounce it, or pretend it isn't there.   D'ARCY MCNICKLE, NCAI founder, 1959

Despite overwhelming odds during the last five centuries, Indians have persisted as identifiable ethnic communities. Since contact with Indians, Euro-Americans have tried to incorporate distinct independent Indian societies into Anglo-American social and political systems. Over the years white efforts at Indian annihilation, relocation, assimilation, and bureaucratic domination have forced native groups into new methods of ethnic stratification. Forced assimilation sometimes resulted in the loss of native peoples' political autonomy and control of their resources. Indians, however, have never been passive partners in the incorporation process. They have contributed to the nature of federal-Indian relations by their reactions to white pressures. While Native Americans were infrequently involved in the decision-making process, they often established the terms on which policymakers reached decisions. And after 1944, some Indian leaders began to change the incorporation process, from white dictatorial forms, into a vehicle for their own collective action.

The NCAI facilitated both an intertribal identity, which emphasized Indians as a single ethnic group, and a tribal identity, which emphasized the citizenship of Indians in separate nations. In fact, the NCAI strengthened tribal ties by serving as a stabilizing element. In some cases, it even promoted tribalism where it had rarely occurred, such as in urban areas. Thus the NCAI revived multiple eth-

nicities that sought to promote a single voice. As a result, Indians
have assumed a more active posture in the political mainstream. The
Euro-American tendency to reduce diverse Indian groups to a single
ethnic status also unwittingly contributed to a shared Indian identity.[1] Incorporation changed the indigenous peoples from diverse
and scattered groups with little in common into a national identity.[2]
Encroachment from outsiders brought increased Indian unity as the
Indian world continued to close in on its members. The NCAI was in
part a convergence of native resiliency and forces of assimilation. Despite numerous attempts at Indian assimilation, Indian identity did
not die but actually prospered and expanded. By the mid-twentieth
century, the NCAI had successfully turned processes of ethnic diversi-
fication into a shared national identity.

An old adage says: "One can never put one's foot in the same river
twice." Since river currents and time constantly move forward, it is
never the same water or experience twice even though it is the same
river. Obstacles such as rocks, riverbanks, curves, and bends constantly shape and alter the body of water as it flows ever onward to
its destination. The history of federal-Indian relations is analogous
to the mythical river in the ancient adage. Native Americans have
adopted, adapted, and altered the course of relations with policymakers, yet they have rarely had the same experience twice, though
the patterns were often similar. But the river is always the same: the
federal government. If one is to fully understand the present course
of any river, one must retrace its path. Twentieth-century Indian
identities are a lot like our imaginary river in that they are directly
linked to an age-old Indian past and the Indian present. Thus to understand the evolution of the NCAI, one must understand the nature
of the federal policies that preceded and helped create it and the Indian activism that followed it.

Within limits, diverse Indian groups began to shape their own political future from the earliest contact with whites. Indigenous collective mobilization to challenge the new outside forces occurred from
almost the moment Western intruders set foot in North America.
Either just before or shortly after initial contact with whites, power-

ful native alliances, such as the Iroquois and Powhatan Confederacies in the early seventeenth century, challenged Euro-American domination. Like their counterparts nearly a century earlier, individuals such as Pontiac and Tecumseh attempted to empower themselves and prevent further white encroachment and loss of autonomy through intertribal alliances. With few exceptions these early Indian movements represented political and military mobilization. In all cases these movements largely failed.

While alliances were important and helped establish a precedent for later intertribal activity, they did not directly lead to the formation of the NCAI. Native American experiences in the latter part of the nineteenth century triggered the first successful national intertribal organization. Unprecedented Indian reform occurred in the last two decades of the nineteenth century. Religious reformers, legislators, and bureaucrats joined hands in a campaign to replace the ineffective reservation system with a more coercive assimilation program. Christian reformers, convinced of their divine mission to spread American culture and to develop the West for the advancement of Christianity, deeply believed that communal landholding hindered the Indians' progress toward "civilization." Consequently, they demanded the individualization of the Indians' holdings. Hostile toward Indian culture, religious reformers set out to destroy Indian traditions and tribal relations and to replace both with white institutions. Through severalty, or individual allotments of land, they intended to force the tribes into an Anglo-American system of tenure and inheritance, which they believed would quickly assimilate the Indians. Operating on the tenet that the destruction of tribal lifestyle brought assimilation, proponents of severalty fiercely advocated the dissolution of the reservations.[3] The policy of rapid assimilation was so overwhelmingly popular that few critics opposed it.[4]

On February 8, 1887, the proponents of assimilation won a great victory. The new measure, known as the Dawes Act, contained ample authority for coercive assimilation and the destruction of tribes as political units. It divided the reservations into allotments that were assigned to individuals, despite Indian sentiment. The federal government held the allotments in trust for twenty-five years. During this period, an Indian could not sell his or her allotment, and local and state governments could not tax it. After officials allotted reservation lands to individual Indians, the federal government could purchase surplus or unalloted lands through an agreement with the tribe and subsequently open the lands to white settlement. Trustees placed the proceeds from the purchase of surplus lands in tribal accounts in the U.S. Treasury, but the money was subject to appropriation by Congress for the education and benefit of the Indians. Once individual Indians accepted their allotments, they became citizens of the United States and of the state or territory in which they resided. Administrators provided Indians a fee-simple patent to their allotment at the expiration of the trust period. Later modifications to the act, such as the Burke Act of 1906, authorized the secretary of the interior either to extend the twenty-five-year trust period or to remove all restrictions on the lease or sale of land before the twenty-five-year period had expired. Policymakers delayed citizenship until all restrictions on Indian property were removed.[5]

Unfortunately, the Dawes Act failed to be the panacea to the Indian problems that its supporters envisioned. Intended to turn Indians into self-supporting and happily assimilated citizens, the act and its subsequent modifications rapidly destroyed any prospects for the Indians' material progress or their satisfactory cultural adjustment to life in the dominant society. Moreover, the Dawes Act failed to destroy the tribe as a political unit. Tribalism continued throughout the twentieth century.[6]

The Dawes Act, the culmination of nearly a decade of reform, produced an ironic twist to national Indian political mobilization. Had assimilationist reformers succeeded in their optimistic goals of private landownership, education, and citizenship, native cultures would have ceased to exist as distinct groups. Yet implementation of the legislation failed to destroy Indian cultures and communities. On the contrary, assimilationist reformers set in motion several forces that indirectly sped Indians along the path to national Indian political mobilization.

Probably no federal program in the late nineteenth century played a larger role in the development of national Indian political consciousness than education. In the 1880s boarding schools emerged as the key component of Indian Commissioner Thomas J. Morgan's efforts to promote rapid assimilation. The philosophy behind such schools involved separating Indian children from tribal influences, indoctrinating them in white values, and providing vocational training. Thus, reformers intended boarding schools to turn tribal members into American individualists and expectant capitalists. Of the boarding schools, the off-reservation schools, particularly Carlisle Indian Industrial School in Pennsylvania, Hampton Institute in Virginia, and Haskell Institute in Kansas, were the most important vehicles in the creation of national political identity. Unfortunately, these schools failed to fulfill most of the reformers' expectations.[7] Ironically, however, they encouraged pan-Indianism.

The off-reservation boarding school experience promoted intertribal cooperation through several crucial developments. It advanced the use of English, supplying individuals from different tribes with a common language. It brought together in one location a multitribal population. In the process, intertribal dating relationships produced marriages across tribal lines and fostered Native American solidarity. Indian students learned both from firsthand and classroom instruction the mechanics of white institutional agencies. Indian pupils benefited from access to mass transportation (trains and later automobiles) and mass communication (mail service and newspapers). Student experiences at schools encouraged later generations to evaluate and define what it meant to be Indian, as participants shared many common problems and goals with each other and their younger members. From these boarding school experiences, a new generation of Indian leaders emerged, armed with new political and cultural weapons.[8]

Peyotism, another important Indian response to outside pressures, appeared to ease the assault on tribalism in the late nineteenth century. Since Euro-American contact, demoralized Indian groups had often turned to religion as a vehicle to counter cultural upheaval.

Throughout much of the eighteenth and nineteenth centuries, Indian communities turned to messiahs or prophets to articulate dreams of renascences, just as the Western world had done. Via rituals, ceremonies, and sacred power, leaders such as Handsome Lake of the Iroquois, Tenskwatawa of the Shawnees, and Wovoka of the Paiutes and others offered adherents prescriptions for coping with existing problems. The common thread in these and many movements was spiritual power. The movements represented attempts by the oppressed to regain control of the chaotic world around them. Participants in these movements could, at least temporarily, reestablish Indian control over Indian lives and slow the erosion of Indian autonomy. Perceived in this way, these movements were both religious and political.[9]

Of all the Indian religious movements, the most significant, at the least the longest lasting, has been peyotism. The Peyote religion spread from the southern plains in the late nineteenth century. Rooted in religious practices among pre-Columbian Mexican peoples, peyote practitioners sought spiritual power from the hallucinogenic effects produced by buttons from the peyote cactus. Peyotism offered Indians an important alternative to Christianity while also incorporating many elements of that religion. By the end of the early decades of the twentieth century, physicians, the Bureau of Indian Affairs (BIA), missionaries, and Indian defense leagues sought legislation to prohibit Indian use of peyote. Opponents of peyote charged that the drug led to dangerous and immoral behavior. Peyotists, on the other hand, received support from James Mooney of the Bureau of American Ethnology and other anthropologists who cited its harmless effects. Opposition to peyote led to the incorporation of the Native American Church (NAC) in Oklahoma in 1918 to gain the protection of First Amendment rights. Numbered among the active peyotists often were graduates of the boarding schools.[10] While NAC is intertribal in the sense that it has cut across regional boundaries, it is a religious denomination with numerous local variations and not the national Native American religion. Powwows, particularly on the plains, also contributed to the expansion of a specifically Indian identity. Thus, shared experiences and perceptions from peyote usage and the powwows formed additional links in the construction of a national Indian identity.[11]

Outside exclusive tribal settings, powwows spread in the early twentieth century to celebrate "being Indian." Crossing intertribal lines, powwows advanced pan-Indianism through song, dance, costumes, ceremonies, giveaways, prayers, and speeches in native languages and English. Powwows started as a religious ceremony of the Pawnees, sometime before the mid-nineteenth century. The dance spread westward across the Great Plains tribes, where each tribe learned it from its neighbor. As the dances spread to new tribes and locations, they took on new distinctions. Powwows initially gained the largest support among the tribes in Oklahoma. By the mid-1950s, tribal members began traveling between reservation and urban communities to participate in powwow contests. Powwows represented the most public expression of Indian identity in the twentieth century. While the powwow fostered cultural revitalization and pan-Indian activities, it lacked a political agenda.[12]

By 1911 the dream of the first successful, though limited, national Indian political organization became a reality. In April, six well-educated and professional Indians met in Columbus, Ohio, to organize the first national Indian political organization, the Society of American Indians (SAI). Present at the organizational meeting were Dr. Charles A. Eastman, Sioux; Dr. Carlos Montezuma, Yavapai; Thomas L. Sloan, Omaha; Charles E. Daganett, Peoria; Laura M. Cornelius, Oneida; and Henry Standing Bear, Sioux. Dr. Fayette A. McKenzie, a non-Indian professor of sociology at Ohio State University, hosted the Columbus meeting. Planners extended membership opportunities to both Indian and non-Indian. However, only the former had voting rights and office-holding privileges. Headquartered in Washington, DC, the organization pursued a general platform that called for better Indian educational programs and improved living conditions. SAI leaders sought many other Indian reforms that coincided with contemporary Progressive ideals. Like many Progressives, these Indian leaders promoted Indian assimilation. They also tended to ignore reservation needs, and one faction sought not only to immediately abolish the BIA, but reservations as well.

Despite the successful beginning of the SAI, factionalism crippled and ultimately destroyed the organization. Conflicts over representation in the organization, leadership, criticisms of the BIA, and the volatile peyote issue divided the Society's members. The organization held its final conference in 1923. In the end, the SAI failed to resolve its internal conflicts and to transcend the boundaries between reservation and urban Indians. By promoting assimilation and ignoring tribalism, SAI leadership alienated the mass of Indians on reservations. Opponents of the SAI also charged that non-Indians controlled the organization. Yet, the failures of the SAI should not overshadow its accomplishments. In a society still ambivalent and indifferent about Indian rights, the SAI was the first significant movement toward national Indian organization.[13] Moreover, Indian activists in later years undoubtedly learned important lessons from the movement's experiences.

Arising at almost the same time as the SAI, urban Indians across the country united in fraternal associations modeled on those of the whites. In organizations such as the Tepee Order of America, urban Indians stressed a common Indian experience. Founded in New York City in 1915, the Tepee Order arose as an adult, secret fraternal organization modeled after Freemasonry. With branches in several large cities, the Tepee Order hoped to promote awareness and interest in Indian history and culture. Its early advisory board included SAI founders Eastman, Montezuma, and Sloan. Organization officers held titles such as Head Chief and Medicine Man. While the charter called for Indians to serve as officers, non-Indians also were eligible for membership. Like the SAI, the Tepee Order solicited the support of prominent non-Indians. Resentment by Native American members of the role of non-Indians in the organization and a lack of financial support brought the Tepee Order to an end in 1927. The sudden emergence of the Tepee Order and other lesser-known organizations such as the Grand Council Fire of American Indians, the Indian Association of America, and the Indian Confederation of

America provided Indians with valuable associative and political experiences and set a precedent for later pan-Indian urban activity. While the pan-Indian movement continued to develop through these and other organizations, it drew membership from both Indians and non-Indians.[14]

Following the passage of the Indian Citizenship Act (1924), Gertrude Simmons Bonnin (Zitkala Ša) in 1926 organized the National Council of American Indians (NCAI). Bonnin, former Carlisle teacher, secretary of the SAI, and an author, sought to organize Indians politically to protect and advance their civil rights. While living on the Unitah Ouray Ute Agency in Duchesne, Utah, Bonnin witnessed widespread usage of peyote. Disgusted with the peyote ritual, as were several of her other SAI counterparts, she actively campaigned against the growing peyote religion. Serving as editor of Society of American Indian's *American Indian Magazine* in 1918–19, she not only condemned peyote but promoted Indian rights and citizenship for all Native Americans. Dressed in traditional buckskin, she also pushed her message of opposition to assimilation policies on many public speaking tours. When SAI disintegrated after 1920, Bonnin sought another avenue to champion her reforms.

With her husband Raymond Bonnin, she founded the National Council of American Indians as a means to express the growing twentieth-century Indian identity movement. Short on funds and staff help, the Bonnins singlehandedly lobbied Congress and the BIA to correct Indian injustices. Sharing office space with the American Indian Defense Association, they also sought to empower Native Americans politically through voting blocs. In an attempt to attract reservation support, the Bonnins founded several chapters of the council throughout Indian country. Despite their efforts, however, the organization failed to attract either significant reservation or urban support. Near the close of the Progressive era and throughout the early 1920s, Indian reform, like reform in general, had lost its zeal. Lacking a large Indian mandate, Indian protests such as legal issues, sovereignty questions, and civil rights remained on an individual tribal basis rather than on a national scale. In the end Bonnin's NCAI never attracted widespread Indian support and lasted only until the mid-1930s.[15]

During the 1920s the government began to abandon its aggressive assimilation policies in favor of increased interest in the preservation of Indian resources. Most studies to this point have seen these changes as a reaction to several important factors. In 1928 the Institute for Government Research published the influential Meriam Report. Critical of the previous allotment policies, the report noted the bleak reservation conditions of poverty and suffering and weaknesses in education and health care. The Meriam Report marked a significant shift in federal-policy philosophy toward the Indians. Although it saw a need for Indians to adjust, it also recognized the cultural diversity of the various tribes and recommended that the government encourage rather than destroy Indian values.[16]

John Collier's emergence as an Indian reformer further bolstered the findings of the Meriam Report. Born in Atlanta in 1884, Collier later moved to New York City to help recently arrived immigrants adjust to urban life. Filled with the ideals of a young, radical social-justice progressive, he became repulsed by the excessive individualism and materialism of the impersonal industrial revolution. Like many contemporary thinkers, Collier believed that the industrial revolution, conservative Social Darwinism, and self-interest had created a society that made people isolated and alienated. Instead, he sought a return to spiritual and moral values of the preindustrial American community.

Collier's first encounter with Indians developed after a stopover at Taos, New Mexico, in 1921 that interrupted he and his family's camping trip to Sonora, Mexico. After witnessing the dramatic Christmas rites staged at Taos Pueblo, he saw the Indians' communal lifestyles as a model to enrich the entire nation. By preserving tribal cultures, Indians would not only continue an attractive lifestyle but bring to all Americans a sense of community and shared obligations that he believed once existed in European traditional communities. From a practical perspective he associated Indian cultural survival with retention of their land base. He also recognized that Indians would ultimately become acculturated, but he rejected the forced assimilation of previous governmental policies.[17]

Collier's campaign against the assimilationist course in Indian policy led him to advocate an alternate outlook—cultural pluralism. After his appointment as BIA commissioner in 1933, Collier had hoped to translate into policy his vision of a renewed tribal life and to create a Red Atlantis. He settled for much less in the Indian Reorganization Act (IRA) of 1934. Although weaker than Collier originally proposed, the IRA was central to New Deal Indian reform.[18] This watershed legislation extended to Indians a tribal alternative to assimilation. In a reversal of the goals of the allotment advocates, this important measure ended land allotment, provided mechanisms to revitalize and strengthen tribal governments, and promoted economic development on the Indian reservations. To accomplish its goals, the IRA allowed the organization and chartering of tribal governments and businesses.[19]

Implementation of the IRA proved difficult. The success of the IRA hinged on whether the Indians voted to endorse the reform measures. In practice the IRA often represented nothing more than a paper tiger, as many tribes failed to support the heart of Collier's reform measure. Sixty percent of the Indians in referenda on the IRA rejected the adoption of constitutions and the formation of tribal councils.[20]

Several other factors also explain opposition to the IRA. Previous experiences with broken treaties and promises led many Indians to avoid participation in IRA tribal governments. Other Indian leaders favored assimilation because they feared that tribalism would lead to segregation.[21] Even when approved, tribal factionalism often made the operation of tribal governments problematic. When tribes approved the act, mix-bloods often seized control of IRA councils and excluded full-bloods for their own political ends.[22] Several Native American leaders capitalized on the confusion of the program to advance their own political interests. Crossing tribal lines, Joseph Bruner and his American Indian Federation (AIF) sought to repeal the IRA. Established in 1934, the Oklahoma-based AIF charged the IRA with retarding Indian assimilation and condemning native peoples to poverty and dependence. Created to remove Collier from office, stop or slow the IRA, and abolish the BIA, the AIF drew support nationally from individuals with diverse opinions. AIF president Bruner, a wealthy Creek Indian, himself the product of an assimilationist education, and Oklahoma supporters urged legislative adjudication of Indian claims through a final cash settlement and an end to federal wardship over Indian affairs. Much of the strong call to abolish the BIA came from the earlier influence and ideas of Carlos Montezuma. The AIF viewed Collier's programs as increasing rather than decreasing federal control over Indians. Several progressive and landless Oklahoma members of the AIF criticized the Indian New Deal because they feared a return to the communal tribal lifestyle and an end to individual initiative. Important non-Oklahoma members of the AIF included Seneca Alice Lee Jemison; Thomas Sloan, prior president of the SAI; Adan Castillo, president of the Mission Indian Federaton; and Jacob C. Morgan, a Navajo leader.

AIF leadership attracted support from conservative elements. Using extremist right-wing protest language and smear tactics, the anti-Indian New Deal message of the AIF drew attention from conservative members of Congress as well as antiblack, anti-Semitic, and even fascist protesters. Right-wing groups ranging from the Daughters of the American Revolution to the Silver Shirts of America helped the AIF in its attack of the New Deal programs. The red-baiting methods of the AIF drew national attention. Tired of the attacks, by 1938 the Interior Department struck back by infiltrating the AIF, spying on its meetings, and seeking FBI surveillance of the organization's leaders.

Dissension within the rank and file of the AIF destroyed its long-term success. Failure to accomplish its goals caused the organization to splinter. Bruner's promotion of final cash awards of claims forced many traditional supporters and also non-Oklahoma leaders from the organization. After 1939 the AIF became little more than the personal instrument of Bruner and his Oklahoma followers until the organization's end in the mid-1940s. By the beginning of World War II the AIF represented few Indians and had lost national representation and influence.

The legacy of the AIF remains difficult to measure. The AIF clearly represented a more important national Indian political organization than was previously thought. While never a tightly organized protest movement or an organization that represented widespread Indian populations, the AIF nevertheless forced Collier to move cautiously in matters of policy. Although not successful in its goals, the AIF effectively protested the repeated government error in trying to apply sweeping, uniform policy changes to peoples as diverse as Native Americans. To many Indians, the Indian New Deal simply represented further federal interference in Indian affairs. Ironically, the condemnation of the BIA by the AIF helped advance an end to the federal trust relationship movement following World War II. While AIF members promoted Indian self-determination, their actions had produced the opposite result, namely, termination of the trust. Moreover, regardless of whether the AIF was a deliberate or an accidental pan-Indian movement in its broadest sense, founding members of the NCAI later had to deal with Collier's critics before they could establish their own organization.[23]

By the end of the 1930s, the Indian New Deal, as had Franklin D. Roosevelt's New Deal program, lost momentum. In the waning years of World War II an embattled John Collier confronted opposition that kept him on the defensive. The war discouraged cultural pluralism by promoting a sense of national unity and thereby a renewed emphasis on assimilation. Despite the formal end to Collier's reforms, the legacy of the Indian New Deal remained. For Native Americans, Collier's increasing problems created both opportunities and problems. Although Collier's programs met with limited success, his self-government policies spurred Indians' renewed interest in their own affairs. Debates over the merits of the IRA helped spark interest in a national Indian organization and brought new hope to thousands of Indians. Whether they opposed or supported the IRA, Indians around the country gathered to discuss the program's merits.

Groups such as AIF brought together Indians of varying outlooks to fight Collier's programs and to revise Indian policy. Even as IRA programs faltered, several Indian leaders pursued a national organization to promote shared interests with other Indians.

Recent scholarship reveals that Collier's Indian New Deal programs failed to live up to expectations. In essence, the IRA failed to provide means for complete Indian self-determination. Instead of allowing the Indians the freedom to make choices, Collier often exercised his power to do what he thought best for them. The measure contained many statements that allowed tribes to act only with the approval of the secretary of interior, which in practice meant Collier or other non-Indian administrators. Besides Indian opposition to the IRA, Collier faced serious challenges from western representatives such as Burton K. Wheeler of Montana, Sen. Dennis Chavez of New Mexico, and other interest groups trying to reform Indian policy. In the end Congress failed to provide adequate funds to bring long-term prosperity to most reservations.

Several historians maintain that the Indian New Deal never increased the freedom of Indians from the BIA. Some reservations benefited from relief programs, but others experienced problems adapting to a market economy. The IRA also failed to solve problems of heirship or factionalized allotments of Indian lands. Moreover, Will Carson Ryan Jr. and Willard Walcott Beatty, Collier's education directors for the BIA, failed to prepare students to live off, as well as on, reservations. Collier's programs therefore provided only limited prosperity or self-sufficiency.[24]

Despite his idealism or his administrative and propaganda skills, Collier tended to attack complex problems with simplistic solutions. In particular, he often failed to consult Indian groups about policy changes. Against the backdrop of the emerging Cold War and following a conservative backlash among Indians and whites in the early 1940s and during World War II, Collier eventually retreated from his reforms. Today, more than fifty years later, historians continue to debate Collier's success in bringing about lasting freedom, prosperity, and self-government for Indians.[25] Despite the fact that they are often factionalized and family run, however, the IRA tribal councils remain to this day important political and legal constructs.[26]

Collier left indelible imprints on Indian affairs. The IRA contained several important provisions to encourage Indian sovereignty, political equality, and tribal self-government. The Indian New Deal stopped the disastrous allotment policy of the previous generation. Moreover, many of Collier's programs directly or indirectly promoted pan-Indianism and national Indian political participation. Most importantly, the Indian New Deal encouraged the preservation of Indian culture and ethnic identity. Federal preferential hiring of Indians, although seldom in key positions, changed the composition of the Indian Bureau and provided to Indians valuable political experience. The tribal councils, despite their shortcomings, also provided a training ground for a new generation of Indian leaders. The same councils introduced participants to such non-Indians ideas as written constitutions, formally elected representatives, fixed terms of office, written laws, published proceedings, and majority rule. Although patterned after white models, the IRA councils drew Indians into the larger political arena. Other significant provisions of the IRA included federal aid for economic and education programs.[27]

Collier also encouraged Indian unity through regional, national, and international conferences. He sponsored regional conferences in 1939-40 in Minneapolis, Minnesota; Billings, Montana; Carson City, Nevada; and Phoenix, Arizona, to promote intertribal communication. Excited by the prospects for solidarity, participants at the meetings sought a permanent Indian institute and annual national Indian conventions. In addition, Collier actively promoted pan-Indianism throughout the Western Hemisphere. He encouraged intertribal contacts between groups in North and South America to discuss common Indian problems. In 1939, for example, Collier appointed Arthur C. Parker, Louis Bruce, Archie Phinney, David Owl, D'Arcy McNickle, and Ruth Muskrat Bronson as delegates to a Canadian conference on North American Indians, jointly sponsored by the University of Toronto and Yale University.[28] All these influential Indian leaders, except David Owl, became founding members of NCAI.

Participation in an inter-American conference in Patzcuaro, Mexico, in 1940 further fostered Indian solidarity.[29] More importantly, both conferences served to direct U.S. tribal interests to shared problems and the need for intertribal organization and cooperation. Following the Toronto deliberations, D'Arcy McNickle, Ruth Bronson, Archie Phinney, and others met occasionally to champion the creation of a national Indian organization.[30]

World War II also contributed to the rise of pan-Indianism in a different but important way. The war years reshaped not only the nation but the West in particular. For the purpose of this book, the geographic limits of the American West rest on political boundaries and start with the eastern borders of the Great Plains states—the Dakotas, Nebraska, Kansas, Oklahoma, and Texas. Since prior to 1941 more than 75 percent of federally recognized Indians lived west of the Mississippi, any changes in the development of the region naturally affected most the Indian nations. (The largest Indian populations in 1940 were centered in Arizona, California, Minnesota, Montana, New Mexico, Oklahoma, South Dakota, Wisconsin, North Carolina, and Washington.)[31] For many Indians, World War II provided their first significant opportunity to participate in the larger economy. The outbreak of World War II redirected federal resources in ways that benefited many western Indians. As the war ended, new Indian leaders such as the NCAI arose to protect and expand their new gains.

Without question, the West benefited from New Deal relief and recovery reform measures.[32] Indeed, the region during the New Deal profited from more per capita federal expenditures than any other section in the nation at large. Yet Roosevelt's reform measures did not allow the West to escape its subordinate economic position.[33]

Far more extensive changes followed. The wartime years propelled the West from economic colonialism into a national postindustrial pacesetter. Within four years, the West moved from an underdeveloped region based on the production of raw materials and semiprocessed goods to a modern diversified economy.[34] Federally financed factories and shipyards along the West Coast and construction of military bases and supply depots throughout the region were chief instruments in loosing previous economic shackles. As massive federal funds poured into the region after 1941, westerners assumed an increasingly larger role in government and became key players in deciding their own destiny. Throughout the region, metropolitan centers of corporate capitalism emerged in response to the wartime demands. Most of the urban growth centered on the West Coast and in such cities as Phoenix, Denver, Dallas, and Houston.

By contrast, the plains and northern states lagged far behind in economic and urban development. Because of the wartime changes, the region became "two Wests": an urban West centered along the coast and a rural West that prevailed in the vast interior. Moreover, the centers of power also changed. Whereas eastern forces once controlled the West, wartime economic development prompted the urban West to dominate the rural West.[35]

The rise of the urban West and wartime experiences forever altered the lives of most Native Americans. Wartime employment opportunities sparked a large wave of Indian migration to off-reservation jobs. The nearly forty thousand who worked in urban war industries often plied skills learned in the Indian Civilian Conservation Corps (ccc). Many Indians obtained temporary or seasonal jobs and returned to the reservation after short stints. Others who worked in the West Coast war plants and shipyards or large interior cities integrated into mainstream society. In both cases the Indians benefited economically and gained valuable job experience.[36]

National unity fueled by the war effort also thrust thousands of Indians into military service. Caught up in the patriotic fervor of wartime nationalism, roughly twenty-five thousand Indians served in the armed forces. Because of the Citizenship Act of 1924, all Indians came under Selective Service legislation. Never in American history had such large numbers of Indians fought side by side with white counterparts. Indian soldiers often distinguished themselves on the battlefield. The war produced not only Indian war heroes, but greatly accelerated the movement toward assimilation. Military service acquainted Indians with the consumer culture and introduced them to steady incomes; their service also brought them the respect due military men and more equal treatment that they had previously known among whites.[37]

The war also caused profound reductions in BIA services to Indians. In 1942 the BIA moved its Washington DC office to Chicago, a move that served to curtail Collier's influence in Congress and the federal government. Needing funds to fight the war, Congress quickly dropped Indian New Deal programs and slashed the BIA budget. Numerous Indian Service employees left the BIA for military service or for better economic opportunities. The severe disruptions in BIA staff and programs left Indian affairs in disorder. As New Deal programs faltered on some reservations and as the BIA came under attack, Indian leaders turned to each other rather than to the government for help in solving their own problems.[38]

Throughout most of American history, Indians have sought to organize themselves into more complex intertribal units. Perhaps the most significant theme in these intertribal movements has been the participants' attempt to retain their own sense of identity. Indeed, their greatest efforts have been to define their identity among themselves and within the larger white society. By the mid-twentieth century, a new and different Indian organization emerged in direct response to earlier policies and previous intertribal efforts. Its early leadership had experienced firsthand the impact of allotments, reservation life, boarding schools, the Depression and the New Deal, and both World Wars.

As will be seen in the following chapters, the cycle of Indian intertribal political mobilization that had begun at the time of Euro-American contact completed its evolution in the mid-1940s. In the aftermath of the IRA and World War II, a new generation of Indian actors took advantage of newly opened political doors. Eager to secure the rights to which they were entitled, returning Indian veterans and urban Indians entered the political mainstream. Borrowing much of its philosophy, early personnel, tactics, and organizational structure from the Indian New Deal, some Indian leaders hoped to establish a broadly based, nonpartisan organization to improve the status of Indians. While many of these leaders had championed the New Deal, they also correctly realized that the long-term success of any new Indian political organization required inclusion of those who opposed Collier's reform efforts.

2. THE CONSTITUTIONAL CONVENTION

Now I know that you can't put the same blanket over everybody because when you do that you are going to pull it off of somebody else. The same blanket won't go over everybody at the same time, but if you use some judgment you can spread the blanket out so that the one that is a little bit colder can get warmth from it.

BEN DWIGHT, NCAI Constitutional Convention Keynote Address, November 1944

The postwar period gave Indians the hope that life would be better than it was before the war. Indian participation in the war effort, both as soldiers and as laborers, propelled them into mainstream society. White perceptions of Indians and Indians' views of whites often changed because of this contact. Widespread exposure to mainstream society and a higher standard of living as well as the new respect that the war had brought to Indian veterans meant that Indians would never again accept the lower status they had endured before the war. In particular, Indians became more sensitive to several issues and forms of discrimination during and immediately following the war. Such concerns as voting rights, BIA controls, and prohibition of drinking became especially important. By war's end, Indians were prepared to secure rights both as U.S. citizens and as members of domestic-dependent nations. Wartime experiences, coupled with the legacy of the Indian New Deal, convinced a new generation of Indians of the need to organize in order to make their voices heard in Congress and elsewhere.

In early spring 1944 Collier encouraged greater Indian political activism among BIA employees in Chicago. Collier's assistant commissioner, William Zimmerman, also strongly encouraged national Indian mobilization. Because of Collier's and Zimmerman's efforts to encourage communication, Indian employees met periodically to discuss common interests. They were careful, however, to avoid using paid government time for such meetings. These informal evening gatherings at restaurants and a local library led to discussions of the need for a broadly based national Indian organization. While Collier encouraged Indian organization, he never participated directly.[1] Although bureau employees largely founded the NCAI, Collier's influence was obvious. Planners never intended, as critics later charged, that the new organization serve as a tool to promote or defend the gains of the Indian New Deal.[2] McNickle and his colleagues planned from the outset to launch the NCAI and then step down.[3] Thus, the motivation to organize simply came from prominent Indian leaders who saw the need for a united front. Individuals such as McNickle, Phinney, Ben Dwight, Mark Burns, and other politically astute Indians had long campaigned for a national Indian organization.[4] Collier merely served as a timely facilitator of communication between the BIA and the Indians. Surviving founding members of the NCAI recall that although the idea for the NCAI did not originate with Collier, the planning went on with his blessing.[5]

Credit largely goes to three individuals for founding the NCAI: McNickle, Phinney, and Charles E. J. Heacock. Well known as an Indian activist and author, McNickle arguably was the best-known leader of the three. Born in 1904 on the Flathead Reservation, he spent most of his career in Indian affairs. His strong determination and practical mind carried the NCAI through its formative years.

Archie Phinney, Nez Perce and superintendent of the Northern Idaho Indian Agency, played a larger role in the formation of the NCAI than most scholars have documented. Born in 1904 in Culdesac, Idaho, at the Nez Perce Reservation, Phinney had long envisioned a national Indian organization that would champion Indian rights. His strong academic training and his experiences in the Indian Service led him to a greater appreciation for cultural diversity and ensured his comfortableness in a non-Indian political world. He started his higher education at Haskell Indian Institute and went on to the University of Kansas, where he graduated in 1926 with a bachelor of arts degree. While working as a clerk in the BIA in Washington DC after graduation, he took night courses in ethnology at George Washington University. Longing to return to school full-time, he quit his job in 1928 to enroll in graduate school at Columbia University in New York. He studied anthropology under Franz Boaz. Working between 1932 and 1937 on a project cosponsored by Columbia and Leningrad, Phinney taught and studied at the Leningrad Academy of Sciences in the Soviet Union. While overseas, he assisted Soviet minority groups in economic rehabilitation and self-help. After he returned to the United States and the Indian Service rehired him as a field agent, he was anxious to apply his knowledge and energy toward helping his own people. By 1938 Phinney began with other BIA employees to explore the idea of a new Indian organization.[6]

Curious about earlier intertribal efforts, Phinney began making inquiries into previous Indian movements. Interested in the bylaws, structure, and reasons for the failure of the Society of American Indians (SAI), Phinney in 1942 wrote Arthur C. Parker for insight into his participation in the alliance. Parker immediately supplied the requested information and blamed the demise of the SAI on the self-interest and the poor leadership of Thomas L. Sloan. He wished Phinney well in his pursuit of a more permanent national Indian organization.[7] Praising the earlier efforts of the SAI, Phinney claimed the new Indian coalition needed a more aggressive and militant agenda than previous Indian intertribal organizations. Unless planners could achieve that goal, he said, "we might as well affiliate with some ladies' aid society."[8]

Satisfied with the potential for a more assertive organization, Phinney proposed an outline for a national intertribal organization. He appropriately termed the purpose of the new organization "ethnic democracy."[9] Pleased with Phinney's efforts, Charles E. J. Heacock, important pioneer member, called him the "guiding genius and founding father" of the movement.[10] Phinney's vision included the creation of an organization on regional levels that reported to a national headquarters in the organization division of the new BIA office. Modeling his plans after Collier's staff meetings and regional conferences, he hoped the new organization would serve as an Indian branch of the BIA.[11] McNickle vehemently disagreed. He rightfully believed that Phinney's proposal would create an organization that would appear as nothing more than a tool of the BIA. McNickle wanted instead an organization built and led completely by Indians, without the assistance of outside help. Collier and his assistants shared McNickle's view.[12]

Phinney's close friendship with McNickle led to many other discussions in the early planning stages about the nature, structure, and course of the new organization. The two Indian leaders, however, shared fundamental differences in relation to the structure the organization needed. Phinney preferred to keep tribal councils out of the organization, for he feared that they were not capable of considering issues beyond reservation boundaries. He therefore supported individual memberships as opposed to representatives from the tribes. McNickle, however, believed that the councils should be the heart and soul of the organization. He wanted to restrict individual memberships to off-reservation Indians and not allow those Indians a vote in national conventions.[13] Phinney also felt that an elite should govern the organization through its embryonic stages. Trusting in the principles of democracy, McNickle preferred to let the majority select the leaders. Walking the middle ground, Charles E. J. Heacock, BIA statistician, believed that regardless of the course taken, a natural elite would automatically rise to the top leadership positions. Not taking any chances, Phinney asserted that "only about four of us should engineer policymaking at Denver [site of the first convention.]"[14]

Nearly as important as McNickle and Phinney in the founding of the new intertribal organization, Heacock became the third point in the planning triangle. Born in 1904 on the Rosebud Reservation in South Dakota, he started work in 1935 at the BIA. With a degree from the University of Nebraska and a master's in chemistry from State College, South Dakota, he held several positions within the BIA. Heacock became a significant sounding board for McNickle and Phinney. Usually more extreme than McNickle, Heacock often sided with Phinney in ideological debates.

Heacock raised several concerns about the plausibility of a national Indian coalition. Though highly assimilated himself, he worried that the more assimilated members would always dominate and often exclude the more traditional elements. Thus, he feared that a national organization might not always reflect all Indian sentiments. Yet reflecting his own biases, he believed that only the educated elite should lead the organization. He also felt that the only way such an effort could succeed was if it joined forces with other civil rights movements and organizations.[15] His plan included making the organization a branch of Collier's Inter-American Institute. This would help ensure that Indian BIA employees formed the nucleus of the new organization.[16] Phinney initially agreed with him on the need to link the organization to an established program, and he proposed tying into the National Indian Institute or to a specially created division of the Indian Service.[17]

Within a year, Phinney changed his mind on linking the new Indian organization to a Collier program and shifted toward McNickle's position. Ernest E. Maes, secretary of the National Indian Institute, welcomed the idea of increased Indian leadership in his program.[18] Phinney, however, opposed the idea. Lest they miss the "chance of [their] Indianist lifetimes," Phinney warned, it would be a mistake to cling "to the shirttail of the Institute." If the organization was to succeed and represent all Indians, he felt, it needed freedom from the Indian Institute. Moving closer together in attitudes, McNickle wholeheartedly agreed with Phinney.[19]

McNickle raised some questions with Phinney in 1942 over the prospect of launching such a large movement. He conceded that if Phinney's plans were "too ambiguous and perhaps premature," then maybe they should instead focus on organizing intertribal organizations in regions instead of on a national scale. Confident of national success, Phinney pushed forward with his plans. In early summer 1943 McNickle still had doubts about the viability of uniting Indians in a common league. Commissioner Collier, however, had gradually changed his opinion on the need for such an organization. He now believed it truly represented Indian leadership, and he felt the timing was good.[20]

In January 1944, nearly thirty BIA employees attended a preliminary meeting held away from governmental offices to explore ideas for launching such an organization. Participants selected Heacock to chair the informal sessions. Delighted by the response of those present, Heacock chose a working committee and made plans to meet in early February in Chicago.[21] When the groups met a second time, roughly seventy people attended, and the participants selected nine temporary working committee members until the election of permanent officers. Phinney, McNickle, and Heacock headed the list. Heacock continued as acting chairman of the council.[22] Noting that most of the committee represented Indians from the southern plains, Midwest, and East, McNickle urged members also to select representatives from the Southwest and Northwest. He cautioned the founding members not to establish their organization in Oklahoma until it had successfully gotten off the ground. "Oklahoma is a hell of a place to organize anything," he said," and it is a particularly bad place to organize Indians."[23] He correctly anticipated the need for critical support from some of the influential tribes in the Southwest and Northwest. During a trip to the larger reservations in the Southwest in the spring of 1944, McNickle successfully met with tribal representatives to sell the working committee's ideas for an all-Indian organization. Without leadership backing from the Oklahoma tribes, however, the organization had little hope for success.[24]

The ad hoc committee met again in May to complete plans to launch the organization. At this point, McNickle decided to invite the American Association on Indian Affairs (AAIA) to help get the organization started.[25] McNickle thought it best to avoid accepting help from Indian reform organizations such as the Indian Rights Association and the Home Missions Council because he felt they were unprogressive and supportive of coercive assimilation. He considered the AAIA, a predominantly white reform organization, an exception, truly sympathetic to the needs of Indians.[26] Created in 1937, the AAIA resulted from a merger between the American Indian Defense Association, founded in 1923 by John Collier, and the National Association on Indian Affairs (NAIA). In 1946 the American Association on Indian Affairs changed to its present name—the Association on American Indian Affairs. Oliver LaFarge, anthropologist and author, served as the first president of the organization. Since the late 1940s, the AAIA, like the NCAI, has continued to work to protect and secure the constitutional rights of Indians.[27]

On May 23, 1944, Dr. Eduard Lindeman, a member of the executive committee of the AAIA, met in Chicago with the ad hoc committee to offer counsel for launching the new Indian organization. Lindeman advised the founders that their group should remain all-Indian, politically nonpartisan, and independent of white groups involved in Indian reform work. He also suggested they avoid factional reservation politics. Perhaps more importantly, he cautioned the group to remain free of any association with the BIA. Lindeman then promised to try to solicit funds from AAIA to help the new organization get started.[28] Phinney warned McNickle, however, not to let the AAIA have any control or power over the upstart organization. "With trusty tomahawk, not on bended knee, we exploit all along the way," he claimed," and in this way we can also use the good knowledge of Felix Cohen and others."[29] Phinney rightfully understood that all too often in the past non-Indian groups undermined previous Indian associations and pressed their own reform agenda.

To ensure equal representation at the national convention, the ad hoc committee proposed a plan. Using the regional field organization of the BIA as a model, the plan proposed to divide the country into nine geographical areas. Although the regional field organization was divided into ten regions, the working committee excluded the Alaskan region from the initial proposal because of distances to the convention site. The remaining nine regions included Eastern, Great Lakes, North Central Plains, Northwestern Plains, Pacific Northwest, California, Inter-Mountain, Southwest, and South Central Plains. Based upon the Indian population of its geographical area, each region would send an apportionment of delegates to re-

gional conventions. Each regional convention then would select proportionate numbers of delegates to send to the national convention.
Since the Inter-Mountain region contained the smallest Indian population, planners hoped to use that region as the basis to decide the
numbers of delegates from the other regions. Preliminary figures
called for 133 delegates to attend regional conventions from which
33 delegates would be selected to the national convention. The ad
hoc committee then nominated various individuals to serve as area
leaders to oversee their respective geographical areas.[30] Two months
before the constitutional convention, however, charter leaders abandoned the plan. To ensure greater participation across Indian country, convention planners favored representation based on individuals, tribes, or groups rather than on region. McNickle and Phinney
had reached an important compromise.

With the background work of the ad hoc committee completed,
on May 25–27, 1944, D'Arcy McNickle joined twenty-one other Indians in Chicago to complete plans for a national Indian organization. The closeness to the Indian Bureau made Chicago the logical location. Under the direction of temporary chairman Heacock, the
founders convened at a local YMCA on South La Salle Street.[31] Besides
Heacock, McNickle, and Phinney, Mark L. Burns, Ruth Bronson, David Dozier, Ed Rogers, George LaMotte, Kent Fitzgerald, Roy Gourd,
Erma Hicks Walz, Lois Harlan, and Ben Dwight shouldered much
of the burden for the success of the Chicago meetings.[32] Two-thirds
of the planners claimed either Cherokee, Chippewa, or Choctaw
descent. Nearly all worked for Collier and the BIA. As John Rainer,
former executive director of NCAI, later recalled, "[These individuals]
were like Washington and Jefferson for us."[33]

The first day of the meetings addressed questions concerning
membership and the purpose of the new organization. Participants
in the sessions agreed to limit membership solely to Indians. Decisions about whether the polity should represent individuals or tribes
remained unanswered. Of considerable importance was the expediency of bringing returning Indian veterans into the new organization to profit from their experience and broadened outlook. Equally

important were debates over whether the new Indian organization should align itself with other minorities. While the planners unanimously sympathized with the plight of other minorities, they concluded it might not be in their best interest to align themselves with other ethnic interest groups. The leaders privately hoped that the work of a national Indian organization would advance the interests of other groups with similar problems. While tempted to merge efforts with other minority groups to push for broad improvements, planners could ill-afford to abandon the fight for unique rights and the special needs of individual tribes. Through alignment with other minority groups, they risked becoming too readily identified by policymakers as just another poor group. Special legal relationships and treaty rights made them different.[34]

Planners devoted the final two days of the Chicago meetings to the nuts and bolts of the new organization. Before the meetings adjourned on May 27, conference participants accepted several important measures. Except for minor changes, they unanimously adopted a provisional constitution and preamble. Preparing for the national convention, Phinney and Heacock patterned the constitution and bylaws after the charter of the Federal Employees Union No. 780 in Chicago, a union to which some Bureau employees belonged.[35] The preamble stressed both civil and tribal rights by declaring that the common welfare of Native Americans required the preservation of cultural values, the defense of legal rights, and the education of the public.[36] Officers were then chosen and committees appointed until successors could be elected at the national convention. Mark L. Burns, Chippewa and Indian Bureau's field representative in Minnesota, was selected temporary president. Heacock and Ed Rogers, Chippewa, were chosen as first and second vice-presidents. The provisional executive committee included six individuals—Ben Dwight, Oklahoma Choctaw, D'Arcy McNickle, Flathead, David Dozier, Flathead, Ruth Bronson, Cherokee, and Arthur O. Allen and George LaMotte, Chippewa.

Following the Chicago meetings, the group organized under the new constitution as the National Council of American Indians and selected Denver, Colorado, as the location for the first national convention.[37] They chose Denver as the site because of its central location to much of Indian country.[38] The planning committee then selected November 1944 as the date for the constitutional convention.

To secure a successful beginning to the organization, its planners elicited critical reservation support. In October 1944, one month before the convention, Mark Burns called on reservation leaders to participate actively in the constitutional convention. Cautious tribal leaders sought greater political power through a larger Indian forum, but they also risked jeopardizing their own individual needs and the flow of federal benefits. Burns tried to convince them that the benefits outweighed the risks. He also tried to allay their fears that although bureau employees dominated the early phases of ncai, the new organization was not an instrument of John Collier. Affiliation with Collier had become an image problem that plagued ncai for years.[39] ncai promoters further challenged Indian leaders across the country to "talk Indian organization, sleep Indian organization, and eat Indian organization."[40]

As the Denver convention approached, convention organizers continued to struggle with the role the bia employees played in the early planning of ncai. Planners debated the political wisdom of inviting Commissioner Collier to the national convention. Critics feared his presence at the convention might intensify existing fears that the new organization was a tool of the Bureau. Proponents of the idea, however, maintained that the commissioner's attendance at the constitutional convention would bring visibility and credibility to the new organization.[41] Commissioner Collier's hectic schedule resolved the dispute. Previous commitments prevented him from attending the charter convention, so instead he sent a note of best wishes that was read during the afternoon session on opening day.[42]

Less than one month before the constitutional convention, Archie Phinney started having serious doubts about whether the new organization could succeed. He worried that because of a lack of tribal funds few delegates would make the trip to Denver. More importantly, he still had misgivings about whether tribal delegates could make the transition from local reservation problems to a more global Indian agenda. He hoped strong leadership could overcome these potential setbacks. He also held to his belief that individuals, as well as tribal representatives, should feel comfortable in participating in the new organization.[43] While McNickle shared Phinney's concern about tribal leadership's ability to operate on a larger scale, he rightfully believed that the organization would have to live and die on reservation support. Learning from the mistakes of the sai, McNickle promised to raise limited funds for Indians who would not otherwise be able to attend.[44]

Neither fears that the new organization was a tool of Collier nor concerns about tribal funds prevented a sizable turnout at the constitutional convention. Interest in creating a national Indian organization drew the largest pan-Indian gathering in American Indian history. Nearly eighty delegates from twenty-seven states, representing fifty tribes, met at the Cosmopolitan Hotel in Denver, Colorado. The delegates attending represented a fair cross section of Indian leadership west of the Mississippi River. As Phinney had hoped, the participants had come as individuals, not as tribal appointees. The largest tribe, the Navajos, however, failed to participate. Since the inception of ncai, Navajo leaders have refused to relinquish any tribal authority.

Although the existing biographical data on some delegates remain sketchy, scholars have pieced together enough information to create a general profile of the founding members of the ncai. Although many representatives came from urban areas, the convention drew better-than-expected reservation-based support. On the whole, the convention attendees represented an equal blend of young and old, full-bloods and mixed-bloods, and highly educated and less formally educated Indians. Not surprisingly, the greatest participation came from the more assimilated tribes of Oklahoma and the northern plains states, particularly from the Sioux Nation. The Oklahoma delegation was so large that the participants reserved an entire railroad coach for the trip.[45] Among the founding members was an impressive array of Indian leadership—anthropologists, lawyers, business people, elected state and federal officials, tribal leaders, and even a former professional baseball player George Eastman (Santee Sioux). Present were prominent individuals such as Napoleon B. Johnson, district court judge from Oklahoma, Edward L. Rogers, attorney from Minnesota, and Dan Madrano who held a seat in the Oklahoma legislature. Nearly half of the founding members had served on IRA-chartered tribal councils. Several had graduated from Carlisle Indian School, Haskell Institute, and from four-year colleges. Roughly 80 percent of the charter members had some ties to the BIA. In contrast to the youthful Bureau planners of the NCAI, the charter delegates represented an equal number of young and older Indians. The delegates fell into two nearly equal age groups: those twenty-eight to forty-five and those forty-six to sixty-five.[46] Showing the long experience of some charter members, at least four individuals—Albert Exendine, Jesse Rowlodge, Henry Standing Bear, and Arthur C. Parker—had also been founding members of the SAI. The delegates were largely men. While women comprised only 10 percent of the registered delegates in 1944, their numbers continually increased until 1955 when they represented more than 50 percent of NCAI membership.

The convention opened with a bang. Fifteen years later, D'Arcy McNickle recalled that evening:

> Basil Two Bears (Standing Rock Reservation) was asked to give an invocation in Sioux, which he did. But he ended his prayer with what must have been an old Sioux warwhoop, telling us to get in there and give the Bureau hell. Well, it happened that the National Reclamation Association was meeting in the other half of the ballroom, with only sliding doors between the two meetings, not much to obstruct the sound. The Reclamation Association came pouring out of the hall to find out who had been stabbed.[47]

After Two Bears' dramatic invocation, the atmosphere at the convention remained charged. Acting President Mark Burns was unable to preside because of illness, but his vice-president, Charles E. J. Heacock, assumed control of the meetings.

In the opening sessions NCAI founders quickly worked to quell rumors that the new organization was Bureau controlled. Ben Dwight, attorney, former Choctaw chief, and aide to Sen. Robert S. Kerr, set the tone in his keynote address to the convention. Despite some initial doubts himself, Dwight reassured the audience that the Bureau planners had "not lost their Indian hearts" and sold out to Collier. Instead, he said, they admirably founded NCAI to represent the collective interests of all Indians.[48] Peru Farver, a BIA employee and Oklahoma Choctaw, further defended the founders' actions in the creation of NCAI. In a paternalistic tone he suggested that it was only logical that the more politically sophisticated Indians "use the tools of organization" to advance the interests of "those who are not so fortunate." Critics of the Bureau planners' role in NCAI, however, warned the founders not to press their stewardship too far. Henry Standing Bear, an elderly and respected Oglala Sioux, cautioned the founders to toe the line or face the consequences. Oklahoma Supreme Court Justice Napoleon B. Johnson, later the first president of the NCAI, took a more moderate approach. He maintained that despite the forces who criticized NCAI, the convention provided Indians an opportunity to organize.[49]

As the convention progressed, several delegates suggested a plan to put the controversy forever to rest. They proposed an amendment to the NCAI constitution that would prohibit Indian Service employees from holding positions in the new organization.[50] The membership of the NCAI, however, voted down the proposal. The delegates wisely opted to use the experience and leadership skills of the BIA employees. Nevertheless, Councilmen Phinney and McNickle resigned their positions the following year in response to the criticism. In 1945 McNickle supported a resolution to forbid BIA employees from holding elected positions in NCAI. The resolution passed at the Second NCAI Convention, held in Browning, Montana, in 1945.[51] Surviving the first major crisis, planners had skillfully shifted custody of leadership from themselves to the floor of the convention. With the question over Bureau domination of the NCAI temporarily quelled, the delegates spent the remainder of the convention establishing the governing structure and a platform for the new organization. Under the chairmanship of Ben Dwight, they adopted a constitution and a name, defined the organization's membership requirements, elected officers, and specified goals.

Establishing a distinct Indian identity remained a top priority. Delegates limited membership in the new organization to people of Indian descent, either as individuals, groups, or tribes. Non-Indians could participate as nonvoting associates. Phinney's ideas for individual and group participation had prevailed over those of McNickle. The floor of the convention then changed the original name of the organization from the National Council of American Indians to the National Congress of American Indians. Some historians have asserted that the delegates changed the name to pattern the organization after white legislative bodies.[52] The official transcript of the constitutional convention and interviews with founding members, however, suggest that delegates wanted to avoid confusion with Gertrude Bonnin's 1920s organization that had borne the same name.[53]

The Denver convention ratified the Chicago planning committee's constitution and bylaws with few changes. The preamble reflected the broad commitment of the NCAI to both individual and tribal rights:

> We, the members of the Indian Tribes of the United States of America in convention assembled on the 16th day of November, 1944, at Denver, Colorado; in order to secure the rights and benefits to which we are entitled under the laws of the United States, the several states thereof, and the territory of Alaska; to enlighten the public toward a better understanding of the Indian race; to preserve cultural values; to seek an equitable adjustment to tribal affairs; to secure and to preserve rights under Indian treaties with the United States; and to otherwise promote the common welfare of the American Indians—do establish this organization and adopt the following Constitution and By-Laws.[54]

The Denver Convention then created ten permanent committees and elected an executive council made up of four officers and eight councilmen. The new executive council, the Congress's governing body, reflected the influence of the assimilated tribes of Oklahoma—

a pattern that would continue for nearly a decade. Throughout the first eleven conventions, delegates elected council members from the floor of the national conventions, a practice that often resulted in leadership by the more educated and urban Indians. Realizing the inequities in reservation leadership, the NCAI revised its constitution in 1955 to ensure that the executive council included one voting delegate from each member tribe. Unlike the Oklahoma-dominated experience in the founding period, more equal representation assured that in future years no group of individuals dominated the proceedings or leadership positions. Judge Napoleon B. Johnson, a Cherokee from Claremore, Oklahoma, and boyhood friend of humorist Will Rogers, served as the first president. Delegates also elected Dan Madrano, a Caddo, as their first secretary. Edward L. Rogers, a Minnesota Chippewa, was elected vice-president. As treasurer, voters selected George G. LaMotte, a retired Wisconsin Chippewa living in Chicago.[55]

To counterbalance the influence of the more assimilated officers, the executive council reflected the organization's strong reservation-based element. Five of the eight members came from reservations: Stephen DeMers, a Flathead from Montana; Henry Throssell, a Papago from Arizona; William Firethunder and Luke Gilbert, Pine Ridge and Cheyenne River Sioux respectively from South Dakota; and Howard Gorman, a Navajo from Arizona and one of only a few Navajos who joined NCAI. D'Arcy McNickle and Archie Phinney represented the original founders of NCAI.[56] Arthur C. Parker, early twentieth-century Indian activist, rounded out the council. Although Parker brought marquee status to NCAI, his role in the new organization appears to have been slight.

On November 18, 1944, delegates passed eighteen resolutions that became the platform of the NCAI for the upcoming year. The resolutions addressed three broad themes: sovereignty, civil rights, and political recognition for all Indians. From these resolutions emerged two immediate concerns: the establishment of a claims commission for tribes to litigate old land claims against the government and the securing of voting rights for Indians in New Mexico and Arizona.[57]

By passing broad resolutions the founders had skillfully mapped a political strategy that would appeal to all Indians. By steering a moderate course, NCAI leadership lessened the risk of alienating the reservation Indians from urban Indians, the more assimilated from the less assimilated, and older Indians from the younger. Ben Dwight in his keynote address to the delegates articulately summarized the need of NCAI to walk the middle ground:

> Now what has been my personal opinion as to what this organization should do? I think we should come out of here with three things done. I think that we should write a program, you may call it a platform, call it anything you like, but come out of here with your ideas put into written form. Come out of here with decisions of common interest to all the tribes of the United States, that being the program or platform that will meet the wishes of a majority of the Indian people, where one group can help another. A program that is flexible. A program that is general in nature. Of course, under that program a part of it may be applied in one jurisdiction that may not be applied in another, but a working skeleton that will fit the needs in a general way, of all the Indians in the United States, and that can be operated harmoniously so that it will be of benefit to all the Indians in this country. Now I know that you can't put the same blanket over everybody because when you do that, you are going to pull it off of somebody else. The same blanket won't go over everybody at the same time, but if you use some judgment you can spread that blanket out so that the one that is a little colder can get warmth from it. We can write a program that is general in nature that can fit our needs so that every tribe in the nation can follow it. We have full-bloods, we have mixed-bloods, we have Indians of 1/64th and on up.[58]

The passage of the resolutions signaled an end to the Denver convention's proceedings.

The shared blanket of the NCAI essentially stretched too far and tore in half before it realized its potential. Factionalism in early 1945 threatened to destroy the NCAI less than six months after its inception. Calling George LaMotte, treasurer, and Dan Madrano, secretary, "two sour lemons," McNickle accused the officers of being "phony publicity hounds." McNickle and others had pleaded with

Madrano to fulfill his responsibilities and publish the inaugural NCAI newsletter. Despite numerous promises that he would print the paper, Madrano failed to get a single issue out. Realizing the urgent need for publicity for the new organization, McNickle asked Heacock to publish the paper.

McNickle also complained that LaMotte and Madrano had pulled an unauthorized publicity stunt. Acting without the approval of the executive committee, LaMotte, in May 1945, arranged for the NCAI, with the aid of local groups, to sponsor a reception, luncheon, broadcast, and parade to honor Ira Hayes, noted Pima war hero, at Soldier Field in Chicago. Directing most events on the program, LaMotte personally led the parade of seventy-five Indians dressed in traditional attire as they staged a reenactment of the flag raising at Iwo Jima in front of sixty thousand people. McNickle complained that Madrano and LaMotte had used the event for self-promoting purposes. Claiming the episode encouraged stereotypes and produced bad publicity for the NCAI, McNickle threatened to quit unless NCAI president Johnson more tightly controlled the pair. Trying to soothe McNickle's anger, Heacock comforted him that the "Hayes" stunt, although it was unauthorized, actually provided the NCAI with positive publicity. Cautioning McNickle not to draw attention to the split in the NCAI hierarchy, Heacock asked him to bide his time until elections at the next convention.[59]

Internal divisions continued the following year within the leadership ranks. Heacock complained that "a lot of ineffectual debating, sprinkled with carousing around as in former times" hampered committee meetings. Disgusted with the progress of the NCAI, several officials threatened to quit the organization. Trying to unite the organization through questionable and radical means, Heacock suggested to Phinney that someone write a short article in the NCAI newsletter raising the question "What good are the mixed bloods in the Indian Service to the Indian People?" He hoped that placing the more assimilated Indian BIA employees on the defensive would unite all Indians in a common purpose. Yielding to the sounder advice of others, he never wrote the article.[60]

Throughout 1944, Heacock and McNickle continued to shoulder the organizational burden for the new Indian political instrument. Heacock by mid- to late 1945 began to feel that the Oklahoma Indians should increasingly expend more effort to make the NCAI work. Noting the strong Oklahoma contention at the first convention, he argued that "the Oklahoma forces were the best vehicle we had at the moment to push NCAI into the national scene."[61] Heacock's insights proved correct.

By the next convention in November 1945, the NCAI had survived its inaugural year. Having worked out early difficulties, the organization rapidly grew as the Oklahoma Indians assumed larger leadership roles. Unfortunately, it also lost two of its most important founders. By 1946 poor health forced Phinney to withdraw from the NCAI, and in 1949 a brain aneurysm left Heacock physically impaired and no longer able to participate in NCAI activities.[62]

In the immediate postwar years the NCAI quickly came to occupy a watchdog position similar to the National Association for the Advancement of Colored People (NAACP), the Chinese Benevolent Association (CBA), and the Japanese American Citizens' League (JACL), the League of United Latin American Citizens (LULAC), and the Congress of Racial Equality (CORE). Founded in the first half of the twentieth century, these organizations also promoted ethnic identity and civil rights. While the end of World War II increased expectations that second-class citizenship for Indian people would end, it did the same for these other ethnic groups. Unfortunately, the immediate aftermath of war produced a return to apathy and intolerance for ethnic politics. In an important way, however, the NCAI was different from these other twentieth-century ethnic organizational efforts. While most other ethnic groups during the period promoted integration into the mainstream society, the NCAI advocated a distinctive Indianness that fit conservatives, progressives, educated, uneducated, and others. With support from non-Indian reform groups such as the AAIA, the Indian Rights Association, and others, the NCAI pressed for an Indian agenda.[63]

Surviving an uncertain beginning, the broad blanket of the NCAI had stretched forth to include a variety of interests and viewpoints. The historic constitutional convention represented an act of faith and belief in the common interests of all Indians. Collier's IRA, the boarding schools, and the wartime experiences of Indians had helped shape a new generation of Indian leaders with considerable acumen in dealing with the dominant society. When the constitutional convention ended on November 18, 1944, Native Americans had successfully created a new political voice that would eventually echo throughout the chambers of Congress and elsewhere. Hotel lobbies and annual conventions now replaced the council fires of past generations. The mood of the postwar nation and Cold War forces would quickly test the strength of the shared blanket of the NCAI and challenge the new Indian political voice.

3. PRISONERS IN THE HOMELAND

We [Indians] are forgotten men in the land of plenty.
We are prisoners in the land of our birth.

ROBERT YELLOWTAIL, 1948

The end of World War II ushered in a new era for most Americans. In the postwar years the nation witnessed a period of unmatched economic growth. Most minorities and lower-income groups, however, failed to share in the new prosperity. Indian people had benefited economically from the war, but they were still a significantly disadvantaged group. Moreover, Indians had loyally supported the war, both on the battlefield and on the home front. Out of that experience came increased expectations for an end to social, economic, and political discrimination. After fighting against tyranny in Europe and the Pacific, Indians faced second-class status as a submerged minority at home. They continued to encounter discrimination in employment, housing, schools, voting, land rights, and in other areas. "We [Indians] are forgotten men in a land of plenty," former Crow superintendent and the NCAI member Robert Yellowtail stated in 1948. "We are prisoners in the land of our birth."[1]

After the war, strong conservative forces prevented drastic reforms in the postwar years and threatened to reverse earlier Indian New Deal efforts. Yet the shifts in postwar liberalism and the drift in the BIA failed to slow the growth of the NCAI. Instead of destroying the emerging organization, the Cold War atmosphere had the opposite effect. It served as a catalyst to help justify the role of the NCAI as a guardian of the Indian people in uncertain times. By the time the NCAI held its second annual convention in Browning, Montana, in

October 1945, membership had risen from eighty to more than three hundred.[2] Satisfied with the progress of the NCAI over the past year, the Blackfeet and Flathead tribes, which hosted the Browning convention, paid the travel costs of the executive council.[3] Congress also welcomed and praised the new Indian voice in postwar Washington DC.[4] The NCAI leadership quickly learned that it was one thing to request Indian participation and sovereignty and another to receive it. Within months following the constitutional convention, the newly founded NCAI actively battled on several fronts to secure, protect, and expand Indian civil rights.

Harry S. Truman's sudden elevation to the presidency in 1945 caught both Truman and the nation by surprise. The president tried both to preserve and to expand the New Deal reforms. The spirit of the times, however, was not reformist. Instead, a conservative movement in Congress backed a reduction in the power of the federal government and its welfare programs, and the end the new chief executive was unable to push the liberal reform tradition into new areas such as Indian housing, health care, and education. Although Truman largely succeeded in preserving and consolidating the New Deal, he failed to persuade Congress to adopt significant parts of his Fair Deal.

Truman made the federal protection of civil rights an ingredient of his reform agenda. He established the first President's Committee on Civil Rights to study race relations. The committee's report, *To Secure These Rights,* called for an end to racial discrimination and segregation of nonwhites from American life. Truman's administration, however, proved unable to push major civil rights reforms. When the persistent racial discrimination and segregation failed to disappear, some ethnic groups devised new tactics and organizations to raise the consciousness of white America. African Americans turned to the judicial system and later resorted to demonstrative protests. Unlike other ethnic groups, Native Americans have a unique, albeit contradictory, relationship in American society. An unusual legislative, judicial, and treaty arrangement treats Indians as both sovereign nations and wards of the government. Indians in the Truman years, representing a much smaller minority than African Americans, turned to ethnic and political mobilization to protect their civil rights and distinctive status.

The Cold War's political and social climate proved decisive. National obsessions with communism sapped the strength of liberalism as global concerns took center stage. Truman's priorities, especially after 1948, favored funding the struggle against the communist menace rather than spending for social reform. Moreover, a bipartisan conservative coalition of northern Republicans and southern Democrats, the same forces that hampered the New Deal after 1938, retained control of Congress. Despite democratic congressional majorities in the 1948 elections, the coalition withstood any drastic new departures in domestic policy. In addition, anticultural pluralism and national concerns over nonconformity and disloyalty undermined liberal efforts to alter the status quo. The nature of the fight against communism contributed to the second Red Scare. Politicians warned Americans that communism silently and secretly destroyed a country from within. Unhinged by fear, millions of Americans enlisted in a postwar crusade that equated dissent with disloyalty. With the outbreak of the Korean conflict in 1950, the United States committed itself to waging a global contest against communism with arms and words.[5]

Postwar shifts in liberalism also affected Indian affairs. When John Collier resigned as Indian commissioner in 1945, the BIA lost much of its direction and entered a period of drift. Although the NCAI urged the appointment of an Indian as commissioner following Collier's resignation, Franklin D. Roosevelt selected William A. Brophy, a non-Indian.[6] Brophy carried on the Indian New Deal but with much less enthusiasm than his predecessor. During confirmation hearings Brophy pledged to observe congressional edicts.[7] Other staff changes produced similar effects. Secretary of Interior Harold L. Ickes, a staunch champion of Collier's policies, resigned in early 1946 over a Truman appointment.[8] Julius Krug, his successor, had little knowledge of Indian affairs and less zeal for diversity, cultural pluralism, and liberal reforms than Ickes. Brophy's extended illness also prevented him from fulfilling his duties from late 1946 to 1948. William Zimmerman Jr., assistant commissioner, acted in Brophy's place, but he failed to protect Indian New Deal gains from being reversed by powerful non-Indian interest groups.

Acting Commissioner Zimmerman's appearance before the Senate Committee on Civil Service in 1947 provided Congress a model for withdrawal legislation. Testifying under court order, Zimmerman responded to the Senate subcommittee demands for a reduction in BIA expenses by offering a plan that divided reservations into three categories. The first group (the Flatheads, Klamaths, Menominees, Osages, the Iroquois of New York, the Potawatomis of Kansas, several California groups, and conditionally, Turtle Mountain), Zimmerman implied, was ready for an immediate end of federal services. The second group of reservations required an additional ten years of BIA supervision, and a third group needed to remain under federal control indefinitely. Zimmerman proposed several criteria for withdrawal legislation: degree of acculturation, economic readiness, willingness to assume independence, and states' eagerness and ability to provide needed services. Zimmerman even submitted three draft bills for Klamath, Osage, and Menominee withdrawal.

Unfortunately, Zimmerman had played an unintentional but important role in the move toward termination. He had presented conservatives with a basis for a "phased approach" to withdrawal. He later recognized his mistake, but conservatives were more concerned with cutting BIA expenditures than revising Zimmerman's plan. Following Zimmerman's testimony, a legislative consensus emerged that favored a selective withdrawal for individual tribes. The "phased approach" became the cornerstone of the termination policies of the Eisenhower administration.[9]

The anticommunist spirit of postwar America demanded conformity and tended to discourage the preservation of Indian culture and the communal lifestyle of Indians. Opponents of Collier's policies had always charged that the Indian Reorganization Act was communistic. In an era of Cold War tensions, policymakers could ill-afford to ignore such accusations.[10] Postwar liberalism endorsed the persistent federal-policy theme of Indian assimilation into the mainstream of American society. Conservative demands to force Indians to conform and assimilate promoted a reduced federal role in Indian affairs and an end to federal Indian services through Zimmerman's plan.[11]

Understanding the obvious threat to Indian sovereignty and culture, the newly founded NCAI used all its talents to protect the distinct Indian lifestyle. Far ahead of their time, and unique to the period, NCAI leadership took immediate steps to promote female officers within its ranks. Gender discrimination during the postwar period frequently denied women positions of political leadership and an equal role in the political process. Recognizing the important role that Native American women have often played in tribal politics, NCAI delegates at the Montana convention in 1945 adopted a resolution to elect annually at least one woman to the executive council.[12] That important decision repeatedly paid dividends as time went by, for some of the most significant leaders of the NCAI were women from the ranks of the council.

One such woman was Ruth Muskrat Bronson, an Oklahoma Cherokee and former BIA education official. One month after the constitutional convention, the executive council named Bronson their volunteer secretary. Over the next several years Bronson served as executive secretary, editor of the NCAI *Washington Bulletin,* lobbyist, and jack-of-all-trades. Her tireless efforts, usually without pay, kept the organization afloat in its initial years.[13]

Substantial funding from the Robert Marshall Civil Liberties Trust allowed Bronson to open a Washington DC office to provide legal aid to tribes and serve as a center for lobbying activities.[14] Until the NCAI could establish its own office, she worked out of her Georgetown home. A few years later the NCAI opened its first permanent office in Dupont Circle nearer downtown Washington.[15] Within months after its inception, Bronson and other NCAI leaders testified in both houses of Congress, held regular meetings with the Bureau, met with other reform organizations, and contacted the White House.[16] The lobbying campaigns followed the same general theme. In Bronson's words, the Indians wanted "self-determination."[17] The NCAI urged policy-makers to avoid making changes that affected Indians without first consulting their representatives.

The earliest campaigns for Indian rights by the NCAI, however, centered not on images and symbolism but on land issues. In early 1945 the NCAI provided legal aid to the Northwestern Bands of Shoshone Indians in their land suit against the federal government. After a decade and a half of litigation, the Court of Claims concluded that the tribe relinquished title to millions of acres during treaty negotiations. When the NCAI intervened for the Shoshones, the tribe lost a close appeal in the Supreme Court. James Curry, the general counsel of the NCAI, filed an *amicus curiae* brief for a rehearing. The Supreme Court refused to rehear the case since the Shoshones had failed to prove legal title to the land to the court's satisfaction.[18]

This setback merely fueled the desire of the NCAI for a more efficient means to adjudicate Indian land claims. Following the Shoshone decision, the NCAI turned toward creating an Indian claims commission. The idea for such a commission, however, was not new. In the nineteenth century many tribes had land claims against the United States. The unsolved claims continued to embitter federal-Indian relations. Most of the grievances grew out of treaties or other unfulfilled federal contracts. In 1855 Congress created the Court of Claims for citizens to file suits. Although not citizens, some tribes gained access to the new court between 1855 and 1863. In 1863, however, Congress revoked this right to adjudicate claims with Indian tribes after some tribes sided with the Confederacy during the Civil War. Legislation involving the Choctaws and other tribes in 1881 permitted tribes once again to sue before the Court of Claims through passage of separate jurisdiction acts.[19] The process pleased no one because each individual claim was agonizingly slow and settlement uncertain. Each suit placed a heavy load on Congress, federal administrators, justice officials, and the tribes and their attorneys. Moreover, from 1881 to 1946, only 35 of the 219 claims filed with the Court of Claims won awards.

The inability of the court to speed up action on the claims created the need for more efficient procedures. In 1928 the influential Meriam Report criticized the existing method of resolving Indian claims. Instead of a court to process claims, the report recommended an independent commission. Significant effort to establish a commission was expended during Collier's administration. Bureau administrators, Indians, and others hoped that a commission would be more liberal in legal interpretations than the court had been. Despite Bureau support, several bills to create a claims commission during the period died in Congress.

The depression years and World War II sidetracked legislators from the claims issue until 1945. Since its inception the NCAI had made settlement of claims a top priority. Early in 1945 the legal department of the NCAI drafted a claims commission bill that Oklahoma congressman William G. Stigler, himself part Choctaw, introduced to the house as H.R. 1198. A three-member commission was appointed by the president to oversee the claims process. The bill required at least one member of the commission to be an enrolled Indian, that is, an Indian officially recognized and given a tribal I.D. number during the Dawes period. Tribes could select attorneys of their choice and appeal decisions to the Supreme Court.[20]

Henry M. Jackson, a Democrat who chaired the House Indian Affairs Committee, held hearings over a four-month period.[21] Congressman Stigler and Karl E. Mundt, a Republican from South Dakota, also served on the committee. Many leaders from the NCAI testified in support of Stigler's claims commission bill at the hearings. During the proceedings NCAI members Ben Dwight, attorney for the Choctaw, W. W. Short, president of the Choctaw and Chickasaw Confederation, Dan Madrano, secretary, and others called on the federal government to keep its treaty promises, protect Indian sovereignty, and fulfill its obligations regarding the unsettled claims.[22]

From these hearings came a revised bill that was introduced by Jackson before the House of Representatives in October 1945 as H.R. 4497. Importantly, House committee members dropped from the measure the requirement that an Indian serve on the commission. By this deletion, committee members lost a historic opportunity to change drastically the tribunal that heard Indian grievances. Despite this significant exclusion, NCAI leadership championed the bill as a just means to preserve treaty rights and other agreements. Prior to the bill's being placed on the house calendar for a vote, the NCAI wrote thousands of letters to politicians, reform organizations, and administrators seeking support for the measure. The executive council also held three conferences in Washington DC to champion the legislation's passage. Gov. Robert S. Kerr of Oklahoma and the Federated Women's Clubs of America strongly supported the NCAI in their struggle. Lobbying efforts of the NCAI ensured passage of the significant new measure. In late spring 1946, House members forwarded the claims bill to the Senate for approval.[23]

H.R. 4497 became law in August 13, 1946. The new Indian Claims Commission Act provided for a three-man commission to hear lawsuits, and it gave tribes five years to file claims.[24] Congress endorsed the law as a means to usher in a new era in Indian affairs. Napoleon B. Johnson, president of NCAI, D'Arcy McNickle, and other prominent founders of the NCAI visited the White House for the signing of the bill into law by President Truman.[25]

Ironically, legislators, bureaucrats, the NCAI, reformers, and others all claimed victory for the new measure but for diametrically opposite reasons. Pres. Napoleon B. Johnson called the Claims Commission Act the "most important, equitable, and constructive Indian law ever passed by Congress." Reformers also praised the act as a reward for Indian contributions in World War II.[26] For the NCAI, the new law maintained treaty rights and tribal sovereignty. White policymakers, on the other hand, supported the act as a means to hasten assimilation. Advancing Indians down the path of assimilation required the adjudication of long-standing tribal claims. Policymakers also hoped final settlements would reduce the number of entitlements going to Indian groups and lessen their dependence on the federal government. This new legislation served as a harbinger of a dangerous Indian policy looming on the horizon. While on the one hand it corrected centuries of injustice, it also provided for resolution of Indian claims as a means toward ending federal responsibility to the Indian population.

Unfortunately, the tragic experience of the Unitah and Ouray bands of Ute Indians in Utah illustrates the polarized views held by proponents of the new act over the act's intent. In July 1950 the new commission awarded the Utes $18 million for unresolved claims. Shortly after the settlement was reached, disagreements erupted between full-blood and mixed-blood members of the bands over how best to spend the proceeds. Sen. Arthur Watkins of Utah and Ernest Wilkinson, the Ute claims attorney, bullied the Unitah bands into accepting their version of Indian self-determination. Watkins insisted that the Utes not use their cash settlement to develop tribal resources on a dated reservation system. Instead, he used his influence as chair of the Indian Affairs Subcommittee to withhold claims money until the Utes accepted termination. Pressured by these outside sources, the Ute tribe permanently divided itself into full-bloods who retained membership in the tribe and mixed-bloods who became "sacrificial lambs" to the termination movement. Here, Watkins's and Wilkenson's perceptions of the role of the claims commission replaced the Indians' vision of the new act.[27]

Resolving complex native land disputes and protecting tribal groups from special interest groups had not been simply a matter of signing new legislation. Some Indian litigation exceeded the limited powers of the newly created commission. Few places in the postwar period tested the commission's restricted authority more than Alaska. Led by Ruth Bronson and Jim Curry, the NCAI cooperated with the Alaska Native Brotherhood in 1946–47 to protect fishing, trapping, and timber rights of Alaska natives. Alaska natives, who included American Indians, Eskimos, Inuits, and Aleuts, largely remained outside the concern of federal policies and programs. These natives generally organized socially into villages and small communities. Unlike Indians of the United States, policymakers seldom subjected Alaska natives to treaties, reservations, and federal attempts at forced assimilation.

Not until the immediate postwar years did significant changes occur to warrant concern over recognition of Alaska native rights. The threat to Alaska native interests came with the intensified attempts to exploit Alaska's abundant natural resources. Exploration and development of oil, gas, timber, commercial fishing, and other natural resources in the postwar period increased non-Indian settlement and non-Indian demands for statehood for the territory. Several attempts, including salmon-trap legislation sponsored by nonnative fisheries, to usurp Indian land and offshore rights failed to pass Congress. As the movement for statehood grew, the federal government neglected its obligation to protect the rights of Alaska natives.

Few economic developments in Alaska threatened native rights in the territory more than the Tongass Timber Act of 1947. When Russia sold Alaska to the United States in 1867, the treaty failed to define aboriginal occupancy and possessory rights. The Organic Act of 1884, which created the territorial government of Alaska, also did not clarify the Indians' right to unrestricted possession, occupancy, or use of the land. Taking advantage of the murky Indian titles, in 1909 Congress established the Tongass National Forest, appropriating nearly sixteen million acres of land claimed by the southeastern Alaska natives. During the next twenty-five years, the Tlingit and Haida Indians charged that the Forestry Service and timber interests violated their land rights. The Indian Reorganization Act of 1934 and its companion, the Alaska Reorganization Act of 1936, allowed the secretary of interior to set aside reservations to protect Indian land. Strong opposition from fishing, timber, and mineral interests slowed efforts to create the reservations. Secretary of Interior Harold Ickes, however, failed to fulfill the government's obligations to the natives. In 1944–45, the Department of Interior held hearings in Hydaburg, Kake, and Klawock, Alaska, to decide aboriginal possessory rights. Despite the hearings, the secretary of interior by 1947 still had not established Indian boundaries. Instead, pulp companies lobbied Congress to pass the Tongass Timber Bill. The legislation permitted a consortium of West Coast newspaper publishers access to Indian timber in Tongass Forest for a paper-pulp mill.[28]

The Tongass Timber Bill (H.R. 205) of 1946 authorized the secretaries of agriculture and interior to sell land and timber to corporate interests in the Tongass National Forest without Indian consent. In essence, the bill allowed Congress authority to extinguish native title. Revenues from the sale of the timber were to be placed in escrow until the Indians could prove absolute title to the land. The Tongass Timber Bill attracted many white supporters. Besides lumber interests and chambers of commerce, Alaska's territorial governor Ernest Gruening, territorial delegate E. L. Bartlett, and Undersecretary of the Interior Oscar Chapman felt that no "unnecessary obstacles," meaning Indian rights, should stand in the way of territorial economic development. Assistant Interior Secretary Warner W. Gardner, the Department of Agriculture, and the Justice Department supported the measure to promote the pulp industry in southeastern Alaska. Aboriginal titles, however, represented a major obstacle to their plan. Although the Tongass Timber Bill provided corporate interests with congressional protection, the pulp companies feared the risks of development with the strong prospect of further litigation.[29]

The Alaska natives in 1946 continued correctly to believe that they had aboriginal title to the Tongass National Forest. Debates in southeastern Alaska centered on discussions over the creation of three reservations in Hydaburg, Barrow, and Shungnak. Whites in the territory generally opposed the reservations on the grounds that they delayed native assimilation into the mainstream society and impeded economic development in the region. Indians generally supported the reservations as a means to establish clear boundaries to Indian lands. Some NCAI leaders also expressed concern that failure to protect Alaska natives' lands through reservations threatened to establish a dangerous precedent for United States Indians.[30]

The NCAI became involved in the struggle over the Tongass National Forest in late 1946. The southeastern Alaska natives, who were members of the NCAI, called on their organization for support. In October 1946 Ruth Bronson visited southeastern Alaska with financial support from the American Civil Liberties Union (ACLU) to work out a strategy for the defense of Indian rights.[31] At the request of the

Alaska natives, James E. Curry, who was legal counsel for both NCAI and the Alaska Native Brotherhood, visited southeastern Alaska to help the Tlingit and Haida Indians in filing land claims.

As the Tongass Timber Bill drew closer to passage, the NCAI tried to defeat the measure. Delegates at the fourth annual NCAI convention, held in Albuquerque, New Mexico, in 1947, called for the federal government to stop the sale of Indian lands and timber and set aside reservations. Convention resolutions also protested non-Indian fishing and packing firms operating on Indian lands. Bronson and her associates tried to make the public more aware of the crisis in Alaska. In several articles Bronson called the new legislation "an American version of the Nuremberg laws. . . . It is racial seizure of property for private interests," she claimed, "which should be viewed with alarm by all American citizens." Recalling the experiences of Indians in the United States, she argued that American national honor was again at stake. Concerned about the potential for another land run such as in Oklahoma in 1907, NCAI member Ben Dwight warned that "special interests" were again trying to steal Indian land. Representatives of the four largest native villages in southeastern Alaska then traveled to Washington DC in the summer of 1947 to confer with Bronson, Curry, and Napoleon B. Johnson in an attempt to defeat the bill. Curry and the NCAI refused to accept counterproposals. Speaking on the Indians' behalf, he rejected a compromise by Secretary Krug to pay natives 10 percent of the proceeds from the sale of timber if they relinquished possessory rights.[32]

Despite the untiring efforts of Curry, the NCAI, and reform allies on behalf of the Alaska natives, the bill passed in the closing session of the 1947 Congress. The bill became Public Law 385.[33] The leaders of the NCAI placed much of the blame for the passage of the bill into law on Secretary of Interior Krug, whom they believed had sold out Indian interests to the large timber corporations. In a draft copy of the *Washington Bulletin* Bronson denounced Krug as "a faithless guardian bent on plundering his ward's estate. . . . The dangers of a teapot dome," she further argued, "did not pass away with the removal from office of Albert B. Fall."[34]

Numerous reform groups and individuals had joined the Alaska natives and the NCAI in their unsuccessful bid to stop the timber bill. They included several church organizations, the ACLU, the AAIA, the IRA, and the General Federation of Women's Clubs.[35] The native Alaskans were not without supporters in the BIA and the Department of Interior. William Warne, assistant secretary of interior, and William Brophy, Indian commissioner, opposed the forfeiture of lands without Indian consent and compensation. Brophy's prolonged illness and Warne's lone voice could not prevent passage of the bill.[36] Speaking for the NCAI, Bronson also thanked former Secretary of Interior Harold L. Ickes for his efforts to champion native Alaskan land rights.[37]

Although the Tongass Timber Act authorized the sale of Indian timber in the region, the measure left the question of setting aside reservation lands unresolved. According to the Alaska Reorganization Act of 1936, the secretary of interior still had authority to create reservations in the Tongass region. Special interest groups and politicians led a movement to repeal the 1936 act. In 1948 Nebraska senator Hugh Butler, chairman of the Public Lands Committee, Albert A. Grorud, clerk of the Senate subcommittee on Indian Affairs, Utah senator Arthur Watkins, and Montana congressman Wesley D'Ewart proposed legislation (S.J. 162 and H.R. 269) to repeal the 1936 act authorizing the secretary of interior to create reservations. The NCAI, the Alaska Native Service, the BIA, and the Department of Interior opposed the bill. In Senate hearings proponents of the bill attempted to harass and bully Curry and Bronson. Both stood firm. Following the hearings, the critics of the measure defeated Butler's bill.[38]

Secretary Krug sought options to solve the reservation impasse. He appointed a National Advisory Committee on Indian Affairs to advise him and officials of the BIA on policies relating to Indians. Included on the ten-member committee were two members of the NCAI, Bronson and Louis R. Bruce. Bronson, who served as secretary for the committee, requested that any resolutions passed by the Advisory Committee not be binding to the organizations represented by the participants.[39] Without consulting the committee in the winter of

1948–49, Krug prepared to sponsor the Krug Indian Land Confiscation Bill to extinguish all native land claims in Alaska. He suggested that if Indians relinquished claims to the land, in return the government would provide sufficient land for them to live on. Opposition by the NCAI and other reform groups and his own Advisory Committee on Indian Affairs forced him to drop the measure.[40] On November 30, 1949, his last day in office, Krug finally signed the order that created the three reservations in Hydaburg, Barrow, and Shungnak.[41]

Operation of the first pulp mill did not begin until 1954. Policymakers failed to resolve the issue fully until the early 1970s. In 1971 Congress took another step toward resolving native land claims through passage of the Alaska Native Claims Settlement Act. The law provided natives legal title to forty million acres and to nearly $1 billion in compensation. The act also authorized the creation of twelve regional economic corporations and numerous village corporations. In exchange, the natives dropped all claims and forfeited most of the reserves.[42]

While taking a stand in Alaska, NCAI leaders learned important lessons about unity and self-determination. Speaking at the 1948 NCAI Convention in Denver, Curry commended the delegates for their efforts to protect Indian rights. Their courageous efforts on behalf of Alaska's natives reminded him of the Sinn Feiners, who had fought for freedom in Ireland; the Jews, who preserved their homeland in Israel; and the farmers who protested in the United States to defend their livelihood.[43] Delegates would later use the lessons learned during the struggle over Alaskan rights in the struggle to defeat the coercive termination policy of the next decade.

In the immediate postwar years federal construction of new dams in the West created still another threat to Indian sovereignty, land resources, and the NCAI. New dams constructed in the Northwest after the war did not involve major relocations of Indians, but dams built on the upper Missouri River threatened six reservations. After severe flooding on the Missouri River in spring 1943, Col. Lewis A. Pick of the Army Corps of Engineers designed a plan for flood prevention. The Bureau of Reclamation quickly announced its own proposal.

While officials debated the merits of both plans, Pick conducted negotiations with William Glenn Sloan of the Department of Reclamation in October 1944, and the two concluded the infamous Pick-
Sloan Plan. Under the proposal, the corps would construct levies and
five major dams below Sioux Falls, and reclamation would build
smaller dams in the upper basin. Congress approved the Pick-Sloan
Plan in 1944.[44]

The Pick-Sloan Plan affected twenty-three Indian reservations.
Although some reservations benefited from it, the plan also hurt
tribal communities on the Missouri River and in the Dakotas. The
Indians at Fort Berthold in North Dakota dealt with the corps first
and learned important lessons in negotiations. The Garrison Dam
flooded the most valuable part of the Fort Berthold Reservation. The
relocation of the Three Affiliated Tribes (Arikara, Hidatsa, and Man-
dan) caused by the reservoir threatened to disrupt life severely on the
reservation. In addition, relocation upset established communal and
kinship ties and jeopardized strong attachments to land and sacred
areas.[45]

Although the Three Affiliated Tribes protested construction of the
Garrison Dam, the corps went ahead with the preliminary work at
Fort Berthold. Corps engineers proposed to move the reservation to
another site on lands "comparable in quality and sufficient in area" as
compensation for flooded lands. On May 25, 1946, the tribal business
council of the Three Affiliated Tribes offered an alternate site for the
dam near the northern boundary of the reservation. The corps de-
clined the proposal. In December 1946 the corps offered substitute
lands several miles below the proposed dam site.[46]

Representatives from Fort Berthold and the NCAI participated in
hearings in Washington DC in mid-December to negotiate a settlement. James Curry, the NCAI general counsel, recommended that the
tribes reject the substitute lands. After the Fort Berthold council rejected the proposal, the only option was a monetary settlement for
land flooded by the dam. An assertive corps marred negotiations
with the council and dictated events. The BIA also lacked the motivation and political influence to safeguard Indian needs. In 1948 leaders

from the Three Affiliated Tribes accepted a cash settlement, and in 1950 Congress appropriated $7.5 million as compensation for the flooded lands.[47] Francis Horn, Curry's law associate, recalled years later that the NCAI and the Three Affiliated Tribes took a severe beating in negotiations with the more experienced and assertive corps.[48] The NCAI and Sioux leaders benefited from Fort Berthold's experiences with the corps. In later negotiations involving Sioux reservations they maneuvered more lucrative settlements.

Settling land claims represented the first of many contests fought by the NCAI over Indian civil rights in the postwar era. The heavily Indian-populated states of Arizona and New Mexico often became the sites of other clashes. Even after passage of the Indian Citizenship Act of 1924, Arizona and New Mexico in 1945 refused to permit Indians the right to vote. New Mexico denied the ballot to Indians because they were "not taxed." In Arizona, state officials disenfranchised Indians because of their status as federal wards.[49] In the prewar years Bureau officials questioned the legality of voter discrimination in these holdout states. The war, however, interrupted any further action.

When the war was over, the NCAI, other Indian reform organizations, and federal administrators launched an aggressive crusade to enforce Indian voting rights in both Arizona and New Mexico. Their campaign efforts had an almost immediate impact. In 1948 in New Mexico a Pueblo veteran tested the state's constitution that withheld the ballot. Led by noted attorney on Indian affairs Felix Cohen and general counsel James E. Curry of the NCAI, a special panel of federal judges gathered in Santa Fe in July 1948 ruled that the New Mexico constitution violated the federal constitution.

The Arizona Supreme Court reversed earlier decisions and legalized Indian voting. In 1948 a Mohave-Apache Indian veteran appealed to the state court for the right to vote. The NCAI championed the petition by filing *amicus curiae* briefs for him, and Curry represented the Indian plaintiff.[50] To bring pressure to bear on Arizona officials, the NCAI and the ACLU also sponsored another case involving Indians from the San Carlos and Fort Apache Reservations in the

U.S. district court in Phoenix.[51] In August 1948 the Arizona Supreme Court extended the franchise to Arizona Indians by decreeing that they were not wards or dependents because only their property was under guardianship. Both decisions represented significant victories for Indians. Attorneys for the NCAI called the verdicts a "smashing victory for civil rights of our oldest minority."[52]

While Indian voting rights represented a significant step toward equality, the Navajos and Hopis in New Mexico and Arizona and the NCAI faced a more serious crisis. During the New Deal, federal officials destroyed large numbers of Navajo livestock to prevent soil erosion. Destroying the stock weakened Navajo subsistence and contributed to a state of dependency.[53] Postwar unemployment and overpopulation on the two reservations also developed after workers and veterans returned from the war. Blizzards further strained resources when insufferable weather pounded the region in the winter of 1947–48. Lacking public assistance from state agencies, the Navajos' impoverished economic condition left the tribe with an uncertain future.

News reports about the Indians' plight led to private and federal humanitarian efforts. As a result, the Department of Interior faced pressure to develop a long-term recovery program. Department officials focused most of their attention on the desperate plight of the Navajos. Studies revealed that more than one-third of Navajo families earned an annual income of less than $750. The reservation lacked sufficient health care and educational facilities as well as an adequate economic infrastructure.[54]

By 1947 the NCAI became heavily involved in the Navajo crisis. In the early months of that year, other reformers asked the NCAI to participate in the Coordinating Committee on Indian Affairs, a reform coalition consisting of the ACLU, the AAIA, the IRA, the General Federation of Women's Clubs, the Home Mission Council, and the New Mexico Association on Indian Affairs. The committee met to promote Navajo irrigation, relief, health, and education rights.[55] Indian and non-Indian reformers charged that the federal government had failed to fulfill its treaty obligations to the Navajos.

In particular, these critics focused on Article vi of the Treaty of 1868, which promised a teacher and a school per thirty Navajo children between the ages of six and sixteen. Instead, by 1946 the government provided educational facilities for only 25 percent of all Navajo children. Lack of formal education prohibited the Indians from competing in the workplace.[56] "The Navajo is not a museum piece," Elma Smith, a Navajo teacher, argued. "He should be given his liberty from the prisoner of war status he has held 80 years after the final treaty was signed."[57]

Meeting in convention in Santa Fe in December 1947, NCAI delegates heard Navajo chairman Sam Ahkeah blame the BIA for the conditions of the Navajos. During the conference Johnson and Bronson met with Ahkeah in the hotel lobby to discuss the Navajo plight and strategies to remedy it. Following the conversation, Elizabeth Chief, a Native American social worker from Shiprock, New Mexico, visited nearby hogans to observe firsthand the deplorable conditions. Not surprisingly, delegates in the closing session of the convention passed a resolution to seek a Navajo relief and rehabilitation program.[58]

Inspired by Truman's Marshall Plan to provide relief to Europe, Secretary of Interior Julius Krug in 1948 proposed the basis of the Navajo-Hopi Rehabilitation Bill. Twin bills introduced in both houses in early 1949 proposed a ten-year program, costing $88 million, to attempt to ease the poverty. NCAI leadership worked diligently to pass the relief measure. Their efforts drew the attention of the son of a noted Oklahoma humorist and humanitarian, Will Rogers Jr. Impressed by the NCAI, he testified for the organization in Congress in favor of the legislation.[59] Not new to Indian affairs, Rogers, himself part Cherokee Indian, established the American Citizens League in Los Angeles to help urban Indians. Speaking to the Denver delegates in 1948, he promoted the relief bill as a step toward Indian self-determination. Treating Indians with "dignity and honor and fairness," he said, requires Indian participation in the legislation process.[60]

Passage of the measure had appeared certain, but two obstacles had to be dealt with. The first hurdle involved the question of Indians' eligibility for social security benefits in Arizona and New Mexico. The issue centered not around retirement benefits, but aid for the elderly, dependent children, and the disabled. Although federal aid supported such programs, individual states decided eligibility. As with voting rights, both Arizona and New Mexico denied Indian participation in the program. Ruth Bronson and NCAI attorneys worked closely with the Social Security Administration in 1947 to file a discrimination suit against both states. They also threatened to withhold federal funding from Arizona and New Mexico until they complied with federal law. Judges scheduled the lawsuit in the District Court of the District of Columbia.

Before the case went to court in 1949, officials from both states, the Federal Security Administration, and the Bureau met privately in Santa Fe to resolve the situation. While the NCAI requested participation in the meetings, negotiators denied them access. Hoping for a successful outcome to the meetings, the NCAI began instructing Indians in both states on how to file social security applications. Under a gentleman's agreement, all parties at the private discussions reached a compromise. The Department of Interior agreed to assume the states' share of the cost to extend social security benefits to Indians. The Department of Interior also agreed to boost the federal share of social security payments from the standard 60 percent to more than 90 percent in Arizona and New Mexico. The two states maintained that they could not afford public assistance to the Indians. The NCAI, however, rejected this argument as racial discrimination. Federal officials resented the additional expense but accepted it to protect passage of the rehabilitation bill.[61]

Just as federal proponents of the measure reached an important compromise over the social security question, another serious controversy surfaced. In May 1945 Representative Antonio M. Fernandez of New Mexico proposed an amendment to section nine of the rehabilitation bill. He wanted to place both the Navajo and Hopi Reservations under state civil and criminal jurisdiction. Sensing an opportunity to limit federal reimbursement in New Mexico and Arizona, Senate members also added a rider to the bill in late summer 1949.

The rider reduced remuneration to 80 percent of the normal share of public assistance payments to Indians. Moreover, it represented a growing movement to transfer federal responsibilities of the tribes to the states. While some tribes welcomed state jurisdiction, others believed it violated treaty rights and sovereignty.

The amendments aroused immediate protests from the NCAI and other critics. Even though the bill attempted to provide relief to both tribes, the NCAI felt that Fernandez's amendment would set a dangerous precedent. It would uniformly provide for the transfer of services to states without Indian consent. In essence, it would destroy tribal integrity and place Indians at the mercy of states unprepared or unwilling to assume these services. Bronson called the rider "a piece of faithless political manipulation." She feared that state jurisdiction threatened tribal sovereignties, treaty protections, and legal immunities.[62] Former commissioner John Collier also ridiculed Arizona and New Mexico for their refusal to pay their share of public assistance costs. He further warned that the bill would lead to forced assimilation.[63]

Despite these objections to the amendments, Secretary of the Interior Krug submitted the revised bill to Congress in 1949. The measure passed quickly through both houses. After the bill cleared Congress, the NCAI in early October sent a telegram to President Truman, urging him not to sign the amended measure into law.[64] On October 17, 1949, Truman vetoed the bill. The president supported the rehabilitation provisions but disapproved of the amendments allowing state jurisdiction over the reservations. Truman, responding to the opposition of the Navajo tribal council, found that not only was section nine ambiguous, but it also conflicted with the principle of "self-determination in matters of local government." While the president believed that Indians should assimilate into the mainstream, he also thought that they should not be forced to do so through legal intervention. "It would be unjust and unwise," he said, "to compel them to abide by State laws written to fill other needs than theirs." In his veto message to the Senate, he vowed to support a bill without the section nine amendments.[65] When Congress omitted the Fernandez amendment, the bill passed in early 1950, and the rehabilitation programs improved the Hopi and Navajo economic conditions.[66]

The successful efforts of the NCAI to aid the Navajos did not come without a price. Scholar and former NCAI executive director Vine Deloria Jr. noted that the Navajos not only failed to recognize the significant efforts of the NCAI on their behalf but later snubbed the organization. Other tribes, according to Deloria, later regretted NCAI assistance to the Navajos. They felt the help detracted from other needed Indian causes. Yet, Deloria acknowledged, "Without the early work of NCAI there would probably be no Navajo tribe today."[67]

The postwar Hopi and Navajo crisis had other profound consequences on the NCAI. When the economic crisis on the Hopi and Navajo Reservations arose in 1948–49, the NCAI launched a fund-raising campaign to aid the stricken tribes. The position of the NCAI as a political organization, however, prevented it from enjoying tax-exempt advantages for its contributions. To bypass this problem, the NCAI created the NCAI Fund to serve as the tax-exempt, fund-raising arm of the organization.

The idea for the fund initially was that of Will Rogers Jr. In the summer of 1948 he went to Taos, New Mexico, to search for someone to help his wife, Collier, in establishing an organization to raise funds to aid the Navajos. While in Taos, Rogers meet John Rainer, a full-blood Taos Pueblo Indian and principal of a local junior high school. Rogers convinced Rainer, who later became the first salaried executive director of the NCAI, to move to California.[68] With the help of Collier Rogers and the future Indian commissioner, Robert Bennett, Rainer created the fund-raising organization. The venture succeeded only after they attached the organization to the NCAI.[69]

Rogers's upstart organization conveniently provided the NCAI with the tax-exempt status it desperately needed, and the organization incorporated the fund on April 29, 1949. Ruth Bronson, D'Arcy McNickle, and Napoleon B. Johnson served as the original trustees. The charter allowed the trustees authority to select future board members. It also broadly defined the purposes of the fund as an instrument to help the NCAI to aid Indians through "educational and charitable means."

On October 4, 1949, less than six months after incorporation, the trustees significantly reorganized the fund. In a tactical move they changed the name of the organization to Americans for the Restitution and Rightings of Old Wrongs (ARROW) and dropped the name of the parent organization from its title. Amending the charter, the trustees excluded any reference to the NCAI. Yet the NCAI retained complete control over ARROW. The new charter allowed the NCAI business committee authority to elect the trustees of ARROW and in 1950 its executive officer. Doubtless, NCAI attorneys Curry and Francis (Lopinsky) Horn recommended these steps to prevent IRS objections to the tax-exempt status of ARROW.[70]

From the beginning, ARROW and the NCAI suffered a stormy marriage. In the earliest days Ruth Bronson worried that Collier Rogers, a non-Indian, would not subordinate her interests in ARROW to the NCAI. "It was as if she had erected a gigantic stage on which she was to be the sole star and supporting cast," Bronson said. The executive director also expressed concern that the NCAI needed to divest itself from Rogers's leadership to compete effectively for limited funds with the newly created American Indian Fund of the AAIA.[71] Will Rogers, president of ARROW, finally relented to the pressure from NCAI leadership to remove his wife from directorship of ARROW. Like its parent organization the NCAI, it was considered essential that ARROW be an all-Indian organization. In the early years prominent Indian leaders such as John Rainer, Robert Bennett, and Louis R. Bruce Jr., later Richard M. Nixon's Indian commissioner, ably led ARROW. Through their leadership the fund-raising arm of NCAI sponsored many service and educational projects and successfully competed for grant money.

With conflicting goals, ARROW slowly began to usurp power from the NCAI. After 1953 the organization's board of directors moved to elect its own trustees rather than rely on the NCAI business committee. In effect this move permanently strained the legal relationship between the two organizations. No longer wanting to remain in the shadow of the NCAI, ARROW now sought more independence. In February 1954, however, NCAI Executive Director Helen Peterson admonished ARROW to be a "supporting arm" of the NCAI and "stand in the background." By 1957 tension between the NCAI and ARROW had strained relations beyond repair and caused the organizations to sever ties with one another. Within a short period NCAI created the NCAI Fund to replace ARROW.[72] Still, ARROW had served an invaluable role in financially sustaining the NCAI through its early troubled times.

The successful beginning of the NCAI inspired new Indian organizations. Within a short time following its inception, the NCAI welcomed several state and regional organizations as allies. Moreover, newly formed organizations such as the Arizona Inter-Tribal Council and the Affiliated Tribes of Northwest Indians proved fertile training grounds for later NCAI leadership. While the NCAI slowly matured and gathered strength, opponents of tribal rights, such as Nebraska senator Hugh Butler and Nevada senator George Malone, tried to discredit it by falsely linking it with communist groups. Curry later maintained that Comm. Dillon Myer inspired the attacks.[73]

An experienced administrator, Myer had directed several federal programs, including the War Relocation Authority (WRA). As director of the relocation program, Myer supervised the internment of 120,000 Japanese-Americans from the Pacific Coast into detention camps in the interior West. He used his authoritarian managerial style to run the camps in an atmosphere of forced compliance. When critics later attacked his methods, he characteristically remarked, "I never have been bothered when it comes to carrying on a job that I feel that I am responsible for."[74]

Myer approached his appointment as commissioner of Indian Affairs in 1950 with the attitude of a professional bureaucrat. Despite inexperience in Indian affairs, Myer would provide the policies, leadership, and personnel to diminish the role of the BIA and to compel Indians to accept a new lifestyle. With little consideration for previous practices, Myer expected Native Americans simply to cooperate with the new program. Showing his experience as an administrator, he immediately consolidated his power. Before accepting the appointment, he secured permission to report directly to Secretary of Interior Oscar Chapman, an old friend. This move allowed Myer to replace John Collier holdovers with his staff from the WRA. Converting branch directors in the Washington office into staff positions, he further strengthened his power. On the surface his reorganization seemed to decentralize the BIA and strengthen area offices, but in reality Myer rigidly controlled the area directors. Rejecting radical plans to abolish the BIA and to force Indians into assimilation, Myer helped carry out a program aimed at ending federal services to the Indians.[75]

The NCAI initially welcomed Myer's appointment and promised to support him. Speaking before the NCAI in Bellingham, Washington, in August 1950, Myer pledged Indian consultation and "Indian self-determination." At Bellingham, Myer failed to seek Indian input, however, in defining what self-determination meant in practice. To Bronson, Napoleon B. Johnson, and others, Indian self-determination differed greatly from Myer's use of the term. While many NCAI members tired of the federal regulations keeping them as wards, they did not want a complete end to federal supervision of Indian affairs. Instead, they desired federal trusteeship that included improvements in education, health care, and employment opportunities before the federal government relinquished its responsibilities. Their self-rule stressed tax-free land, Indian self-government protected by legal rights, economic development on reservations, and Indian consultation in the shaping of policies.[76]

Following the convention, Ruth Bronson asked Myer for a clarification of his remarks. "I believe it is your duty and obligation," she challenged him, "to determine the extent to which Indian people may participate in their government." Myer's actions later revealed that his view on Indian self-determination differed greatly from those of Bronson and many other Indians. Myer, like most Americans of the time, believed that democracy meant individualism but also conformity. To Bronson, "the faint hope" that Indians "might have some realistic voice in their own government became just another mockery."[77]

While verbally Myer acknowledged self-determination for Indians, his actions betrayed a different view. Events surrounding the NCAI and Mescalero Apache Reservation in New Mexico in 1949–50 served to prove that he was reluctant to allow Indians control in their own destiny. Pressures from the Mescalero Apache business committee forced the NCAI to intervene in a dispute between the committee and their superintendent, John Old Crow. The business committee charged Old Crow, part Cherokee and involved in the NCAI, with interfering in its right to self-government. Specifically, committee members accused the superintendent of misuse of funds and dictatorial methods. In September 1949 the committee passed a resolution demanding the removal of Old Crow from the reservation. Within days Old Crow fired the business committee. Some tribal members feared that Old Crow would interfere in free elections to create a new committee.

Following appeals from the business committee and Old Crow, the NCAI decided to investigate the committee's charges. In a resolution passed at Bellingham, Washington, in 1950, the NCAI established a special commission to look into the matter. After gathering considerable information on the dispute, the committee, comprised of Ruth Bronson, Ben Dwight, the NCAI business committee, and Lawrence Lindley, secretary of the IRA, published their findings in late 1950. The special committee found Old Crow guilty of violating the tribe's right to govern itself, and it demanded his removal. After conducting his own investigation, Myer refused to remove Old Crow.

Myer's actions greatly disturbed John Rainer, the new executive director. Using the incident as a rallying cry, Rainer sent copies of the NCAI investigative report to tribes across the country. While attacking both Old Crow and Myer, Rainer feared the incident set a dangerous precedent and threatened tribal sovereignty. Indeed, the event not only strained relations between the NCAI and Myer, but illustrated that the commissioner's rhetoric failed to match his actions. Myer had made his point: Indians did not run the BIA, he did. Unfortunately, as Rainer had predicted, the incident signaled the beginning of a pattern. In the months ahead, Myer's dictatorial style would challenge Indian legal rights, integrity, sovereignty, and the right to exist as separate cultural units.[78]

Following the stressful campaigns in the immediate postwar period, the NCAI underwent several changes in leadership. In 1949 Bronson's husband's ill health forced her to step down as executive director of the NCAI. Louis R. Bruce Jr., a Mohawk/Oglala, replaced Bronson. Outside commitments, however, forced Bruce to resign one year later. Thirty-seven-year-old John Rainer, secretary of the Board of Trustees of ARROW, replaced Bruce in 1950. In 1951 Bronson returned to her old position for a short stint. Her husband's persistent illness, however, forced a second resignation. In 1952 Frank George, a Nez Perce from the Colville Reservation, replaced Bronson. Bronson's contributions to NCAI in the founding years were immeasurable. She alone carried much of the burden for the early survival of the NCAI by performing countless duties. When she departed in 1952, she had helped the NCAI survive many battles. After leaving, she remained an activist for Indian rights until her death in the 1970s. Although several individuals filled the position of executive director of the NCAI, Napoleon B. Johnson was president from its inception until 1953.

Johnson, Bronson, and others had successfully promoted ethnic solidarity. In the fight to promote oneness, cultural symbols played an important role. The theme of the fourth annual convention of the NCAI at Santa Fe, New Mexico, in 1948 was vaguely reminiscent of Lincoln's famous 1858 "House Divided" speech. The convention theme stressed the significance of a united front: "One for All, All for One, United We Endure." In a symbolic gesture the officers of NCAI created a "Treaty of Peace, Friendship, and Mutual Assistance." The document served as a symbolic instrument to erase past tribal differences and to unite the tribes in a common future. Modeled after earlier federal Indian treaties, all member tribes of the NCAI signed the treaty.[79]

From the beginning the annual conventions used symbols such as the treaty to promote ethnic identity, not only to member tribes, but to the public as well. Convention planners arranged Indian dances, parades, Indian beauty pageants, and art displays, and sometimes constructed Indian villages at the host site.[80] The symbols changed over time, but they reflected efforts to mobilize membership through a shared past and to draw outside attention to the Indians' plight.

In these critical early years, the NCAI scored both significant victories and suffered serious defeats, but most importantly it survived. Addressing the St. Paul Convention in 1951, D'Arcy McNickle attributed the successful beginning of the NCAI to specific, practical, and reachable goals.[81] Before 1944 Indians had rarely presented a unified or formal position to Washington. After World War II they reached a new level of sophistication. Founders of NCAI learned to operate within the political and legal structure, using the same rules and techniques employed by policymakers in Washington. Through the NCAI many tribes used the political arena to confront pressures intended to usurp their resources and to cope with the exigencies of modern life. Although divided by tribal differences, the NCAI provided a means for Indians to take collective action on issues involving treaty rights, sovereignty, and civil rights.

Inconsistencies and drift in the federal treatment of Indians marked the immediate postwar period. Bronson best summarized the directionless Indian policy. "To search for the determined historical objective of the American Government in its dealings with the Indians since their pacification," she said, "seems to me like searching on a dark night for a black cat that isn't there."[82] The period of indecision in Indian affairs ended in 1950 with the appointment of Dillon Myer as Indian commissioner. Unfortunately for Bronson and other Indians, the black cat would get even darker.

4. ATTORNEY CONTRACTS
AND THE PRELUDE TO TERMINATION

If the Indian people henceforth are forced into Court defended only by attorneys selected by, and therefore subservient to, the Indian Bureau then we Indians will have lost our battle before we even start. RUTH BRONSON, 1950

On a cold January morning in 1952 nearly two hundred individuals crowded into a small chamber to participate in hearings at the Interior Department. "During the war we were regarded as men," Manuel Holcomb, Santa Clara Pueblo governor, testified, "but the war is over now, and the Commissioner thinks we are savages again." At issue, Commissioner Myer wanted stricter regulations to govern contracts between tribes and their lawyers. In the middle of the hearings, Popovi Da, former governor of the San Ildefonso Pueblos, yelled out a loud "war whoop." Da, a former worker on the Manhattan project, then tensely described Indian participation in construction of the bomb. His point: If federal officials had confidence in Indians to work on the war's greatest secret, then the BIA should now trust them to choose their own attorneys. The Indian-attorney contracts dispute threatened Indian civil rights and self-determination and hastened the drive for termination of federal guardianship over Indian tribes.[1]

Like other ethnic minorities, Native Americans have long battled legal discrimination. Indians, however, have a unique historical and judicial status. Following the historical decisions of Chief Justice John Marshall in the 1920s and 1930s, lawmakers treated Indian nations both as wards of the federal government and distinct political communities with inherent tribal sovereignty. Marshall's famous trilogy—*Johnson* v. *McIntosh* (1823), *Cherokee Nation* v. *Georgia* (1831), and *Worcester* v. *Georgia* (1832)—ruled that tribes were largely autonomous groups subject to federal jurisdiction but not state control. Following the decisions, proponents of Indian rights claimed that tribes retained all the powers not relinquished to the federal government by treaties, agreements, statutes, or the Constitution. In other words, these "reserved rights" (or residual powers) provided the basis for tribal governance on reservations.

Tribal authority, however, often rested on case law. Several precedent-setting cases adopted the view that Congress exercised plenary powers over Indian affairs and concluded that tribes possessed only limited authority. In *United States* v. *Kagama* (1886), *McBratney* v. *United States* (1882), and *Lone Wolf* v. *Hitchcock* (1903) the Supreme Court disregarded tribal authority in favor of congressional power. In effect, *Lone Wolf* suggested that Congress never acted in bad faith toward Indian tribes. Congress thus could unilaterally restrict or abolish tribal governments, dispose of Indian lands, and abrogate treaties and agreements. But without congressional action, or unless Congress delegated jurisdiction to the states, tribes in the twentieth century reserved the inherent right to govern themselves. In the many instances where Congress failed to provide specific guidance, the courts continue to this day to interpret questions of sovereignty.[2]

Throughout most of the history of federal-Indian relations, lawmakers have modified tribes' legal status to correspond with changing policy goals. Current law entitles Indians to both the full benefits of citizenship accorded all American citizens and the rights and limitations accorded tribal members. Without legal protection to safeguard those liberties, the non-Indian society often threatens Indian rights and sovereignty. As do all American citizens, Indians rely upon lawyers to assert their legal rights. For Indians, lawyers must also translate the theory of tribal sovereignty into practice. Reforms of the Indian Reorganization Act (IRA), however, not only established the tribes as legal entities, but empowered tribal councils with the right to freedom of counsel. Obtaining lawyers knowledgeable and interested in defending Indian rights, however, has been difficult.[3]

In the late 1940s, capitalizing on the IRA legal reforms, lawyer James E. Curry represented both the NCAI and numerous individual tribes. He brought to the NCAI not only valuable legal experience, but an ardent commitment to Indian rights. His dedication to Indian causes quickly drew recognition from the NCAI. "His skin may be that of a white man," NCAI chaplain Aaron Hancock said in 1948, "but we know that his heart is Indian."[4]

Curry first began his law practice in the Midwest, distanced from large Indian populations. After receiving his law degree from Loyola University in 1930, Curry practiced in Chicago. His employment in the BIA, Interior Department, and other government agencies after 1936, however, alerted Curry to the Indians' situation. In 1950 he left government service and opened a private practice where he could represent both Indian and Puerto Rican clients. Under arrangements devised by D'Arcy McNickle at the annual convention in Browning, Montana, the NCAI hired Curry in 1946 to be its attorney. Seeing the benefits of contacts with so many tribes, the attorney agreed to work without compensation until the legal committee of the NCAI could pay him. With financial aid from the Robert Marshall Civil Liberties Trust, the NCAI paid Curry his back fees in 1951 and placed him on the payroll.[5]

In early 1947 Curry employed Frances Lopinsky Horn to help him in his work with the NCAI and individual tribes. After graduating from the University of West Virginia School of Law, Horn had worked briefly with the National Labor Relations Board and other government agencies before joining Curry. The young lawyer soon became a valued associate in Curry's Washington office. As a capable and eager attorney, she helped prepare legal briefs and legislative summaries and even assumed the managerial duties of Ruth Bronson while the NCAI executive director was away in Alaska.[6]

While Curry worked closely with Horn, his competitive nature often led him to be suspicious of the motives of other Indian lawyers, particularly his chief rival, Felix Cohen. Having served as colleagues in the Department of Interior, Curry invited the well-known Cohen to join him in 1948 as a legal counsel for the NCAI. Second thoughts about Cohen's role in the organization and concerns that he might usurp his power led Curry to withdraw his offer. Moreover, Cohen had no interest in a joint appointment as NCAI general counsel. Instead, Cohen took his legal expertise to the American Association for Indian Affairs (AAIA). Partially for that reason, Curry never fully trusted the motivations of the AAIA. Later in 1948, the NCAI attorney was disgruntled when Cohen was one of several prominent Indian lawyers seeking appointment as commissioner of Indian Affairs. Fearing that this would curtail his own influence, Curry suggested in confidential memos that the NCAI adopt resolutions in their convention to prevent his competitor's nomination. By the summer of 1948 Curry and Cohen had severed professional ties.

By 1949 Curry became particularly worried that Cohen was trying to wrestle control of the NCAI in order to place the interests of the Indian organization second to the AAIA. His insecurities and jealousies led him to recommend that the NCAI not invite Cohen to the annual conventions. Executive Director John Rainer worried that the competition between the two lawyers would divide Indians into two camps. Rainer had just cause for his concern. In late 1949 Curry pressured the NCAI to adopt a resolution that called for an investigation into Cohen's legal activities with the tribes. Curry maintained that Cohen, as former acting solicitor of the Interior Department, illegally used his prior connections to secure new claims work. Officials at the Justice Department, however, failed to find evidence that Cohen was guilty of any wrongdoing. The matter simply served to further divide the two attorneys and place them on the defensive. As each attorney carved out his own sphere of influence within the Indian community, controversy surrounding changes in federal-Indian attorney contracts forced the two rivals to become cautious allies.[7]

Federal concerns over potentially lucrative Indian legal practices at the Indians' expense arose following the Indian Claims Commission Act of 1946. When Congress paved the way for the adjudication of Indian land claims (and as the tribes' need for counsel increased), aggressive lawyers rushed to obtain contracts. Federal officials worried that opportunistic, unscrupulous attorneys would take advantage of the situation. Few attorneys in the postwar period worked any harder than did Curry in amassing Indian contracts. Not only did he represent the NCAI, but his contracts with individual tribes stretched from the southwestern United States to Alaska.

Friends and colleagues recall that although Curry could be headstrong, even abrasive, he was "dogged in his efforts" to represent the best interests of Indian people. While his intense personality often drew applause from friends and Indian clients, it also alienated him from the BIA and powerful non-Indian interests.[8] When Curry unwisely decided to challenge both the BIA and powerful western interests in Nevada, he found himself in an unwinnable battle. Moreover, the affair raised serious concerns about the limits of federal guardianship.

The issue between Curry, the BIA, and the state of Nevada came to a head in the early 1950s over Pyramid Lake Paiute land claims. These claims stemmed from the creation of the Paiute reservation, named the Pyramid Lake Reservation, in 1859. Tribal members had never signed a treaty surrendering control over considerable amounts of land outside the reservation boundaries. Federal officials, however, sold most of that land to homesteaders in 1924 without having acquired legal title to it. When the homesteaders did not make payments on the land, the federal government failed to evict them. During the New Deal, the Paiutes sued the government for compensation for the confiscated lands. Like most other Indian land claims in the early twentieth century, the case soon bogged down in the federal courts. Passage of the Indian Claims Commission Act of 1946 brought new hope to the Paiutes for a just settlement to the land-claims case. When the Paiutes searched for a law firm to represent their interests in Washington, NCAI leaders introduced the tribe to Curry. Although Curry, the NCAI, and the Paiutes picked the specific legal battle, the BIA and western politicians selected the battleground.[9]

In agreeing to represent the interests of the Paiutes, Curry immediately faced the antagonism of Nevada senator Pat McCarran, who had been challenging the Paiutes' land claims for years. Known among his colleagues as a fierce and crusty politician, McCarran wielded substantial influence in Nevada and throughout the West.

He invested considerable time and energy in the 1930s and 1940s in supporting legislation to block Indian interests in Nevada and in protecting white homesteaders on the Pyramid Lake Reservation. Perhaps more importantly, McCarran was also a close ally of the new Indian commissioner, Dillon S. Myer.

Myer's appointment had brought not only a new BIA attitude, but a shifting political alignment. The new commissioner joined forces with conservative interests and effected a reversal of Collier's programs. In particular, the new administration held strong ties with western congressional leadership. Besides McCarran, Myer already knew Sen. Clinton P. Anderson of New Mexico, former secretary of agriculture and influential member of the Interior Department and Insular Affairs Committee. Myer's associate commissioner, H. Rex Lee, shared strong Mormon ties with Arthur Watkins, also of Utah.

As a close friend of McCarran and other western interests, Myer decided to intervene in the tribal hiring of private attorneys. NCAI attorney Curry became his prime target. In late 1943 the U.S. Supreme Court ordered the eviction of several white squatters from Indian lands at Pyramid Lake. Before the court carried out the action, McCarran and Myer moved to block the settlers' expulsion. Following the court's decree, McCarran introduced several bills in Congress that would force the Paiutes to sell reservation lands to the settlers at a fraction of their worth. In effect, the bills would have provided title to 2,140 acres of valuable Indian irrigation land to five white ranchers.

As members of the NCAI, the Paiutes urged the Indian organization to help them defeat McCarran and the illegal homesteaders. Working through Curry, the NCAI opposed McCarran's measures and demanded compliance of the 1943 Supreme Court decision to evict the homesteaders. Hoping that direct action would carry the day, Curry and E. Reeseman Fryer, superintendent of the Carson City Agency, early in 1949 recommended that the tribe take physical possession of the disputed land. The Indians followed their advice and fenced off the Indian property. For the moment, the NCAI and the Paiutes headed off McCarran's plan.

When McCarran failed to skirt the court's ruling through delays, he and the settlers tried another course. The settlers shut off the water supply to the disputed lands by controlling irrigation facilities outside reservation boundaries. McCarran, working through Myer's office, further blocked Fryer's efforts to develop the lands for Indian use as stipulated in the court decree. When those tactics failed to stop Indian efforts and it appeared that the homesteaders' removal was certain, McCarran had Superintendent Fryer transferred from the Carson City Agency.[10]

Since his arrival as superintendent at the Carson City Agency in the late 1940s, Fryer had championed the Paiutes' claims. He received praise for his efforts as superintendent from both the Paiutes and the NCAI. While holding the line on Indian rights, however, Fryer represented an obstacle to McCarran and the white interests at Pyramid Lake. The powerful Nevada senator sought to have the superintendent removed and took his case to his close friend Dillon Myer. Without consulting Oscar Chapman, his superior, Commissioner Myer ordered Fryer's transfer.

Seeing the obvious political implication of Fryer's removal from the Carson City Agency, the NCAI immediately protested Myer's decision. Mounting evidence convinced the NCAI that McCarran strongly influenced the superintendent's removal from Pyramid Lake. Upon hearing about the superintendent's transfer, NCAI leaders Rainer and Bronson went to see Commissioner Myer to protest his decision. Myer denied that McCarran had played any role in the decision and implied that Fryer had initiated the transfer. Questioning the truthfulness of Myer's statement, Rainer then telegrammed Fryer to ask if he had requested the transfer. Fryer denied that he initiated the transfer and called it a "repudiation" of his obligation to defend Indian rights.

Following Fryer's reply, Bronson paid another visit to the commissioner, who told her that he had transferred Fryer according to the wishes of former Commissioner John R. Nichols. NCAI representatives then tried to see Chapman, but he was in Puerto Rico. When the NCAI failed to get satisfactory answers from Myer, Rainer made an appointment to see Dale E. Doty, assistant secretary of the interior. He hoped to ask for a delay in the transfer until Myer more fully justified his decision. The following day the executive director also sent President Harry S. Truman a telegram, urging him to intervene on behalf of the Indians.[11]

The persistence of the NCAI paid off. On October 10, 1950, President Truman granted Bronson an interview. Following the appointment, the president overruled Myer and blocked the transfer. Throughout the controversy Myer's version of the events conflicted with that of the NCAI. Although the AAIA joined the NCAI in expressing concern about the circumstances surrounding the transfer, AAIA President Oliver La Farge tended to believe Myer. In a confidential memo to AAIA members La Farge claimed that "the N.C.A.I. officers in Washington are an extremely excitable group of Indians, inclined to simplify everything into dramatic black and white." Yet, contradictions in Myer's account supported the NCAI's interpretation of events. With support from the General Federation of Women's Clubs, the IRA, the AIAA, former Indian Commissioner John Collier, former Interior Secretary Harold L. Ickes, and the national media, the NCAI officers and Curry had succeeded in getting Fryer reinstated.[12]

Following his reinstatement, Fryer resigned as superintendent of Pyramid Lake. "Like any superintendent worth his salt," Fryer wrote Rainer, "I would remain in the Indian Service only if I knew I could do creditable work. This requires the support of the Commissioner."[13] In Fryer's view the commissioner ignored his responsibilities to the Indian people. The superintendent left the BIA to accept a position as director of the Division of Health, Education, and Welfare Projects in the State Department. Before he left, he worried that Indians would view his resignation as a retreat and an embarrassment to the NCAI. He offered to delay his departure. He knew that he had become a symbolic pawn in the struggle over the "purposes for which NCAI made the fight." The organization regretted his departure but wished him well in his new duties. In a final gesture, Fryer thanked the NCAI for their support and "magnificent work."[14]

Fryer, Curry, the NCAI, and other Indian reform groups may have won the first round, but the larger struggle lay ahead. McCarran was not finished trying to defraud the Indians of their land at Pyramid Lake. In 1950 the crafty politician tried yet another strategy. He tried to drive Curry out of the practice of Indian law. In his efforts to nullify Curry's influence, the Nevada senator's friendship with Myer paid handsome returns. Clearly, both McCarran and Myer strongly disliked Curry. The young attorney frequently represented a prickly thorn in the commissioner's side. He consistently kept the BIA on the defensive with new demands from the NCAI and the Indian tribes. When the Indian lawyer failed to get satisfactory responses to his inquiries and charges, he did not hesitate to take his complaints to higher-level administrators. Myer, as much as McCarran, wanted to be free of the meddling of Curry and fellow mavericks. In order to retain greater control over internal affairs and prepare a program to end federal wardship, Myer decided to restrict the limits of lawyers' authority with the tribes in as clear a fashion as possible.

Soon after his appointment, Commissioner Myer revised the guidelines by which the BIA regulated attorneys' contracts with the tribes. He found the policy written during the IRA unacceptable because it established different rules for federally recognized and non-federally recognized tribes. In particular, attorney contracts were subject to compliance with the provisions of IRA constitutions and charters. More specifically, Myer disliked these regulations because they afforded tribes the right to select and pay independent attorneys without BIA supervision. Only the selection of attorneys and setting of fees were subject to the secretary of interior's approval. Essentially, Myer felt the IRA attorney guidelines provided recognized tribes too much legal tribal authority and Indian self-rule.

Under Myer's new provisions the BIA had unlimited authority to govern the contracts of Indian lawyers. To justify his action, Myer invoked a 1872 statute that required the commissioner's approval of attorney contracts. He also maintained that as trustee he had a legal and moral obligation to watch over and protect the interests of his charges.[15]

The specific details of Myer's new regulations in November 1950 contained several controversial points. The regulations no longer permitted fixed retainer fees in claims contracts. Payment for attorney services were contingent upon successful recovery, and the courts or the Indian Claims Commission set compensation. Solicitation or brokering of contracts by any attorney would cause the cancellation of all further contracts by that attorney. More importantly, the BIA disallowed contracts for periods longer than three years, and the commissioner could cancel a contract with a tribe's consent without giving notification or cause. The guidelines also discouraged the hiring of attorneys from Washington DC in favor of local attorneys. Such actions made attorneys more accountable to the commissioner than to the tribes. In essence, Myer denied Indians their constitutional right to an independent attorney protected by the Fifth Amendment. Hoping to catch Curry in his trap, Myer had now set the bait.[16]

Myer's policy statement drew immediate protest from a variety of sources. As expected, Curry filed a formal appeal objecting to the change in policy. Insisting that he barely eked out a subsistence as an Indian lawyer, Curry maintained that the only misdeed he was guilty of committing was not being a "yes-man for the Indian Bureau."[17] Clearly, he had a legitimate grievance against the Bureau's new contract regulations. In the six months before his November 1950 guidelines, Myer had rejected seven of Curry's pending contracts or amendments to contracts. The commissioner complained that the lawyer already held fifty-six contracts with thirty-seven Indian tribes or groups. Thus on the surface Myer claimed Curry had become a contract broker, and as commissioner he was unlikely to approve any more of the attorney's agreements. Myer's real agenda, however, was to quell Curry's ardent defense of Indian self-rule, slow his prosecution of Indian claims, and prevent Curry and the NCAI from embarrassing his administration further.[18]

Assistant Secretary Dale E. Doty, Myer's immediate superior, and others questioned the commissioner's authority to issue the guidelines without prior approval of the secretary of interior. Doty also worried that the new regulations interfered with the Indians' right to self-determination.[19] Led by such well-known Indian attorneys as Charles L. Black, Theodore H. Haas, and Felix Cohen, fifteen law firms also distributed a lengthy memorandum protesting the illegality and immorality of the new regulations. The American Bar Association joined the others in condemning Myer's regulations.[20] In a lengthy rebuttal Myer defended his new regulations as fulfilling his trust responsibilities to the Indians.[21]

The new guidelines appalled the NCAI and other Indian rights groups. Recognizing the obvious threat to Indian sovereignty, Executive Director John Rainer accused Myer of forcing upon Indians "drum head justice" similar to that used in military tribunals. Fearing the threat to Indians' civil rights, Rainer further objected to Myer's tacit assumption that Indians were incapable of making wise and rational decisions about matters that affected them.[22] Rainer and other NCAI members correctly perceived potential pitfalls in the new proposal. Organizations such as the NCAI relied heavily on their attorneys and representatives in Washington to monitor the BIA and Congress.

The hiring of tribal attorneys on a case-by-case basis left the Indian communities vulnerable to the passage of detrimental legislation without their knowledge. Attorneys employed under the new regulations also owed their loyalty to the BIA, and not Indians, the NCAI charged. "If the Indian people henceforward are forced into Court defended only by attorneys selected by, and therefore subservient to, the Indian Bureau," Ruth Bronson argued, "then we Indians will have lost our battle before we even start." Bronson also saw the possibility of "political spoliation of Indian property, on a scale greater than hitherto known."[23]

Critics such as the NCAI and other Indian reform groups opposed the new regulations because they reduced tribal autonomy in selecting lawyers.[24] In its struggle against Myer NCAI solicited and received support from many organizations interested in minority civil rights. The NCAI, with the Indian Committee of the American Civil Liberties Union (ACLU), the Institute of Ethnic Affairs, the AAIA, the National Council of Negro Women, the Japanese-American Citizens League, the National Jewish Welfare Board, the Congregational Christian Churches, the National Association for the Advancement of Colored People, the American Jewish Congress, and B'nai B'rith, requested a meeting with Chapman concerning the contract controversy. The secretary denied their petition.[25]

Seeking more visibility, Curry and the NCAI in late 1950 appealed to Harold L. Ickes and John Collier for assistance. Criticizing the continuing paternalistic relationship of the federal government toward Indians, Bronson wrote Ickes that the Indians' "muscles of resistance are not yet fully developed. . . . They need to be fed with the vitamins of a few successful experiences in self-determination," she continued, "before they will be strong enough to carry on a tough fight, or even to hold the line for long." As Bronson articulately noted, and Ickes agreed, Indian civil rights and self-determination included the Indians' unrestricted choice of legal counsel.[26]

Ickes and Collier responded to the call for help by offering to "hog-tie Myer" as quickly as possible. In addition to his letters to Chapman, Ickes kept up a constant assault against Myer and McCarran in his *New Republic* column. In May 1951, the former secretary of interior denounced the Indian commissioner as "Hitler and Mussolini rolled into one" for refusing Indians the freedom to select their own attorneys. The issue provided the former secretary with "arrows he could shoot at the Truman administration on the Indian administration."[27] Ickes even went so far in his defense of Curry that he agreed to serve as the Indian lawyer's pro bono legal counselor.[28] In January 1951 Collier also berated the BIA for sabotaging Indian progress toward democratic self-government.[29]

The harsh protests raised by Indians and allies forced Chapman to examine the growing controversy. In December 1950 he appointed a three-member committee to advise him on the delicate matter and to review the many complaints. Chaired by Associate Solicitor W. H. Flanery, the rest of the committee included Arthur E. Demaray, director of the National Park Service, and Joel D. Wolfsohn, Chapman's assistant. Wolfsohn's appointment represented a bad omen to Myer.

The assistant secretary, although friendly, "was cutting my throat regularly," Myer maintained. His doubts about the appeal board's possible recommendations led him to ask Flanery to review the committee's findings and prepare a response before the recommendations were passed on to Chapman.[30]

Myer's misgivings were well founded. In February 1951 the board recommended reinstating four of Curry's canceled contracts. The committee did not find evidence that the Indian attorney had failed in his responsibilities to the tribes. Reprimanding Myer, the committee advised the secretary to seek legal counsel over attorney contracts from the solicitor on the authority of the Interior Department. Following the board's recommendations, Chapman approved the four Curry contracts and requested legal advice from the Solicitor's Office.[31]

Curry won yet another skirmish, but the widening war threatened to engulf him. The two adversaries, Curry and Myer, would soon meet in a final showdown in a conflict involving the Pyramid Lake Paiutes. In November 1950 Curry, working with former Nevada Sen. E. P. Carville, extended his contract with the Paiutes for a ten-year period. The extension far exceeded the three-year limit mandated by the BIA at the time. Myer delayed approving the contract. While the commissioner sat on his decision, the Pyramid Lake Paiutes urged the NCAI not to let the contract expire lest the tribe fall into the "hands of McCarran factors."

The NCAI reacted by sending telegrams to President Truman and Secretary Chapman that requested they intervene on the tribe's behalf.[32] In response McCarran and his forces circulated false information that charged the NCAI with ties to communist organizations. Taking advantage of Red Scare fears, George Malone of Nevada attacked the NCAI from the floor of the Senate. Albert Grorud, a disbarred Montana attorney and clerk on the Senate Indian subcommittee, assailed the NCAI in memos sent to tribal groups. The tactics of McCarran and his allies put the NCAI on the defensive at a critical time.[33]

In March 1951, as the time grew closer for Curry's original contract to expire, Myer suggested that he would approve a modified contract.

Myer demanded a reduction in the term of the contract from ten years to two. He also required a cancellation of the contract by the tribe, with the commissioner's consent, with sixty days notice and provisions for the employment of local counsel. Finally the commissioner required an agreement that Curry submit semiannual reports to the tribe and to the commissioner documenting services performed.

Curry rejected the modifications and appealed to Chapman to override the commissioner. Myer proposed to extend the original contract indefinitely, until Chapman resolved the appeal. The Paiutes agreed, but Curry rejected the offer, hoping to force Chapman to take a stand. As a result, and despite pressing legal problems, the Paiutes went without an approved attorney contract after April 1951. Realizing the importance of his decision, Chapman again asked the Solicitor's Office for a legal opinion. In July 1951 Solicitor Mastin White upheld Myer's decision. Citing several reasons for his ruling, White maintained that department heads should rarely overrule subordinates. Chapman agreed and denied Curry's appeal. Myer had outmaneuvered Curry.[34]

After White's memorandum, Secretary Chapman instructed Commissioner Myer to reexamine and revise his policy regulations on tribal attorneys. The amended regulations, which appeared in August 1951 in the *Federal Register,* differed little from the earlier guidelines. Upon the recommendation of a special committee of the American Bar Association (ABA), the organization severely criticized the new guidelines and urged their withdrawal. Former Secretary Ickes once again attacked the commissioner in a *New Republic* column.[35] Perhaps the heaviest assaults against Myer and White came in a series of letters from Ickes to Chapman in the fall of 1951. Referring to the commissioner as "a little tin Hitler," Ickes called for Myer's removal. Mincing few words, the former secretary also questioned White's integrity. Hoping for a last-minute change of heart, Ickes challenged Chapman to reconsider his decision in the Curry case. "It occurs to me that your Solicitor and your Indian Commissioner have become so desperate in their desire to destroy Mr. James E. Curry,"

Ickes wrote Chapman, "that they are willing, if necessary, to destroy you, and with you, themselves." In February 1952, before Chapman could respond, however, Ickes died.[36]

Throughout most of the next year, newspaper coverage provided ample fuel for the tribal sovereignty battle over the attorney issue. In an article first published in the *Washington Post* and syndicated elsewhere, Drew Pearson, whose father was a former prominent employee of the Department of Interior, defended Myer's actions. He accused Curry of "feathering his nest" at the expense of his clients. Defenders of Curry and critics of the policy of the BIA, presumably sponsored by the NCAI and other Indian reform organizations, attacked Myer and Chapman in dozens of newspaper editorial columns from coast to coast.[37]

Deeming the revised regulations unacceptable and unconstitutional, the NCAI considered enlisting the NAACP in the Indian struggle for civil rights. By the late 1940s, African Americans, like Native Americans, realized that they would have to take the lead in the fight against discrimination. In the early years of the struggle the NAACP, much like the NCAI, carried its own banner into the battle. Instead of attacking Jim Crow head-on, the NAACP had chiseled away at the legal logic of segregation. In *Sweatt* v. *Painter* and *McLaurin* v. *Board of Regents* in 1950, the NAACP lawyers won impressive decisions in overturning segregation in higher education.

Aware of these successes, Ruth Bronson in late 1950 proposed the idea of soliciting the aid of legal staff of the NAACP to prepare a test case for Indians to challenge the proposed new tribal attorney regulations. Not only would the NAACP offer the NCAI strong legal expertise, it would also bring high visibility to the controversy. Although the NCAI apparently decided against formally asking the NAACP for legal help, the NAACP did lend moral support.[38] The NCAI also often sought and received advice from Roger Baldwin, founder and chairperson of the ACLU.

In the midst of criticism from all sides, Myer agreed to deliver the keynote address at the eighth annual convention of the NCAI in St. Paul, Minnesota, on July 25, 1951. His participation in the conference was minimal; symbolically, he bore an olive branch which he hoped could soothe the resentment of disgruntled tribal leaders. In his address, Myer called on the Indian community and the BIA to work together in a spirit of cooperation. He denied the accusations that he was engaging in a cunning, tyrannical endeavor to expand his own power over Indian affairs. In fact, he argued that the opposite was true. He promised to lead "the Indian people out of the shadows of federal paternalism into the sunlight of fully responsible citizens." He also maintained that he was looking out for the best interests of all Indians.[39] The NCAI members, however, disagreed with the commissioner's assessment of the controversy. Resolutions passed at St. Paul denounced Myer's new guidelines and urged the secretary of interior to approve all pending contracts.[40]

In a last-ditch effort to turn the tide of battle in his favor, Curry persuaded a Paiute delegation to visit Washington DC to lobby for a contract extension. Led by Avery Winnemucca, Paiute tribal chairman, the three-member tribal delegation that included Albert Aleck and Warren Toby arrived in the nation's capital in October 1951 to demand a hearing with Secretary Chapman. The envoy met with Myer, Chapman, several members of Congress, and newspaper reporters in an attempt to marshal support for their cause. When their efforts failed to gain an extension of Curry's contract, two of the delegates returned to Nevada. Only Winnemucca remained behind to continue his lobbying efforts.

The Paiute delegation's lack of success signaled the moment of decline of Curry's career as an Indian attorney. Many reform organizations, including the ACLU, the American Jewish Congress, the General Federation of Women's Clubs, the NAACP, the AAIA, the IRA, the Council of Californian Indians, and the New Mexico Association of Indian Affairs, joined the NCAI in demanding hearings on the proposed regulations.[41] In response to the public outcry against the attorney contract regulations, Secretary Chapman decided to hold public hearings for two days in January 1952.

With the secretary presiding over hearings, all the significant Indian reform groups attended the discussions, including the NCAI and

Curry. Executive Director Ruth Bronson decided against having Curry represent the interests of the NCAI at the hearings because of his personal involvement in the case. Instead, the NCAI sent Vice President Frank George as the organization's spokesperson. George correctly noted that the new attorney regulations contradicted the BIA promise of increased Indian sovereignty that Myer had made at the 1950 NCAI convention in Bellingham, Washington. In his defense, Curry testified that BIA officials had crossed ethical lines in preventing him from helping Indians control their own destiny.[42]

Confronted with strong opposition, Chapman abandoned the proposed regulations and appointed a special four-member committee, chaired by Assistant Secretary Dale E. Doty, to make future recommendations.[43] Vacillating in his stance, Secretary Chapman had retreated from his earlier neutral position. The NCAI applauded Chapman's ruling and hoped it would set a precedent for greater Indian self-determination in the future.[44]

Because of Chapman's decision, Curry enjoyed a short period of success, which only made Myer more determined to resolve the question. He asked Democratic senator Clinton P. Anderson of New Mexico, an old friend, to hold congressional hearings on the attorney question. Anderson, an influential member of the Interior Department and Insular Affairs Committee, used his leverage to help establish a five-member subcommittee to investigate the activities of Indian attorneys. The character of the subcommittee foretold its conclusions. Anderson, often a prickly thorn in the side of Indians, served as chairperson. Critics of Anderson suggested that Curry incurred the wrath of the New Mexico senator when he helped Indians secure the right to vote in New Mexico and Arizona in 1950. After they secured the ballot in the early 1950s, most Indians voted Republican; Anderson and his colleagues were Democrats.[45]

Other members of the committee included Sen. Arthur Watkins of Utah, who later became the catalyst behind the movement for termination. Watkins with Anderson had sponsored the Tongass Timber Bill. Montana Republican Zales N. Ecton, Russell B. Long of Louisiana, and Herbert H. Lehman of New York completed the panel.

Anderson and Watkins were the ringleaders, while the other three committee members were along for the ride. Senator Anderson requested that Chapman delay any action on attorney contracts until after the congressional hearings. Objecting to any further holdups on contracts, Frank George, who had been appointed executive director of the NCAI as of 1952, demanded that the Department of Interior immediately resolve the Curry matter.[46]

Beginning January 21, 1952, the Anderson subcommittee met twenty-four times that year. The first investigation examined the activities of Curry. Speaking at the first session of the hearings, Commissioner Myer set the tone by charging the lawyer with misconduct and violations of the "Canons of Professional Ethics." He specifically accused the attorney of solicitation of contracts, claims brokerage, nonperformance of contracts, interference in tribal hiring of other attorneys, and misrepresentation to his clients and the BIA.[47] Instead of a legislative inquiry, the proper forum to investigate Myer's and Andersons' allegations should have been a disbarment hearing.

Ironically some of the most damaging testimony in the hearings against Curry came from former vice-president of the NCAI and former Oglala Sioux tribal council chairman Chief William Fire Thunder. He claimed that the NCAI retained Curry to provide free counsel for the NCAI tribal members who could not afford to hire regular counsel. Instead of furnishing the tribes with free counsel, according to Fire Thunder, Curry used his position with the NCAI to solicit tribal contracts for his personal monetary gain. The former NCAI officer testified that many tribes, including the Alaska natives, remained hostile to the NCAI after Curry duped them into private contracts with high retainers instead of providing them with free legal counsel. Curry's tactics, according to the former Oglala tribal chairman, had forced Thunder to leave the NCAI in 1950.[48]

Additional negative testimony regarding Curry's relationship to the NCAI came from several others. Roy Mobley, a former legal associate of the Indian attorney, testified that Curry used Ruth Bronson as a front to obtain private contracts for himself. As executive director of the NCAI, Bronson, according to Mobley, had visited tribes in her official NCAI capacity and then recommended that tribes hire Curry as their tribal legal counsel. During her visits Bronson admittedly brought with her unsigned contracts. She helped the tribes fill them out with Curry listed as their tribal attorney. Mobley further charged that Curry loaned Bronson his office for NCAI operations when she was executive director, and placed her on his payroll. Bronson claimed, however, that she had recommended Curry to the tribes because he was an excellent attorney with high standards. Ben Dwight, founding member of the NCAI, considered testifying to help salvage the reputation of the NCAI but decided against being swept into the muddy water.[49]

As the hearings progressed, Curry's influence with the NCAI plummeted. By March 1952 Dwight and the NCAI president, Napoleon B. Johnson, began to consider Curry a liability and to contemplate severing his relationship with the organization. As the year progressed, Dwight became increasingly convinced that Curry was controlling the NCAI for his own benefit. To prevent future non-Indian attorneys from attempting to control the NCAI, Dwight recommended that the organization fire him and hire an Indian attorney. Ruth Bronson and former executive director Louis Bruce, however, preferred to delay any decisions on the lawyer's contract until the Senate subcommittee hearings were completed.[50]

As Dwight and Johnson contemplated terminating Curry's contract with the NCAI, Edward L. Rogers, another founding member of the NCAI and an attorney in Minnesota, protested the Washington lawyer's possible dismissal. Johnson and Dwight did not have the authority to end Curry's contract, Rogers argued; only the full executive committee did. Moreover, Rogers maintained, the lawyer had provided valuable legal assistance to the NCAI. "There is no doubt that Curry's enemies are our principal enemies," the Minnesota lawyer explained. "If we desert him, we are deserting our own cause." Like Bronson and Bruce, Rogers preferred to postpone any action on Curry until the next annual convention in Denver, Colorado, in the fall of 1952. Respecting the opinion of their fellow members, Johnson and Bronson agreed to defer the matter until the convention.[51]

When Curry received word that the NCAI was considering dropping him as its lawyer, he immediately defended himself from his attackers. He maintained that his past success as an attorney in protecting Indian interests had made him a target of powerful, non-Indian western groups. Curry also speculated that the reason that Dwight and Johnson, Oklahoma government employees, wanted him fired was that as the attorney for the NCAI he had alienated the "Oklahoma political crowd."[52]

During the period of the Anderson subcommittee hearings, Sen. Pat McCarran continued the attacks against Curry in Congress. During a Senate debate over an appropriation bill concerning the BIA, McCarran charged Curry with using Winnemucca, chairman of the Pyramid Lake tribal council, as a front to raise money for his legal defense. During Winnemucca's earlier visit to Washington, maintained McCarran, the lawyer allegedly had sent letters signed by Winnemucca asking for donations to aid the Paiutes in their fight to extend Curry's contract. While the letters reported Winnemucca as treasurer of the special fund, the post office listed Curry's box for receipt of the donations. An investigation on the Paiute reservation, according to the Nevada senator, had proved that the tribe had no such knowledge of the fund or how the money had been spent.

McCarran's brief but damaging statement raised further questions about Curry's integrity and legal judgment and left the Washington attorney with few supporters. Curry denied McCarran's statements and maintained that the Paiutes had no choice but to start a defense fund, because Myer had tied up their tribal funds. Not only had Curry paid tribal expenses out of his own pocket, but those who would profit from putting him out of business exaggerated the charges against him.[53]

While the hearings briefly recessed in the fall of 1952, matters grew worse for Curry. On September 24, 1952, the Department of Interior officially nullified his contract with the Paiutes. Following up on the action, Secretary Chapman announced that a special committee of the Department of Interior, as called for following the two-day hearings in January, would investigate misconduct charges. Comprised of three lawyers from the Solicitor's Office, the committee examined the allegations and recommended appropriate action. Believing that the committee was another government ruse to discredit him, Curry called Chapman's action little more than a "kangaroo court."[54]

By the fall of 1952, as his situation grew more ominous and as he waited for the hearings to conclude, Curry had nearly exhausted both his patience and his financial resources. With many of his contracts either canceled or delayed by the BIA pending the outcome of the hearings, the lawyer began soliciting funds from nonprofit organizations to help sustain him.[55] Desperate to salvage his reputation and his practice, he played his last cards. Through the courtesy of radio station WFJL in Chicago, in late 1952 Curry delivered a series of Sunday night discussions on the administration of Indian affairs. Not only did he chastise the government for past treatment of Indians, he saved his harshest criticism for Chapman and Myer. Instead of using their positions to protect Indians' interests, the lawyer charged that the secretary and commissioner were wielding their power to victimize their wards. Curry warned that McCarran and his "stooges in the BIA" seriously threatened Indian rights and properties. The last hope for the Indians' cause, he warned, was for the president to fire Chapman and Myer.[56]

Desperate to prevent his removal as NCAI lawyer, in late 1952 Curry asked D'Arcy McNickle to use his influence with the NCAI members to retain his services. But as the movement within the NCAI to dismiss him gained momentum, Curry agreed to end the contract as of February 1, 1953. In return, his detractors within the NCAI agreed to not release him before the hearings were completed. With the end of his career as an Indian attorney looming large, in October 1952 Curry announced that although he would not cancel existing contracts unless his clients so wanted, he would no longer accept new Indian clients.[57]

When the Anderson subcommittee filed its final report in January 1953, the controversy sped toward a conclusion. The subcommittee reprimanded Curry for deceiving his clients for personal gains, inappropriately soliciting contracts, improperly fulfilling his legal obligations, and disregarding ABA standards. In its statement on Indian self-determination, the report highly criticized the activities of the NCAI and tarnished its image. The majority report, signed by Anderson, Watkins, and Long, praised Myer's actions and recommended that the attorney general of the United States review Curry's conduct. Senator Lehman, while not disagreeing with the majority's findings, criticized his associates for being more concerned with legal ethics than with the welfare of the Indian clients. In the end, Myer's vision of limited Indian self-determination had won out over that of Curry and the NCAI.[58]

The subcommittee findings finished Curry as an Indian attorney and ended his legal relationship with the NCAI. While his motives represented a combination of public service and private gain, Curry had been unfairly railroaded by Myer and his allies. Though Curry had often represented the NCAI in its early legal battles, such as the voting and social security issues for Indians in New Mexico and Arizona, native land rights in Alaska, and the Paiutes' case, his weakened reputation now made him more of a liability than an asset. Several years after the organization severed contractual ties with Curry, Helen Peterson, NCAI executive director, bestowed a gift of three hundred dollars on Curry for his past services to the organization. Although Curry believed that the NCAI still owed him more in back pay, he graciously accepted the money and called the account even.[59] Within a short time the law firm of Wilkinson, Cragun, and Barker replaced Curry as legal counsel to the NCAI.

The Indian attorney question lost its energy following the findings of the Anderson subcommittee. At the heart of the controversy had been a power struggle between an authoritative and dictatorial Indian commissioner and an equally assertive attorney. The commissioner felt threatened by the actions of private attorneys whom he believed were undermining the authority of the BIA. Ultimately, Myer believed that the tribes should rely on the counsel of the BIA instead of private lawyers.[60] The attorney guidelines, however, not only reversed earlier Indian gains during the Collier administration, but seriously threatened the constitutional rights of all Indians. After gaining the rights of citizenship in 1924, the law entitled Indians to the duties, responsibilities, and privileges that came with their new citizenship status. Paramount to the American legal tradition is the right to legal counsel. By assuming a paternalistic posture through new attorney regulations, Myer violated this fundamental right.

Moreover, the Curry controversy in the early 1950s preceded even more serious actions by Myer that threatened both tribal rights and more general civil rights. Unlike the African-American civil rights movement of the late 1940s and early 1950s, which focused on assimilation and equal rights for blacks, Indian activism in the same period had dealt with protection of special rights and advancement of Indian self-rule. Not necessarily wanting wholesale or full assimilation into mainstream white society like other minorities, the NCAI in the postwar period aggressively fought to preserve not only civil rights, but also those associated with treaties, tribal sovereignty, the distinctive relationship with the BIA, and a separate ethnic identity. While the attorney controversy threatened Indian self-determination and a return to unilateral federal action, it was only a prelude to the much more serious crisis after the mid-1950s. Serving as a necessary step to end tribal self-rule, Myer's actions paved the way for his larger movement, termination of tribes.

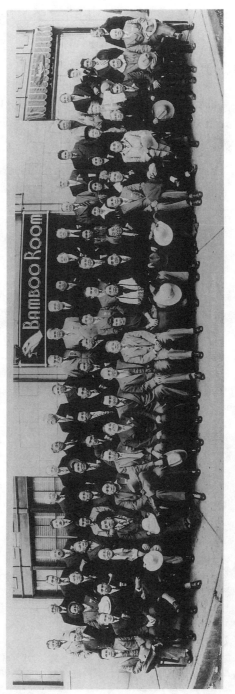

1 Participants in the 1944 Constitutional Convention. Courtesy of the National Anthropological Archives, Smithsonian Institution, Photo No. 98 10202.

2 Willy's Jeep, donated to NCAI and ARROW in 1951 by an unknown benefactor. Used by NCAI and ARROW leaders to travel throughout Indian Country. Courtesy of the National Anthropological Archives, Smithsonian Institution, Photo No. 98 10199.

3 Early NCAI leaders. Left to right: Helen Peterson, D'Arcy McNickle, Joseph Garry, Louis Bruce, Ruth Bronson. Courtesy of the National Anthropological Archives, Smithsonian Institution, Photo No. 98 10200.

4 Helen Peterson meeting with legal consultants during the termination crisis. Left to right: attorneys Frances Horn, Arthur Lazarus, unknown assistant, Helen Peterson. Courtesy of the National Anthropological Archives, Smithsonian Institution, Photo No. 98 10195.

5 Joshua Wetsit posing with Helen Peterson for a publicity photo. Courtesy of the National Anthropological Archives, Smithsonian Institution, Photo No. 98 10201.

6 Presentation of the American Heritage Foundation Outstanding Public Service award to the NCAI in 1957. Left to right: John Rainer, Walter Wetzel, Joseph Garry (representative of AHF), Clarence Wesley. Courtesy of the National Anthropological Archives, Smithsonian Institution, Photo No. 98 10197.

7 Elizabeth Herring and D'Arcy McNickle speaking to future Indian leaders at an AID workshop in the late 1950s. Courtesy of the National Anthropological Archives, Smithsonian Institution, Photo No. 98 10198.

8 Parade of NCAI delegates at the 1962 annual convention in Cherokee NC. Courtesy of the National Anthropological Archives, Smithsonian Institution, Photo No. 98 10196.

9 Discussion of tribal problems. Left to right: Senator Lee Metcalf, Senate Majority Leader Mike Mansfield, Walter Wetzel, President John F. Kennedy. Courtesy of the National Anthropological Archives, Smithsonian Institution, Photo No. 98 10194.

5. TERMINATION OR SELF-DETERMINATION

Today we—America's half million Indians—stand at a fork in the trail. The time has come for all of us to choose the way we will travel. In one direction is the downhill trail we have followed since our lands were invaded more than a century ago. This way, marked by the laws of an often-blind government, leads to ignorance, poverty, disease, and wasted resources. The new trail—the way of self-help—leads toward a better life, toward adequate education, decent income, good health, and wise use of our precious natural wealth. CLARENCE WESLEY, former president of the NCAI

Late in February 1954, Helen Peterson, executive director of NCAI, and her mother collated packets in their basement for an emergency conference on termination of Indian tribes in the United States. Working through the night, the pair produced the materials on a hand-cranked mimeograph machine. Called on short notice, the NCAI emergency conference drew the largest Native American protest in history up until this time and was rivaled only by the Red Power movements a decade later. In the late 1940s through the mid-1950s, the compulsory government termination trend of the period touched a nerve in the Indian community because of its obvious threat to legal and cultural rights. While the termination threat caused internal divisions within the organization, the NCAI withstood the strain. Rejecting the forced nature of the policy and asserting the right of Indian communities to control their own destinies, the NCAI launched an unprecedented drive in the postwar years to defeat or modify the coercive termination program. Peterson's 1954 emergency conference marked a turning point in slowing or stopping the movement.[1]

Despite continual federal efforts since the 1880s to force assimilation of Indians into American society, approximately two hundred and fifty reservations remained in the United States at the end of World War II. During the 1950s the United States government embarked on an ill-fated effort to terminate the federal trust status of Indian reservations. Between 1945 and the mid-1960s the government termination policy affected 1,365,801 acres of Indian land and an estimated 13,263 Indians.[2] In its broadest sense, termination signified a final drive to assimilate the Indians once and for all into the dominant society. In its narrowest sense, termination represented a legal means to abrogate the federal government's trust obligations to the tribes. In particular, it meant the federal government would end its administrative responsibilities for specific tribes as soon as each tribe's circumstances allowed; then it would transfer these responsibilities to state and local governments and distribute tribal assets either to tribes or individual tribe members.

Most scholars who have studied the termination period have reached a consensus on the origins of the movement. Nearly all of them trace the roots of termination to the Truman administration.[3] While the termination movement crested with the 83d Congress, it had started in 1947 when the Senate Civil Service Committee directed the acting commissioner of Indian Affairs, William Zimmerman, to identify and classify tribes based on their readiness for termination. Unfortunately, Zimmerman had prepared the lists without the knowledge and consent of the Indians involved. The acting commissioner later realized his mistake and tried to rectify the error, calling his misinterpreted plan a policy of "extermination" and not "staged termination."[4] Regardless of the error, it was too late, for the "Zimmerman plan" became the cornerstone for the termination policies of the Truman and Eisenhower administrations.

Although implementation of the termination policy is widely associated with the 1940s and 1950s, the idea for a withdrawal of federal services was nothing new.[5] Conservative reform groups and federal policymakers had long advocated the forced assimilation of Native Americans into the mainstream of American society. Historian Kenneth R. Philp links postwar policy shifts to failures of the Indian New Deal. In particular, the reform opponents of John Collier and his philosophy during the 1930s and the immediate postwar years fed the movement for termination.[6]

Postwar changes in liberalism also affected Indian policy. Although John Collier's administration had promoted cultural pluralism, postwar liberalism favored the assimilation of minorities and, with Indians, a reduced federal role and decreased government spending. In a period of rapid economic growth, proponents of termination wanted to remove restrictions on Indian lands and make them fully taxable and alienable. In 1945 O. K. Armstrong voiced many of these sentiments in his widely read *Reader's Digest* article, "Set the American Indian Free!" Practically all the calls to dismantle the tribal edifice, abolish the BIA, and force the Indians into assimilation came from westerners such as senators Burton K. Wheeler of Montana, Elmer Thomas of Oklahoma, and Harlan J. Bushfield of South Dakota.[7]

This new liberal outlook placed a premium on national unity and conformity. The decade after the Second World War demanded that all Americans possess the same societal values. For the dominant population, individualism, competition, capitalism, and private property served as the cornerstones of the American ideal. Many Indians in the postwar period, however, held strikingly different values and mores. According to many tribal traditions and cultures, Native Americans structured their lifestyle around spiritualism, communalism, and community participation. In the Cold War struggle against the Soviet Union, the communal lifestyle fostered by reservations smacked of communism and socialism and ran contrary to the American model of individualism. Anthropologist Nancy Lurie has argued that it was not until the termination movement that many Indians became fully conscious of "the diametrical opposition between Indian and white objectives."[8] Thus termination produced an ideological showdown. Ultimately the campaign of the NCAI to defeat coercive termination centered the education of mainstream society in the needs and rights of Native Americans and America's ethical and legal commitment to protect those rights.

Most well-acculturated leaders of the NCAI initially did not op-

pose the goals of termination—assimilation and equal opportunities—but they wanted to ensure that tribes were prepared for
any new changes.[9] Napoleon B. Johnson, president of the NCAI and
Oklahoma supreme court justice, for example, favored termination
and a full integration of Indians into the mainstream society. "We
look forward to the day when the Indian will have passed out of our
national life as the painted, romantic, feather-crowned hero of fic-
tion," Johnson stated in a 1948 conference address, "and will have added the current of his free, original American blood to the heart of
the this great nation." Johnson and others pursued assimilation
through voluntary termination as a means to an end of Indian sep-
arateness and economic and cultural dislocation. Other NCAI leaders
such as Helen Peterson, executive director, accepted noncompulsory
termination but wanted improved education, health care, job training, and full consultation with tribes before termination occurred.[10]
In essence, Johnson and Peterson sought integration before termination. Experience had also taught, however, that the stated goals of a
policy were often different from the consequences of a proposal.

Whether to accept or reject termination legislation was not a cut-
and-dried decision. Termination was a multifaceted, complex issue
that contained both beneficial and harmful elements. As a result, a
diverse range of opinions from the tribes reached the organization as
to acceptable termination terms. Indian leaders and the tribes welcomed some termination provisions under discussion. Most members of the NCAI agreed that bureaucrats should lessen and remove
some federal regulations regarding Indians and believed in the gradual elimination of the Bureau. For example, most tribal leaders
wanted an end to the Indian liquor law, which they felt discriminated
against them. In reality, an end to some federal control was necessary
before tribes could achieve some measure of self-determination.
These NCAI members disliked federal paternalism, which they
felt hindered Indians' progress. They felt that the BIA had curtailed
land sales, economic opportunities, and Indian self-determination.
Speaking to the NCAI delegates in Denver, Colorado, Will Rogers Jr.

encouraged federal withdrawal to give Indians greater control over their own affairs.[11]

Meeting in Santa Fe, New Mexico, in 1947, representatives passed a resolution that recommended the gradual liquidation of the BIA. It called for the dissolution to proceed in carefully planned phases and for the release of many BIA programs to the states or other federal agencies. For example, almost all of them supported the transfer of Indian Health Services from the BIA to the Public Health Service. Most members also wanted assurances that the federal government would continue to provide and administer special services such as education, housing, and welfare programs. Reservation leaders such as Frank George, however, opposed the dissolution of the BIA. George and other reservation leaders worried that the transfer of federal Indian interests to the states would jeopardize Indian interests. If politicos severed federal ties with tribes, untold stress and substantial economic setbacks would occur.[12]

The question of state jurisdiction over criminal and civil Indian affairs produced much discussion. Some tribes welcomed state criminal jurisdiction on their reservations. While several tribes welcomed state control over civil matters, others worried that it would leave them vulnerable to states that lacked experience in Indian affairs or were unwilling to assume Indian services. Yet several tribes worried that the extension of state criminal jurisdiction over reservations would threaten Indian sovereignty and violate treaty agreements. To offset these concerns, some tribal leaders wanted assurances of Indian consultation before states assumed authority over them.[13]

Congressional initiatives aimed at termination also brought other concerns. Most of the tribal members were anxious over the criteria and regulations for defining tribal rolls. In case of liquidation of tribal assets, the tribes wanted to regulate tribal rolls and set blood quantum requirements. Many delegates also opposed the wording of early congressional termination initiatives because of their negative and uncomplimentary tone. Language such as "emancipation" in the bills carried connotations of slavery and created a false impression that Indians were not already full citizens. Others feared that termination was a step backward because it threatened to negate the advances of the Indian Reorganization Act (IRA). The new measure might abolish tribal organizations, constitutions, and corporations formed under the IRA. Most importantly, termination legislation threatened to allow Congress the opportunity to exercise its plenary powers over Indian affairs whereby Congress could unilaterally legislate on property and alter or nullify treaties and agreements without Indian consent.[14]

Some Indians worried that on the one hand the federal government was reducing federal responsibility, while on the other hand it was expanding federal control. Opponents of termination worried that the expanded federal assistance required to prepare tribes for termination would increase rather than decrease paternalism. Delegates in 1949 passed a resolution resisting a plan to create area offices between the commissioner's post and that of the local superintendent. Opposition to the new level of administration came largely from the tribes in the Northwest. The NCAI garnered support to defeat the proposed area offices from Congressman Compton White of Idaho. However, White's bill to prohibit the offices failed to reach the House floor for a vote. In 1949 Commissioner Dillon Myer had created eleven area offices, seemingly to decentralize administration, but they had also shielded him from tribal consultation.[15]

Land and property remained at the heart of most concerns over termination measures. Some Native Americans saw the potential advantages of the new legislation. Certainly urban Indians saw the likely benefits from the dissolution and disbursement of tribal assets. Small numbers of Native Americans desired a removal, or at least a modification, of trust restrictions over tribal properties and resources. Tribal leaders such as Wade Crawford of the Klamath supported termination as a means to gain control over the tribes' timber resources.

Most members, however, feared a loss of federal custody over Indian land and property. If terminated, their land and properties would be subject to state and local taxation and regulation and no longer under the protection of the BIA. Experience had shown that most Indians who came into possession of title to their lands eventually lost the land. Some worried that the forcing of fee-simple patents on Indians would lead to wholesale loss of lands through tax sales. Most of the members of the NCAI felt that the "emancipation bills" regarding property represented ill-disguised attempts to gain title to Indian real estate and/or tax Indian land.[16]

Obviously it was impossible to create a workable policy that incorporated all Indians' views. What remained for the NCAI was to help design or maintain a policy that best suited the needs of the individual tribes. Exactly how to accomplish this objective was a different matter. Congress often carried out termination legislation that was contrary to tribal views. Differences persisted between tribally supported legislation and congressionally directed termination action. In practice, the 83d Congress passed a blanket measure, prepared in haste and taking little account of individual tribal needs or recommendations. By acting unilaterally, Congress denied Indians rights. Once aware of the sweeping nature of the legislation and the disastrous consequences that confronted them, the tribes prepared to fight back.

Many states with significant Indian populations welcomed the assumption of BIA services. Representatives from "Indian states" convened in Salt Lake City in May 1950 to organize the Governors' Interstate Indian Council (GIIC). The GIIC established committees to assess Indian needs. Committee members generally suggested favorable Indian support for state assumption. They forwarded their recommendations to Congress and to the appropriate governors. Makeup of the committees proved noteworthy. Edward Rogers, Napoleon B. Johnson, Frank George, and Martin Cross, a Gros Ventre from Fort Berthold, all of whom had been founders and leaders of the NCAI, served on GIIC committees. While these leaders seemingly favored a withdrawal of federal services, all would be out of power when the termination movement reached its high tide.[17]

The relocation policy of the period also served as a complimentary program to termination. In the wake of large-scale Indian migrations during World War II, the BIA decided to launch a program to relocate Native Americans to urban areas. Relocation and termination shared a common logic: both fostered assimilation and reduction of government services.[18]

Several termination-minded individuals played key roles in promoting withdrawal in the early phases of the movement. President Truman's commissioner of Indian affairs, Dillon Myer, was the first to push vigorously for termination. Myer, as previously mentioned, purged the BIA of Collier loyalists and replaced them with former WRA colleagues. He then set Indian policy on a new course. Albert Grorud, a special assistant to the Senate Indian Affairs Subcommittee, also performed a significant, but less visible, role in the termination crusade.[19]

In 1952, after intense competition for the position, Pres. Dwight Eisenhower appointed Glenn Emmons, a terminationist from New Mexico, as his commissioner of Indian affairs. Indian support had centered on Henry J. W. Belvin, principal chief of the Oklahoma Choctaws, but by early summer of 1952 the race had narrowed to Alvin J. Simpson and Emmons. Simpson, who chaired the GIIC, later withdrew. The "Emmons plan" seemed to view termination as a long-range goal, and it left passage of termination bills to key individuals in Congress. Republican congressional majorities in 1952 also brought more conservatives into positions of power in Indian affairs.

Sen. Arthur V. Watkins of Utah, however, became the chief congressional architect of the new federal policy. A devout conservative and Latter-Day Saint, Watkins relished the opportunity to participate in the overhaul of Indian policy. Watkins grew up near a Ute reservation, attended Brigham Young University, and graduated from Columbia University Law School. In 1947 he entered Congress and later chaired the Senate's censure investigation of Joseph McCarthy. O. Hatfield Chilson, an Eisenhower official, noted in an interview that Watkins "was the only one I know of who insisted on being on the Indian Affairs Committee."[20]

Chilson also noted an important connection between Watkins' inordinate interest in Indian affairs and his Latter-Day Saint background. Watkins, observed Chilson, "thought he was paying off a debt which the Mormons owed the Indians." Latter-Day Saints believe that Lamanites (Indians) and Nephites (non-Indians) both share a royal heritage. Although a chosen people, Lamanites have suffered injustice and persecution, according to Latter-Day Saints, because of their unrighteous past. The Lamanites, however, will one day "blossom like a rose," when they accept full assimilation into the mainstream society and convert to the true faith.[21] Watkins defended termination in a 1957 article in which he used assimilationist arguments that dated to the 1880s. Indians would advance, he argued, only through assimilation and an end to special federal programs. To Watkins, termination provided a means of equal opportunity and freedom for all Native Americans.[22]

The drive for termination received widespread support from other powerful Utah figures besides Watkins. In 1950 Representative Reva Bosone introduced one of the first resolutions calling for legislation to end federal supervision of Indians. Associate Indian Commissioner H. Rex Lee, a friend of Watkins from childhood, also frequently promoted termination bills. Utah governor J. Bracken Lee endorsed termination as a positive "step in the right direction."[23] Ernest Wilkinson, attorney and former president of Brigham Young University, represented the Paiute communities in Utah and the mixed-blood Utes in their negotiations to end their trust status.

Utah also became the battleground where adversaries fought the first termination campaigns. In 1954, Congress considered general legislation to terminate all the small reservations in Utah, home state of Watkins. The Utah senator was particularly interested in terminating the Southern Utes as a showcase to launch his new legislation. Robert Bennett, an Oneida, a long-time BIA employee who rose to the rank of Indian commissioner during the Johnson years, and a founding member of the NCAI, particularly helped the Utah tribes as they underwent termination. Bennett had started his bureau career with the Ute tribe in Utah, and he hoped that by sacrificing to Watkins and his allies the small Paiute bands and mixed-blood Utes in Utah, who had limited resources, he could protect the Northern Utes, who had more abundant resources.

Bennett reached the decision to offer these small Indian communities as political pawns to the termination tide in an impromptu meeting in a bean field in Utah with two other members of the NCAI. Meeting with Bennett were Reginald Curry, a BYU graduate and Ute tribal leader, and Francis McKinley, also a Ute tribal leader. Bennett, Curry, and McKinley knew that following termination the Latter-Day Saints Church would provide services to the Paiute bands and the mixed-blood Utes.[24]

Once the coercive nature of the new policy became clear, the NCAI united in a concerted effort to oppose forced withdrawal; instead, it promoted alternatives to the shift in policy. Demonstrating near consensus, the NCAI delegates at the 1948 convention in Denver recommended that any withdrawal of federal services to Indians proceed locally on a case-by-case basis rather than as a national policy. The 1948 convention also met the termination threat with proposals to strengthen tribal control over Indian affairs. Having successfully survived earlier criticisms that planners created the organization as a tool of the Collier administration and the BIA, delegates in the same year voted to rescind the 1945 resolution prohibiting Bureau employees from holding office in the NCAI.[25] As the uncertainties and dangers of withdrawal in the late postwar years became more apparent, the NCAI needed to draw from the talents and political expertise of all its members.

As adoption of a termination policy gained momentum, in 1950 President Johnson requested that Oscar L. Chapman, secretary of the interior, assign a permanent federal liaison to work with the NCAI in shaping the new policy. Chapman turned down the request. Through a joint effort with the Association on American Indians Affairs (AAIA), the NCAI two years later arranged for tribal representatives from all across the country to come to the nation's capital to confront Chapman and Myer over the new policies.[26] The meeting had little effect on the new policy course.

Instead of cutting federal services, D'Arcy McNickle, charter member and chairman of the Indian Tribal Relations Committee of the NCAI, outlined a ten-point plan in 1951 to attack Indian poverty.

McNickle roughly based his proposal on Truman's Point Four program. In his State of the Union Address two years earlier Truman had introduced an agenda of U.S. foreign aid aimed at improving the quality of life for undeveloped nations. Like the Marshall Plan, Truman's Point Four program combined humanitarian, anticommunist, and economic objectives. McNickle's self-help proposal called for a domestic Point Four program with greater federal appropriations for Indian reservations. President Napoleon B. Johnson called McNickle's plan the Indian equivalent of the successful "Marshall Plan" that provided aid in the economic reconstruction of Western Europe following World War II.[27]

The termination threat changed the political structure of the NCAI in several important ways. Concern over termination prompted the organization to orient itself more along tribal lines, with less emphasis to be placed on small groups, organizations, and individuals within the tribes. In the struggling infant years of the NCAI, the organization had extended voting membership to urban groups, bands, and chapter affiliates within tribes. By the mid-1950s some urban Indians were attempting to undermine tribal governments. Delegates in 1955 changed the original constitution to limit group membership to federally recognized tribes. New measures accorded tribes more voting power than individuals. Amendments allowed tribes to elect more than one voting delegate, with the number to be based upon the size of the tribe. Delegates also modified participation in the executive council to include all member tribes with their representatives selected by the tribal councils. As with the original constitution, other Indians were still encouraged to join as individuals.[28]

Serious factional disputes within the NCAI concerning forced termination also led to an important change in leadership. Dan Madrano, Frank George, and Sioux attorney Ramon Roubideaux led a small faction that supported voluntary or involuntary termination. Opposition to forced withdrawal by most of the NCAI membership and a lack of the NCAI funds to pay his salary led George to resign before his term was finished. George, who served as a tireless volunteer in the earliest years of the NCAI, however, later claimed that he had resigned under duress. The NCAI leaders at first worried that George's departure would damage the organization's reputation and alienate the Indians of the Northwest at a critical time. Some NCAI officers even worried that Madrano, George, and Roubideaux might try to disrupt the 1953 convention. Neither concern was warranted. To protect the integrity of the organization from possible internal divisions, President W. W. Short considered expelling the former officers.[29] In order to diffuse the situation and officially to end their working relationship with the executive director, the executive council scraped together enough money to pay George part of his back salary. Satisfied with the offer, George departed the scene.[30]

Previously mentioned Helen Louise (White) Peterson, a Northern Cheyenne but enrolled Oglala Sioux, with the given Indian name of "Wa-Cinn-Ya-Win-Pi-Mi" (meaning "a woman to trust and depend on"), replaced George as executive director in 1953. Elizabeth Roe Cloud, activist and wife of noted Winnebago educator Henry Roe Cloud, accompanied Peterson to Washington to help her in the transition. Together they traveled to reservations throughout Indian country in Roe Cloud's late-model Chevy to make contacts and establish Indian needs. Peterson also received tremendous support from Ruth Bronson. She called on her almost daily, and Bronson was willing to share her time and talents with the new director.

Coached at an early age by her grandmother to value Indian land and to be a role model for the Indian community, Peterson proved to be the right leader in a time of crisis. Active in the NCAI since 1948, Peterson was also an adviser to the United States delegation to the earlier noted second American Indian Conference in Cuzco, Peru, in 1949. Her experience in assisting city planners with minority programs in Denver, Colorado, and Rapid City, South Dakota, in the immediate postwar period had paid important dividends for the NCAI. Peterson was to use her diverse background to assert Indian rights, equality, ethnic identity, and to slow the assimilationist movement.[31]

By 1954 the perils of forced termination became apparent to Native Americans on the reservations, and the new policy marked a power shift in Indian leadership within the NCAI. The shift was away from the Great Plains and the Southwest, particularly Oklahoma tribes, toward the tribes of the Northwest. Tribal delegations often worried about the influence of off-reservation Indians looking to benefit from per capita payouts. Reservation Indians were concerned about losing land, water, hunting, and fishing rights. At Phoenix in 1953, W. W. Short replaced Napoleon B. Johnson, who led the NCAI from its inception. While Short served as a president of the NCAI for only one year, he filled an important role during a time of transition. A successful Oklahoma businessman, Short provided the NCAI with financial assistance but more importantly reached out to the reservation community at a critical time.[32]

More significant changes in NCAI leadership came in 1954 with the election of Joseph Garry, a forty-four-year-old, full-blood Coeur d'Alene from Idaho. Garry's heavy recruitment of the Northwest tribes provided the NCAI with support from a strong tribal base during critical years. The great-great-grandson of the noted chief Spokane Garry, the new president of the NCAI was a veteran of both World War II and the Korean War. Before his election to the presidency of the NCAI, he served four years on the organization's executive council. Having earlier served as president of the Affiliated Tribes of the Northwest, Garry was elected to the Idaho state legislature in 1956 and 1958. Handsome, amiable, and articulate, Indian voters named him "Outstanding Indian in North America" in 1957 and 1959. He brought to NCAI a strong dedication to preserving the special relationship between the federal government and the tribes, Indian ethnicity and sovereignty, Indian civil rights, and the reservation community. Perhaps most importantly, he was committed to protecting Indians' land base, resources, and self-determination. In the end, Peterson's and Garry's noncompulsory view of termination won out over the ideas expressed by Roubideaux and Madrano.[33]

House Concurrent Resolution 108 (H.C.R. 108) committed the federal government to coercive termination. H.C.R. 108, approved on August 1, 1953, announced that Indians "should be subject to the same laws and entitled to the same privileges, rights, and responsibilities" as all American citizens. The resolution further recommended the immediate removal of federal guardianship and supervision over selected tribes. To this end, Congress proposed the immediate termination of federal services and supervision for the individual tribes of California, Florida, and Texas. Tribes targeted for termination included the Flatheads of Montana, Klamaths of Oregon, Menominees of Wisconsin, Potawatomis of Kansas and Nebraska, and the Chippewas of North Dakota. The resolution directed the secretary of interior to recommend specific legislation to end federal responsibility by January 1, 1954. The new legislation represented an extremely dangerous situation to the tribes that did not want it. For the tribes targeted for termination, according to NCAI leadership, "it would end federal services without insuring they would be provided by the states; cut off tribal funds; liquidate tribal property; abolish federal protection of Indian land and potentially lead to loss of Indian trust property."[34]

On August 15, 1993, Public Law 280 (P.L. 280), a companion act, extended state laws over selected Indian reservations. The act permitted California, Minnesota, Nebraska, Oregon, and Wisconsin to exercise both criminal and civil jurisdiction over reservations. It also contained provisions to allow other states unilaterally to assume jurisdiction over Indian reservations.[35]

On the heels of H.C.R. 108 and P.L. 280, the December 1953 NCAI annual convention at Phoenix took on particular significance. Convention planners appropriately titled the three-day meeting the "Crisis in Indian Affairs." "We [Indians] are at the crossroads of destiny," Clarence Wesley, chairman of the San Carlos Reservation, proclaimed. "The path we choose today," he continued, "is the road of tomorrow from which there is no turning." The stand of the NCAI against the coercive termination policy generated widespread support from the tribal representatives. In a distinctive symbolic gesture Allie Reynolds, a member of the Creek tribe and well-known pitcher for the New York Yankees, showed his support for the NCAI during this critical time. Planners had scheduled for Reynolds to address the Phoenix delegates. At the last minute, however, other commitments prevented him from attending. Instead, he sent two hundred autographed baseballs to help promote good attendance at the meetings.[36]

During the conference the NCAI stood firm in its opposition to forced termination. In a speech read to the delegates, Commissioner Emmons, who was unable to attend the conference, asked them to put aside past differences between the BIA and the NCAI and unite in creating new policy. Cooperation to Emmons meant unconditional, passive acceptance of the new shift in policy. Opposed to forced and coercive termination, the NCAI urged complete consultation and Indian consent about future policy changes. In essence, the NCAI appealed to a fundamental democratic principle, securing the consent of the governed. As the sweeping nature of the termination threat became imminent, the NCAI braced for the long legal and legislative battle ahead. Fearing Congress might legislate Indians out of existence, D'Arcy McNickle warned that the "battle for civil rights may not yet be won, but the battle for the right to be culturally different has not even started."[37]

Congressional deliberations on the termination bills for individual tribes began on February 15, 1954, when the Senate and House Subcommittees on Indian Affairs opened joint hearings. Pressured by a ridiculous deadline of January 1, 1954, Watkins pushed for draft termination bills even before Congress, state officials, and Indian tribes had had enough time to evaluate properly the benefits and consequences of the measures. Even some westerners like John B. Hart, executive director of the North Dakota Indian Affairs Commission, had reservations about the speed in which the policy was being administered. Hart preferred to delay termination until the federal government worked out the logistics with state, county, and local agencies and, more importantly, supplied funds to such agencies. The twelve bills under discussion included Indian tribes of Florida, Texas, New York, and California, as well as the Klamath, Menominee, Flathead, Makah, Sac and Fox, Kickapoo, Potawatomi of Kansas, and Turtle Mountain Chippewa. Although Watkins usually presided over the hastily organized hearings, E. Y. Berry, chairman of the House Subcommittee, stood in. Like Watkins, Representative Berry of South Dakota was a conservative Republican. As a proassimilationist, Berry had denounced the Indian New Deal as retrogressive.[38] Other terminationists, such as Representatives Wesley D'Ewart of Montana, William Harrison of Wyoming, and A. L. Miller of Nebraska, occasionally attended some hearings but did not take an active role.

Dominating the proceedings, Watkins usually bullied the witnesses by eliciting only the assimilationist responses he was interested in hearing; he even interrupted testimony to assert his own beliefs. Watkins denounced the validity of past treaties and the federal trust responsibilities, and he condemned the failures of the reservation system. As the hearing advanced, Watkins and Berry were not following the previously mentioned "Zimmerman model" for phased termination. The basis for their selection process remains unclear even today. Following the hearings, Congress approved six termination acts during the 1954 session. These included the Menominees, the Klamaths, the numerous bands and tribes of western Oregon, the Alabama-Coushattas of Texas, and the Mixed-blood Utes and southern Paiutes of Utah.[39]

In response to the termination acts, the NCAI immediately went on the offensive to prevent other tribes from being terminated without their consent. The NCAI directed their assault with care, trying to wield influence without bringing the roof down on BIA programs. On February 25–28, 1954, in the midst of the joint hearings, the NCAI called an emergency conference at the Raleigh Hotel in Washington DC. The organization obviously selected the dates and location of the conference to coincide with a break in the termination hearings. The intermission ensured that many Native Americans would be available to attend the conference.[40] Representing more than one-third of the nation's Indian population, delegates from forty-three tribes and twenty-one states and the territory of Alaska were present at the emergency conference. Employees of the federal government, congressional representatives, and lawyers also attended the conference as nonvoting delegates.

Planning the conference with less than three weeks' notice, the NCAI received the generous support of nineteen church or reform organizations. These included the ACLU, the American Friends Service Committee, the American Legion, the American Missionary Society, the AAIA, the Boy Scouts of America, the Daughters of the American Revolution, the Friends Committee on National Legislation, the General Federation of Women's Clubs, the Indian Rights Association, the Institute of Ethnic Affairs, the Japanese-American Citizens' League, the League for Catholic Indian Missions, the Montana Farmers Union, the National Association of Intergroup Relations, the National Council of Churches, the New York Yearly Meeting of Friends, the North Dakota Indian Affairs Commission, and the United Church Women. Commissioner Emmons not only attended the conference but approved the use of tribal funds for delegates to attend. Using their influence in Indian circles, McNickle and Bronson raised the necessary donations for the conference. A generous grant from an anonymous donor also helped the NCAI meet its expenses which totaled nearly fourteen hundred dollars. Noted attorney Theodore Haas also donated his time and legal talents to the conference.[41]

The primary objectives of the conference were to unify Indian support against termination and to provide a forum for public relations. The NCAI admirably accomplished both goals. The NCAI used information from the conference for political persuasion. To achieve its objectives the NCAI hired Annabelle Price, a professional public relations specialist, to organize the media campaign. Price, with Jim Hayes, a member of the American Friends Service Committee, ensured that more than four thousand newspapers and numerous local, regional, and national radio and television stations in the United States and Alaska covered the event. Coverage even included the British Broadcasting Corporation. By most accounts and standards the conference was an enormous public relations victory. Joined by many U.S. reform organizations in its opposition to termination, the NCAI also received moral support from groups in Europe.[42]

The emergency conference educated the public and elected officials concerning Indians' opposition to the changes in federal policy. Perhaps more importantly, however, it functioned to unify the NCAI. When the conference started, some NCAI members still had questions about termination. Proponents of termination had attempted to rush the new policy through Congress before most Native Americans understood its implications. The delegates at the conference listened to legal specialists and tribal and federal officials discuss the ramifications of the pending termination bills. By the time the deliberations concluded, the membership was "100%" opposed to the new measures.[43]

Insisting that forced termination laws violated treaty privileges, the conference delegates adopted a "Declaration of Indian Rights," which called for a continuation of federal guardianship and for the rights and benefits of citizenship. Reservations, the representatives proclaimed, "do not imprison us. They are ancestral homelands, retained by us for our personal use and enjoyment. We feel we must assert our right to maintain ownership in our own way, and to terminate it only by our consent." The NCAI agreed to help tribes, such as the Menominees who consented to the new policy, prepare for immediate termination.[44]

Immediately following the conclusion of the conference, one hundred Indian delegates who remained in Washington overwhelmed Senator Watkins by attempting to attend the Senate Subcommittee termination hearings involving the Salish and Kooteni tribes of the Flathead Reservation in Montana. The senator halted the hearings in the insular affairs committee room and moved them to the more spacious Senate caucus room. The 1954 termination bills were only one of the legislative problems the officers of the NCAI and the Indian people faced. Heirship and competency bills also demanded immediate attention. During 1954 the NCAI also strongly supported the transfer of health services from the BIA to the Public Health Service, because the organization believed the shift would improve health care.[45]

Early in 1954 the NCAI scored several important victories in the battle against forced termination. When Representative Wesley D'Ewart of Montana introduced a "competency" bill in 1953–54, which was intended to lessen Indian land-title restrictions and to force assimilation, the NCAI blocked the measure. The bill called for the automatic fee patenting of allotments when tribal members reached adulthood. Besides providing private interests easier access to buy Indian lands, the proposal represented a form of termination by decree. As the bill neared passage in early 1954, heavy lobbying by the NCAI forced its withdrawal. "Hard work and $425 worth of telephone calls to tribal chairmen to get them to send wires to their Congressmen," Peterson recalled excitedly, "did the trick and it happened right before our eyes!"[46]

The NCAI also modified the first termination bill. In early 1954 Watkins began the hearings with six small bands of Paiutes and Shoshones in his home state of Utah. Since the bands had been too poor to send delegates to the NCAI emergency conference, the NCAI sent a representative to meet with them to learn their wishes regarding termination. While four of the bands showed little resistance to termination, two of the bands, the Skull Valley and Washakie, strongly opposed it. Following the meeting with the Indian communities, the NCAI asked Watkins' subcommittee to delete the two bands from the Utah bill. Before favorably reporting the proposal to the full Congress, the subcommittee dropped the two bands from the bill. Not only did Congress exclude the two bands from the final measure, but it also canceled past debts the two bands owed the federal government. The legislation passed just as the NCAI had requested.[47]

After the two successes, the NCAI proposed in November 1954 at the annual convention in Omaha, Nebraska, a "Point Nine" program as an alternative to the forced termination legislation. The NCAI introduced the plan to Congress as the Point IX Program, modeled after the technical assistance program of the same name for underdeveloped countries. The plan, similar to the one proposed by McNickle in 1951, aimed at restoring lands to tribal ownership, protecting and developing reservation resources, providing occupational training, and establishing a revolving credit fund to help Indian communities and businesses become more self-sufficient. Leaders intended the long-term program to provide the Native Americans with a gradual transition into mainstream society and ultimately to make federal responsibility unnecessary. Indeed, the suggestion of the NCAI represented a well-articulated counterproposal to federal Indian policy. Officials at the Department of Interior, however, opposed the proposal because it implied that the government had previously failed to provide such services, and it limited technical and economic assistance to Indians to the amount accorded foreign governments.[48]

Persistent efforts of the NCAI, however, continued to bear important fruit. The unified stand of the NCAI in 1954, with assistance from other reform groups, had generated adequate political pressure to slow, or sometimes even stop, the termination movement until more important shifts had occurred in Congress. The NCAI halted termination of the Turtle Mountain Chippewa, Florida Seminole, Flathead, and Colville Tribes. Even Helen Peterson expressed surprise at the success of the NCAI movement to slow and alter federal policy. Several members of the Senate and House Subcommittees on Indian Affairs changed their positions on the termination bills following the NCAI emergency conference.[49] The NCAI campaign had also served to alert many state officials to the expensive costs associated with turning federal services to Indians over to the individual states.

In 1955 the Democrats gained control of Congress, and in 1957 they increased their majority. Liberal Democrats from the West took control of the Interior and Insular Affairs Committees. Representative Lee Metcalf, Senators James Murray and Mike Mansfield of Montana, and Joseph O'Mahoney of Wyoming lent valuable assistance to the NCAI and Indian groups opposed to termination.[50]

The anxiety of termination and the legal battle against it increased participation of Indians voting in general elections. The NCAI was largely responsible for the increased political awareness and in 1956 sponsored a program entitled "Register, Inform Yourself and Vote," which interpreted issues, provided candidate information, and explained the mechanics of voting to its members. Politicians from western states recognized the effectiveness of the elevated Indian political activity on legislation in their states. Regional legislators quickly learned that the best way to secure Indian votes was to oppose federal action that did not have Indian consent. In 1957 the respected American Heritage Foundation acknowledged the NCAI for efforts on behalf of voting awareness by presenting the organization an award for "outstanding public service."[51]

Changes in the Eisenhower administration also slowed termination. Secretary of Interior Douglas McKay resigned in 1956 to run for the Senate. Eisenhower named former Nebraska senator and White House staff member Fred S. Seaton to the position. Seaton, a moderate conservative Republican, departed from the strong commitment to termination legislation. Seaton's position reflected the influence of the NCAI. With respect to withdrawal legislation, Secretary Seaton announced that termination would proceed cautiously and only with the consent of the tribe involved. The NCAI officers hailed the new position and offered their cooperation with the new shift policy. Forced termination of the previous generation was now dead. In the late 1960s the policy of the federal government shifted from termination to self-determination and direct assistance to the reservations.[52]

The experiences of the Klamaths provide insight into the termination process and the consequences of forced assimilation. The Klamath Reservation remained federally recognized until 1954 when Congress passed P.L. 587, otherwise known as the Klamath Termination Act. P.L. 587 eventually ended the federal government's administrative responsibilities to the tribe and transferred the responsibilities to state and local agencies. The act also provided for relinquishment of federal trust over Klamath land and the distribution of tribal income and assets on a per-capita basis.[53]

Several advocates had suggested a liquidation of Klamath assets. Rich timber holdings had long made the tribe a target for termination. The Klamath termination movement, however, gained momentum after 1945 largely because of the leadership of tribal politician Wade Crawford. Crawford, son of a tribal judge, and his wife, Ida, had been active in Klamath politics for several decades. In 1933 John Collier appointed him as reservation superintendent but fired him four years later because of incompetence and poor relations between the Klamaths and the BIA. Crawford, on the other hand, charged that Collier had communist sympathies, tolerated fraud on the reservation, and tried to force the tribe to adopt the IRA. By 1945 Crawford and a small minority of off-reservation Klamaths promoted termination as a means to gain access to a per-capita distribution of tribal assets. Crawford's insistence that the Klamaths were ready for termination insured immediate action. Crawford and his followers were vehemently opposed by veteran tribal leaders Boyd J. Jackson, Dibbon Cook, Jesse L. Kirk Sr., and Seldon E. Kirk. In 1947 these antitermination forces requested that representatives of the NCAI attend hearings in Oregon to liquidate the reservation. Financial shortages prevented the NCAI from attending the discussions.[54]

Congressional supporters of the Klamath Termination Act hoped the law would appease both tribal factions. The law allowed tribal members the option either to withdraw from the tribe and receive a pro rata share of tribal assets or to remain with the tribe and have their claims to the unsold portion of the reservation placed under private trust. Further, the law provided a four-year transition period lasting until August 13, 1958. Because the Klamaths were not a member tribe, the NCAI was hesitant to pass resolutions for the Klamaths. At the request of the antitermination faction, however, the NCAI in 1956 opposed P.L. 587 and recommended its repeal. Although not voting members of the NCAI, the Klamaths usually sent representatives to every meeting of the organization. In June 1957, at the suggestion of Helen Peterson, NBC-TV aired a special on the termination of the Klamaths.[55]

Carrying out P.L. 587 proved difficult. Efforts by various conservation and lumber interests produced two amendments to the original termination law. The greater revision came in 1958 as Congress agreed to several key changes. New provisions authorized the sale of timber tracts to private buyers through competitive bids equal to or above the market value. Politicos required purchasers to follow sustained yield and cutting practices and other conservation measures. The federal government, through Forest Service officials, would purchase unsold tracts to create a national forest (Winema National Forest). The federal government would purchase the Klamath Marsh and manage it as a wildlife refuge. As a result of the amendments, bureaucrats postponed final termination until April 1, 1961.[56]

Elections in 1958 effectively ended the Klamath Reservation. In that year, 1,659 Klamaths (77 percent) voted to withdraw from the tribe and receive a per capita payment of $43,000. To pay these individuals their share of the estate, the government sold 717,000 acres of the 862,000-acre reservation. The 474 holdouts (23 percent) continued their tribal status, hoping to survive economically on the remaining 145,000 acres. In 1974, however, these last holdouts voted to sell the remainder of the reservation for per capita shares of $173,000 for each member. Klamath termination proved costly to both the tribe and the federal government. One economist estimates that the federal government spent nearly $72.5 million to terminate a tribe that prior to termination had cost the BIA no more than $200,000 annually.[57]

The relocation of Indians from reservations to urban situations produced mixed results. Conservatives contended that industrial jobs loosed Indians from BIA control, provided them access to better education and other social services, and offered a means for ending Indian poverty. Many participants briefly took urban jobs and then returned to the reservation. Critics of the program charged that relocation failed to improve Indians' living standards and exposed them to slum housing, alcoholism, and other social problems.[58] Inadequate relocation services and training often produced poor results. Relocation was, in short, another controversial attempt to support termination and to force Indian assimilation. While relocation did yield successful adjustment and increased prosperity for some participants, the long-range effects of the program have remained unclear. The long-term cultural effects of relocation are unclear as well.

Throughout the termination period the NCAI depended on the support of church and civic groups, various reform organizations, and the media. The NCAI in 1958 nominated Robert McCormick, a television reporter with NBC, for a Peabody Award for his hour-long report in the Kaleidoscope Series: "The American Stranger." The NBC production took a close-up look at conditions on the Menominee, Blackfeet, and Flathead Reservations. Strongly critical of federal policy and the BIA, the show proved a valuable tool to create public interest and awareness about the Indians' situation.[59]

The Association of American Indian Affairs (AAIA) and the NCAI, sometimes cautious allies, learned to work together during the termination period to advance Indian interests. During the early 1950s, Alexander Lesser, executive director of the AAIA from 1947 to 1955, vehemently opposed any cooperation with the NCAI. Oliver La Farge, president of the AAIA, however, demanded teamwork, not rivalry, between the two groups. Lesser's resignation in 1955 and his replacement by La Verne Madigan paved the way for better relations between the AAIA and the NCAI. Committed to the need for a national Indian organization to serve as a single voice for the Indian community, Madigan fostered cooperation with the NCAI. Having cooperated during the emergency conference in 1954, the AAIA and the NCAI in May 1957 arranged a one-day conference for NCAI members and other reform organizations to discuss legal concerns and federal policy. In 1959 Roger N. Baldwin, founder of the ACLU, trustee of the Robert Marshall Civil Liberties Trust (RMCLT), and an NCAI benefactor, suggested a merger between the AAIA and the NCAI. He intended the union to keep the two organizations from working at cross-purposes and to increase the financial stability of both groups. Under the proposal, the RMCLT would provide financial support for five years until the alliance became self-supporting. After careful consideration of the proposal, the NCAI executive council turned down the recommendation.[60]

Several developments during the period, in addition to the termination struggle, proved that the NCAI was sincere in its resolve to improve the Indians' status. In March 1958 the NCAI sent a delegation to Puerto Rico to study "Operation Bootstrap." Puerto Rico had begun the program in 1948 to industrialize and diversify the island's economy through financial incentives such as tax encouragements. In a relatively short time the Puerto Rican government-sponsored program raised the island's standard of living and made it self-sufficient without any costs to U.S. taxpayers. NCAI hoped that a similar program would also produce the same results for Indians. Peterson and Garry led the twenty-four-member delegation to Puerto Rico. After meeting with Puerto Rican governor Louis Muñoz Marin and other island leaders, the group toured health centers, educational and vocational facilities, residential areas, industrial plants, and community improvement projects. The AAIA, the NCAI Fund, the Phelps-Stokes Fund, the Office of the Commonwealth of Puerto Rico, and some tribal councils contributed financial and staff support for the trip. Impressed by the success of Puerto Rico, the NCAI hoped Congress would approve an "Operation Moccasin" program.[61] With the backing of Puerto Rican leaders, Representative E. Y. Berry proposed legislation in 1959 to industrialize reservations patterned on Puerto Rico's "Operation Bootstrap." Legislators held hearings in the mid-1960s, but the measure died.[62]

With support and cooperation from the NCAI, in 1950 D'Arcy McNickle also created an adjunct organization called the American Indian Development (AID) to plan Indian community revitalization. Through summer workshops, McNickle hoped to encourage tribal leaders to make their communities economically more self-sufficient. Participants shared common experiences, ideas, and ethnic solidarity. McNickle's health education project at Crownpoint, New Mexico, in 1953–55 was a spinoff of the successes of AID. Paralleling the development of AID was a series of summer workshops for Indian youth in 1955 conducted by the Anthropology Department at the University of Chicago. In 1959 AID took over control of the workshops. Always a supporter of educational activities for Indian youth, the NCAI welcomed and promoted the growth of the workshops. The success of the workshops held by AID shaped the evolution of the Indian youth movements of the 1960s. By providing a forum to discuss Indian affairs, these summer workshops led individuals such as Clyde Warrior, Ponca orator and leader of the National Indian Youth Council (NIYC), to become activists.[63]

In the late 1960s and early 1970s, participants in these youth conferences and other Indian activists highly criticized the termination policy. Termination, not implemented with the care its earlier promoters envisioned and applied with haste and confusion, failed to deliver its promises. Termination did not end the vast outlays of federal funds. Nationally, the policy failed to simplify the administration of Indian affairs or reduce federal responsibilities in relation to the Indians. Instead, the policy left many Indians burdened with inadequate local services and perplexed by new state regulations. In almost all cases, termination produced land losses, poverty, unemployment, and bitter resentment. In the end, policymakers only terminated about 3 percent of the Indian population and withdrew federal trust status from the same percentage of Indian lands. Though the coercive termination of Watkins and his allies was relatively short-lived, the fear of termination plagued all Indians. "Termination," as historian Donald Fixico aptly wrote, threatened to be "an all-inclusive destroyer of Indian life-styles."[64]

In the mid-1950s, flexing its newfound political muscles, the NCAI had made an important stand in the nation's capital. Native Americans had for the first time in their history politically expressed themselves effectively on a national level in a unified voice that echoed throughout the chambers of Congress and elsewhere. Despite competition with the McCarthy hearings in 1954, Indian leaders had successfully made their wishes known. From this time forward, Indian people demanded a larger role in the formulation of Indian policy. In the process Native Americans learned two valuable lessons that would serve them well in the decades to come: the power of the vote and of the media. During the termination era, the NCAI used the classic political weapon of the citizenry in a democracy: the ballot. The vote on local and state levels became an important resource for pursuing Indian goals. The NCAI also showed itself adept at using the media to communicate broad appeals for support. In the turbulent 1960s and 1970s and beyond, Indians took advantage of these resources to force their concerns into the larger public arena. In particular, by recalling past abuses they were using tactics aimed at arousing sympathy.

Perhaps the Indian protests in the mid- to late 1950s were not as dramatic as the black confrontations over civil rights during the late 1950s and early 1960s. While some African Americans may have preferred complete assimilation, most Native Americans did not. Passage of the coercive termination bills threatened to complete the Indian assimilation that had started hundreds of years earlier. At stake was not only an end to statutory obligations held by the federal government, but special federal protection negotiated in past treaty agreements and the right to a separate ethnic identity. In the end, the persistent desire to preserve culture and identity proved to be the most powerful weapon of the NCAI.

6 . THE NEW INDIAN TRAIL

We gather here not only mindful of heavy burdens, but also full
of hope. We want to believe there is a New Frontier, a New Trail.
Our faith is renewed that with our renewed effort and the cooper-
ation of the Tribes, their friends, and the U.S. government work-
ing together, we will be able to find better solutions to the problems
we face. ANGUS WILSON, Nez Perce Tribal Chairman,
Eighteenth Annual Conference, 1961

Caught up in the hopes and promises of an Indian New Frontier, the
NCAI participated in the 1961 inaugural parade of John F. Kennedy.
Appropriately titled the "First New Frontier—1620," the NCAI float
entry symbolized the hospitality that Indians extended to the first
European settlers to the new world. The heavy snowstorm on inauguration day, however, ruined the float's display of fresh vegetables
and a turkey. Yet, the poor weather did not dampen the spirits of the
Indian participants. Kennedy's pledge to end forced termination and
his promise of a more vigorous domestic Indian policy offered Native Americans across the country renewed hope.

Four Indian groups besides the NCAI entered floats in the 1961
inaugural parade. Besides the "First New Frontier—1620" float, the
NCAI helped plan a second entry entitled "Sacajawea and Lewis and
Clark Blaze Montana's New Frontier." Recalling the relationship between the popular figures of that famous expedition, it evoked images of peace and cooperation in a new era. The Montana tribal delegation, which organized the float, received more than thirty offers
from donors willing to lend their dogs to be part of an Indian camp
display on the float. After sifting through the submissions, the committee selected a dog named "Nixon."

Members of the Rosebud Sioux also entered a float entitled "Rosebud Sioux, South Dakota Centennial 1961." John Rainer from Taos Pueblo, who was a former executive director of the NCAI, vividly recalled the Sioux participation in the parade:

> Bob Burnette [Rosebud Sioux and executive director of the NCAI in 1961–63] was the lead man. The Sioux [are] reported to be good horsemen. There was a group on horseback; unfortunately, they lined them up behind the Marine band. When the parade started, the Marine band began to drum up and play, and the horses got excited. Bob Burnette had a war bonnet on and the horse stood up and threw Bob Burnette to the ground. The horse got away and they were not able to catch him. So, the Marine jeep driver stopped and a couple of Marines got Bob Burnette to come and sit in the back seat of the jeep, and that's how he finished the parade.[1]

Colorfully decorated, the Indian floats pleased President Kennedy as they passed the reviewing stand. The extreme cold weather on inauguration day prevented many members of the NCAI from attending the inaugural balls. The poor weather, however, did not dampen the spirits of the Indian participants. Receiving an award for their float, the NCAI looked forward with anticipation to the new administration.[2]

After Kennedy's election, major changes occurred in federal policy and in Indian thought and action. Indians during the 1960s became more determined, vocal, and sophisticated in trying to achieve self-determination. Before the sudden end of the Kennedy administration, new Indian protest organizations had arisen to challenge the position of the NCAI. Eventually, the NCAI and the new Indian groups had turned a pivotal corner.

The election of John F. Kennedy marked the coming of a new generation of leadership. His administration symbolized youth, ambition, and energy. Capitalizing on his public appeal, Kennedy pledged imaginative approaches to old problems. In particular, his administration brought a new direction to Indian policy. Promising to fight against Indian poverty and to increase Indian self-determination,

Kennedy also rejected the coercive termination policy of the previous decade. With the end of the Eisenhower administration, Indian groups, and in particular the NCAI, welcomed the opportunity to forge an Indian New Frontier.

Politics in 1960 played an important part in both the courses of national leadership and the direction of the NCAI. Much to the surprise of the delegates at the 1959 convention in Phoenix, Joseph R. Garry, chairman of the Coeur d'Alene tribe and influential leader of the Northwest tribes, announced he would not seek another term as president of NCAI. By standing firm against termination, Garry had helped guide the NCAI through a difficult period in Indian affairs. His presidency, which had begun in 1953, had diligently protected Indian land and resources and had advanced Indian civil rights. Not wanting the organization to appear as if it engaged in partisan politics, Garry bowed out to enter the primary in Idaho as a Democratic candidate for the U.S. Senate. Although he had served in the Idaho state legislature since 1956, he lost his primary bid for the Senate seat.

Two candidates competed closely to fill Garry's vacated position in the NCAI. Clarence Wesley, forty-six-year-old farmer and stockman and chair of the San Carlos Apache, won by a slim margin, 353 to 339, over Walter "Blackie" Wetzel, chairman of the Blackfeet tribe. Wetzel, however, disputed the election, claiming that fifteen proxy votes cast by Osage Chief Paul Pitts on behalf of the Oklahoma tribe were unconstitutional. Disallowing Wetzel's protest, the credentials committee of the NCAI certified Wesley as the next president. To preserve the unity of the NCAI, Wetzel formally accepted Wesley's victory. Given the rough-and-tumble world of twentieth-century Indian politics, he preferred simply to wait another year to launch another campaign.[3]

Garry's Senate bid in 1960 caused other divisions within the NCAI. Marceline Kevis, a member of the Coeur d'Alene tribe to which Garry also belonged, complained that Helen L. Peterson, executive director of the NCAI, solicited contributions from Kevis's tribal council to support Garry's campaign. Crying partisan politics, Kevis charged that Peterson violated the NCAI constitution, which prohibited such activity, and he requested that President Wesley fire Peterson. Several newspapers across the country picked up the story and falsely charged that the NCAI had set a goal of thirty thousand dollars to help get Garry elected. Responding to the allegations, Peterson maintained that the letter in question was nothing more than a personal note she sent in an unofficial capacity to a member of the tribal council to show her support of Garry. She further replied that she had always encouraged qualified Indian candidates, despite their political affiliation, to seek political offices. In short, she denied any wrongdoing.[4]

Concerned by the bad publicity, Allen Slickpoo, recording secretary of the NCAI, and other members of the organization also requested that Wesley investigate the matter and remove Peterson from office. Coming on the heels of the difficult struggle against forced termination, Indian unity was more important than ever, and members took seriously the charges against the NCAI. At the request of Wesley, the group's law firm—Wilkinson, Cragun, and Barker—looked into a possible breach of the NCAI constitution. Although the law firm acknowledged that the complaint was a serious matter, it believed the affair was nothing more than a misunderstanding and contended that Peterson had not violated the NCAI constitution. Because she acted as an individual and not a representative of the organization, the law firm recognized Peterson's right to endorse the candidate of her choice. Accepting Peterson's and the lawyers' interpretation of events, Kevis dropped the complaint.[5]

Because of the fear it caused in Indian communities, termination prompted the NCAI to take an active role in the 1960 national elections. The organization encouraged voter registration, education efforts, and the formulation of policies that reflected an Indian viewpoint. Wishing to remain nonpartisan, particularly following Kevis's complaint, the NCAI did not formally endorse either party.

Kennedy's platform in 1960, however, won almost instant approval from most members of the NCAI. During his campaign, Kennedy had pledged to protect the Indian land base and cultural integrity, to foster improved Indian health programs and education opportunities, to encourage reservation economic development, and to end involuntary termination. Kennedy also promised "competent, sympathetic, and dedicated leadership in the administration of Indian affairs." His platform reflected a significant departure from previous Indian policies, and it reflected many concerns of the NCAI.[6]

Most importantly, Kennedy appealed to many members of the NCAI largely because of his willingness to consult with its representatives about the formulation of Indian policy. Frank George, chairman of the American Indian Section of the Nationalities Division of the Democratic National Committee and former executive director of the NCAI, had conferred with Kennedy at his home in Hyannis Port in the late summer of 1960 to assist in the construction of the party platform. Helping his brother create the Democratic platform on Indian affairs, Sen. Robert Kennedy twice in October 1960 also solicited the views of members of the NCAI.[7] When John Kennedy won a first ballot victory at the Democratic Convention in Los Angeles, Clarence Wesley, president of the NCAI, Joseph Garry, former president of the NCAI, and George were on hand to represent the organization.

To treat both parties equally, the NCAI sought participation in formulating the Republican position on Indian affairs. Robert Barker, attorney for the NCAI, appeared before the Republican platform committee to propose planks pertinent to Indian matters. Wesley and Barker also represented the NCAI at the Republican Convention in Chicago. Vice President Richard M. Nixon, the Republican candidate, and his staff, however, disregarded efforts by the NCAI to offer platform suggestions.[8]

Immediately following his November election, president-elect Kennedy renewed his campaign promise to the NCAI to provide a federal program to assist Indians in achieving better health, education, and economic conditions. Guided by intellectuals and academics, the Kennedy administration's impulses for social reform were often purely humanitarian. Pleased with the shift in Indian policy, President Wesley called the Kennedy position on Indian affairs one of the best in the history of federal-Indian relations.[9]

Meeting at Denver, site of the NCAI founding convention, days after Kennedy's victory, delegates reflected strong optimism for a dramatic change in Indian policy. Convention planners fittingly designated the meeting "Self-determination, Not Termination," reflecting the new outlook of the 1960s. Menaced and placed on the defensive by the threat of termination, keynote speaker Francis McKinley, director of Community Services for the Ute tribe, challenged Indians to view "themselves as capable of self-determination." Equally important, delegates challenged president-elect Kennedy to see Indians as capable of self-rule. Hoping for a return to the liberalism of the prewar years, Wesley trusted the new administration would "apply to Indian problems of the Sixties the spirit of the Indian policies of President Franklin Roosevelt and Secretary Harold Ickes." While certainly not all NCAI members preferred a return to the New Deal era, it is safe to assume that all wanted respect for Indian rights and cultural integrity and a larger voice in Indian affairs.[10]

To carry out his campaign promises, Kennedy appointed Stewart L. Udall, representative from Arizona, as secretary of interior. Deeply interested in Indian affairs, Udall called for self-determination and not termination. Highly critical of the Eisenhower administration's Indian policies, he compared forced termination to that of a stern father who lectured his son daily on responsibilities but denied him the opportunities needed to develop. Confidence, independence, and managerial skills, the secretary maintained, came only with experience. Udall favored protection of the Indian land base, credit assistance, and Indian economic development. Just before his appointment as secretary, Udall had praised the NCAI for its practical and constructive programs.[11]

Indian affairs in the early 1960s started with much promise for change. The Commission on the Rights, Liberties, and Responsibilities of the American Indian, an independent research group in 1961, published a summary report on Indian conditions. The seven-member commission consisted of O. Meridith Wilson, president of the University of Minnesota; William A. Brophy, former commissioner; and his wife, Sophie D. Aberle, former superintendent of the United Pueblo Agency. Besides Wilson, Brophy, and Aberle, the commission included W. W. Keeler, principal chief of the Cherokee Nation and respected oil company executive; Arthur M. Schlesinger Jr., distinguished Harvard historian; Karl N. Llewellyn, a University of Chicago professor; and Charles A. Sprague, editor of the *Oregon Statesman*. Reflecting many sentiments of the NCAI, the 1961 report recommended Indian consent and consultation before future changes in Indian policy. Vigorously condemning the coercive termination policy of the 1950s, the report called for the government to provide Indians with rehabilitation programs. Specifically, it made recommendations on health care and education programs. NCAI members hoped it would have the same impact as the important Meriam Report decades earlier.[12]

A more significant report appeared in the summer of 1961 as a result of an earlier task force established by Secretary Udall to study Indian affairs and make recommendations to the new administration. The task force, chaired by Keeler, included Philleo Nash, specialist in applied anthropology from Wisconsin; James E. Officer, anthropologist from the University of Arizona; and William Zimmerman Jr., former assistant commissioner of Indian affairs. Acting Commissioner John Old Crow, part Cherokee, helped the commission and accompanied it in the field.

After conducting hearings with tribal delegations on numerous reservations, conferring with bureau personnel and scholars in Washington, and using data collected from a questionnaire prepared by the NCAI, the commission submitted its report to Udall on July 10, 1961. Focusing on the need for Indian economic development instead of termination, the report encouraged tribal and individual self-determination through federal and state assistance. Secretary Udall endorsed the seventy-seven-page report as a "new trail" for Indians, leading to equal citizenship, self-sufficiency, and full participation in American society. The task force report communicated a mixed message. While encouraging self-determination, it also seemed to endorse goals of termination. The task force also recommended special assistance for Indians not prepared for a withdrawal of federal services. This included economic development on reservations, increased vocational training and job placement, and improvements in the social welfare and health programs of the BIA. Two themes of the report—greater industrial development on the reservations and increased Indian self-determination—served as the basis for Indian policy during the Kennedy administration.[13]

To help fulfill the provisions of the report, on August 1, 1961, Udall appointed Philleo Nash to be the next commissioner of Indian affairs. Nash, a scholar, cranberry farmer, and strong critic of termination, had political experience both as adviser to President Harry S. Truman on minority affairs and as lieutenant governor of Wisconsin. Because of his genuine interest in Indian welfare, rights, and sovereignty, the Indian community welcomed Nash's appointment. His popularity helped the new commissioner to overcome the hostility caused by termination and allowed him to reestablish a closer working relationship between the tribes and the Bureau. Nash did not revoke termination, nor did he promote new legislation to sever ties with more tribes. Instead, he focused his attention on reservation economic development, educational reform, vocational training, and housing.

Nash interrupted his confirmation hearings in September 1961 and flew to Lewiston, Idaho, to address the eighteenth annual convention of the NCAI. His dramatic appearance at the conference set the tone for his administration. Promising increased Indian self-sufficiency, Nash planned to use the task force report as a guide for his program. On September 26, 1961, he appointed task force member James E. Officer as associate commissioner.[14]

Perhaps few events in 1961 signaled the new Indian mood and outlook more than the American Indian Chicago Conference. Organized by anthropologists Sol Tax and Nancy Lurie and the NCAI, the conference brought together more than 450 Indian delegates from ninety tribes for a week of discussion about Indian concerns. At least as early as March 1960, Tax, chairman of the Department of Anthropology at the University of Chicago, had conceived of the idea for such a conference. On his return from the Kingston Conference of the Indian-Eskimo Association in Canada in March 1960, Tax hoped to assemble Indian leaders in a single location to exchange ideas and to develop a new course in Indian policy. The anthropologist envisioned the Chicago meeting as having the same impact that the Meriam Report of the late 1920s had had on subsequent Indian policy. In November 1960, Tax received a sizable grant from the University of Chicago administration and the school's commitment to host the 1961 conference. The Emil Schwarzhaupt Foundation, a New York–based philanthropic organization, and the Wenner-Gren Foundation for Anthropological Research also provided financial support.[15]

In mid-November 1960 Tax decided to enlist the support of the NCAI in planning the conference and writing the initial draft of the policy statement. From November 14 to 18, Tax, along with representatives of sixteen other universities, attended the convention of the NCAI in Denver to map out a program for Indian education. At the conference, Tax approached Helen Peterson and D'Arcy McNickle and other leaders of the NCAI about an Indian conference in Chicago. Peterson and McNickle agreed to submit Tax's suggestion to the resolutions committee. That group and the NCAI delegates passed a resolution fully endorsing the proposal. Having obtained the approval of the membership, the leaders of the NCAI began to discuss with Tax the logistics of the conference. Afterward, they sent president-elect Kennedy a telegram informing him of the upcoming Chicago gathering. Busy making plans for his new administration, President Kennedy did not respond. McNickle and Peterson decided to remain in Denver a few days following the NCAI convention to draft a preliminary proposal for the American Indian Charter Conference (AICC).[16]

McNickle, Peterson, John Rainer, former executive director of the NCAI, Clarence Wesley, and others met in Albuquerque, New Mexico, at the end of 1960 to plan the conference.[17] Working virtually around the clock for several days, the Indian leaders created a general statement that they hoped reflected the views of all Indians. It addressed the needs of the Indian community and made recommendations for changes in federal Indian policy. McNickle was primarily responsible for writing the first draft of the general statement or "charter" that eventually became the noted "Declaration of Indian Purpose."[18]

The new declaration asked for a reversal of termination, economic assistance, resource development, programs dealing with housing, health, education, welfare, law, jurisdiction, and the establishment of a National Indian Commission to replace the commissioner of Indian affairs. The commission was to consist of six members, with half of the members Indian and all appointed by the president.[19] In early December 1960 Wesley sent McNickle's draft to tribal leaders across the country for their reactions. NCAI leaders then planned to discuss the proposed Indian declaration at the upcoming Chicago conference. Pleased with the expedient work of the NCAI and never dreaming his idea would catch on so quickly, Tax now believed the AICC would "really make history."[20]

The participation of the NCAI in the early stages of the AICC caused factionalism inside the NCAI and increased Indian critics outside the organization. The high profile of the NCAI in helping to launch the conference alienated many groups, particularly eastern tribes who did not trust the motives of NCAI. This created a serious dilemma for Tax and Lurie, who needed the organizational skills of the NCAI to support the conference but could not afford to alienate other tribal groups that disliked the NCAI. Just a few months prior to the start of the conference, Lurie, assistant coordinator of the project, expressed her concern to John Ewes, Smithsonian curator:

> We have, however, had a problem in regard to NCAI. It is the best organized and in many ways most representative intertribal organization, but it does have enemies among Indians. Most criticism comes from the highly traditional groups and the eastern tribes. The first group is suspicious of the acculturated Indians who predominate in [the] NCAI and the eastern groups feel NCAI is oriented almost exclusively toward western reservation problems. The nonreservation, nonfederally recognized, and state-reservation groups east of the Mississippi River fear NCAI as stressing western reservation needs so that their peculiar but critical problems are overlooked. We are caught in a curious position of being very grateful to NCAI for sparking AICC and providing the "model charter" to begin discussion, but at the same time we find we must make explicit that NCAI does not dominate AICC.[21]

Few people reflected this polarization between eastern tribes and the NCAI more than William Rickard, president of the Long House League of North American Indians. In mid-January 1961 Tax appointed Rickard as a member of the Indian steering committee of the planned Chicago conference. He also served as chairman of the eastern regional meeting at Haverford College that was preparing for the conference. From the moment of his involvement in planning the AICC, Rickard, a prominent Iroquois, opposed the viewpoints expressed by the NCAI, which he considered too moderate.[22]

When the Chicago conference opened in mid-June 1961, Rickard boycotted the meeting because he found the format of the meeting, modeled on the NCAI annual conventions, too similar to white political institutions. Rickard accused the NCAI of being "influenced mainly by white politicians and lobbyists and that . . . [has] not worked for the best interest of the Indians." During the conference, he also objected to the participants' emphasis on U.S. citizenship, maintaining instead that Indians were citizens of their individual Indian nations.[23] His views reflected the strong "nationalism" of many Iroquois. Rickard, also a member of the Indian Defense League of America, continued his criticism of the NCAI until his death in 1964.

Misconceptions, rumors, and innuendoes about the role of the NCAI in the AICC continued to swirl throughout Indian country in the spring of 1961. As early as January 1961, some groups mistakenly thought that the purpose of the assembly in Chicago was to create a new national Indian organization. Other Indians worried that the conference was a mutual plot of the NCAI and the BIA. Reva Cooper Barse, an outspoken Seneca woman, claimed, with questionable logic, that the conference would be a moneymaker for the NCAI and government. The NCAI planned to charge Indians $10.00 for the right to vote at the Chicago meeting, according to Barse, while whites would only pay $2.50. General Herbert C. Holdridge, self-appointed but largely ineffective Indian reformer, warned Tax that the NCAI was simply using the University of Chicago for selfish gains. Some Oklahoma tribes, on the other hand, worried that the University of Chicago manipulated the NCAI for the self-centered interests of scholars. Both charges proved false.[24]

Robert Burnette, president of the Rosebud Sioux Tribal Council, joined Wetzel in his criticism of the direction of the NCAI. Burnette, caustic adversary of Peterson, Garry, and Wesley, vehemently denounced plans for the AICC. Burnette also complained that midwestern, urban Indians would dominate the conference and that the proceedings would encourage termination. He also believed that Peterson and her supporters lacked confidence in reservation leadership. Wetzel and Peterson would use the Chicago conference, Burnette added, as a wedge to divide the organization in a struggle for control of the NCAI.[25]

Several factors help explain the factionalism within the NCAI concerning the Chicago meeting. To some tribal groups, the NCAI, in form, leadership, and aims, resembled non-Indian reform associations and organizations not representative of many reservation groups. Led by acculturated, well-educated individuals, its leaders were often more sophisticated than reservation leaders. While the NCAI leaders often maintained close tribal connections, they led their lives in the non-Indian world. Although not totally divorced from the tribal world, the NCAI functioned at a national level that was in reality very distant from daily reservation life. No doubt reservation leaders such as Burnette and Wetzel badly distrusted the NCAI leaders who seemed far removed from tribal identity and reservation problems. Moderate methods, timing, and the perceived arrogance of the NCAI middle-class leaders also alienated some reservation leaders. Much as in 1944, the NCAI in the 1960s continued to face the difficult task of striking the delicate balance between class and educational differences within its membership and between tribal identity and Indian identity.

In the months leading up to the AICC, Tax, Lurie, and his other coordinators continued to work closely with the NCAI. The NCAI helped with coordinated communication between tribes across the country and organized regional meetings to debate the format and statement of purpose of the conference. Not only did Tax and the NCAI use the regional meetings to stir interest in the AICC, but also to ensure that the conference represented as nearly as possible the voices of all Indians. Participants sent concerns and suggestions from these regional meetings to Tax, who mailed them in turn to tribal leaders as AICC "Progress Reports."

In early February 1961, John Rainer, Clarence Wesley, D'Arcy McNickle, and Helen Peterson met in Chicago with twelve other Indian leaders as part of an AICC advisory committee to update plans for the June conference. Important changes in the AICC developed out of the February meetings. At this meeting, the advisory committee changed the title of the statement of purpose and the name of the conference itself. Framers dropped the terms "charter" and "convention" and replaced both with "conference." Several Indian leaders found the term "charter" unacceptable because it implied binding actions rather than an assembly gathered to allow Indians to express their opinions. It also evoked the mistaken impression that the BIA might be involved in the conference, an image the NCAI desperately wanted to avoid. Committee members also felt that the term "convention" implied the creation of a new Indian organization rather than a one-time meeting.

Planners agreed upon a new designation, "American Indian Chicago Conference: The Voice of the American Indian," and titled the statement the AICC would produce the "Declaration of Indian Purpose."[26] At the April 26–30, 1961, regional meeting of the steering committee, McNickle, Wesley, Peterson, and Rainer met again with other Indian leaders in Chicago to complete plans for the June conference. Representatives incorporated the recommendations from this meeting into a second version of the draft. Committee planners mailed the revised and final draft to tribal leaders across the country in May 1961.[27]

The participation of the NCAI in the AICC brought the festering divisions within the national organization to the surface. In late May 1961 the Montana Inter-Policy Board urged the tribes in the state to boycott the AICC and to "censure" the leaders of the NCAI who had drafted the statement of purpose. Walter S. Wetzel opposed the relationship of the NCAI and Tax to the Chicago meeting. Wetzel had continued to blame Peterson, Garry, Rainer, and Wesley for his narrow defeat in the 1959 Phoenix election. Reflecting his disappointment, he failed to support the recommendations of the NCAI leadership. Regarding the draft of the "Declaration of Indian Purpose," he specifically opposed the proposed National Indian Commission, and he worried that nonfederally recognized tribes and urban groups would dominate the AICC meetings and undermine the needs of reservation groups. Under the Indian Reorganization Act, the federal government prescribed rules governing federal recognition of tribal status. Ultimately, the commissioner of Indian affairs determined whether a particular tribe met the guidelines and thus was granted federal recognition and allowed to organize under the IRA. Wetzel also expressed concern that the NCAI was advocating the abolishment of the BIA, which he feared would lead to termination and other harmful policies. Sister Providencia, long-time Roman Catholic missionary to the Blackfeet Nation, who had campaigned for Wetzel's election, also worked to discredit the leaders of the NCAI. To little avail, Wesley appealed for unity and cooperation.[28]

The long-awaited conference convened in Chicago June 13–20, 1961. More importantly, the delegates represented a wide range of Indians: federally and nonfederally recognized tribes, conservatives and liberals, urban and reservation, young and old, educated and uneducated. As anticipated by AICC planners and NCAI leaders, the conference resulted in the much discussed and revised "Declaration of Indian Purpose," the dynamic statement of Indian concerns and recommendations. Reflecting the conference emphasis on Indian sovereignty and the preservation of Indian identity, the document began:

> We, the Indian people must be governed by principles in a democratic manner with a right to choose our way of life. Since our Indian culture is threatened by the presumption of being absorbed by the American society we believe we have the responsibility of preserving our precious heritage. We believe that the Indians must provide the adjustment and thus freely advance with dignity to a better life.[29]

If it accomplished nothing else, the AICC, the largest intertribal gathering in decades, generated public and Indian interest in Indian affairs. In mid-August 1961, an AICC delegation, led by Robert Burnette, who became executive director in 1962, presented a specially bound edition of the "Declaration of Indian Purpose" to President Kennedy at the White House. Kennedy called the abstract "a very useful reminder that there is still a good deal of unfinished business." John Rainer and Robert L. Bennett, later Indian commissioner during the Johnson administration, claimed, however, that the document that came out of the conference was too advanced and complicated for most Indians to understand. "The problem with D'Arcy McNickle [author of the document]," Rainer maintained, "was that he was so highly intelligent and thereby way ahead of our time. The other Indians would not understand what he meant by a statement, you know. It took them ten years to catch up with what D'Arcy was trying to say."[30]

Nevertheless, McNickle and the "Declaration of Indian Purpose" had promoted an Indian consciousness and expressed the need for Indians to confront federal policy on their own terms. Inadvertently, the conference led to the emergence of a powerful new Indian protest movement that rivaled the NCAI. Initially, NCAI invited many Indian college students to serve as pages, but they insisted on entering the debates. Following the AICC, these students, dissatisfied with the moderate direction of the AICC, rose to challenge the NCAI and older tribal leaders. Convening in Gallup, New Mexico, later in the summer of 1961, they formed the National Indian Youth Council (NIYC). Impatient with the pace of change and with the methods of the NCAI, the NIYC advocated greater militancy and quickly became a major player on the Indian political scene.

Tired of what they perceived to be NCAI tribal leadership's unwillingness to confront major issues in Indian affairs, the new group brought a confrontational style to Indian politics. Strongly influenced by the Civil Rights movement, NIYC leaders adopted activist rhetoric and identified with reservation Indians. "We are not free," NIYC president Clyde Warrior argued. "We do not make choices. Our choices are made for us."[31] Warrior, Shirley Hill Witt, Mel Thom, and other NIYC leaders denounced whites as fascists and racists and criticized the NCAI and tribal leaders as "Uncle Tomahawks" or "Apples." Throughout the 1960s the NIYC developed a style of protest more in common with Joseph Brant, Pontiac, and Tecumseh than with the NCAI. Modeled after militant black protesters, NIYC particularly involved itself in "fish-ins" and other demonstrations to protect treaty hunting and fishing rights of northwestern tribes.

Clearly the NIYC represented a logical and natural outgrowth of the NCAI. Since its inception, NCAI founders had strongly encouraged the education and training of young Indian leadership. McNickle's AID program and annual summer workshops had started in the mid-1950s, and these and other programs had brought bright, talented Indian youth together to discuss Indian issues. Many founders of the NIYC gained valuable experience and training in the seminars. Moreover, many Indian college students held memberships in the NCAI. While not yet established enough in tribal politics to be voting delegates, the students often watched the proceedings and wanted a more active role. Thus directly and indirectly the NCAI taught new generations of Indian disciples that intertribal action was not only possible but essential on a national level. The entry of NIYC into the political arena marked the passing of yet another era. Two years later, in 1968, the American Indian Movement (AIM) followed the NIYC lead to address problems experienced by relocated urban Indians.

While the NIYC burst onto the scene and helped start the dramatic Red Power Movement, the NCAI struggled to maintain its identity and place in Indian politics. Deep factionalism within the NCAI, made apparent in disagreements over the organization's participation in the AICC, erupted immediately following the Chicago conference and led to new leadership in the organization. At the AICC, Robert Burnette mounted a campaign to take control of the NCAI. Frustrated with the direction of the NCAI leadership, he solicited support from the Indian delegates at the conference to overhaul the NCAI. In early August 1961, one month after the AICC, Burnette, who appointed himself acting chairman for the reorganization of the

NCAI, called a meeting of his supporters in Sheridan, Wyoming. Sheridan assemblees suggested that the NCAI create three new administrative offices at the level of the executive director: directors of finance, legislation, and administration. While providing resources to the headquarters, these new offices would also monitor the executive director. Burnette's group also recommended changes in the leadership personnel of NCAI. In September 1961 Burnette's proposal was placed on the agenda of the executive council meeting preceding the Lewiston, Idaho, convention. Anxious for a healthy discussion of the proposal, its quick dismissal startled Helen Peterson. Noting that he had not authorized a committee to reorganize the NCAI, President Wesley disallowed the recommended changes.[32]

By fall of 1961 Wetzel and Burnette and a coalition of tribes mainly from South Dakota and Montana attempted to take control of the NCAI. When it appeared that they would be successful, Peterson announced her resignation before the Lewiston convention.[33] Had John Rainer been successful in his attempts to regain the presidency against Wetzel, Peterson would not have resigned. When Rainer lost in a close election, she followed through with her resignation. Peterson's strong dedication to Indian identity and civil rights and her selfless commitment to the NCAI had preserved and advanced the Indian organization through its early years of turmoil. Under her direction the NCAI stopped, or at least slowed, the termination movement. Peterson had been the heart and soul of the organization, much as Ruth Bronson had been a decade earlier. Following her resignation, Peterson returned to Denver as the director of that city's Commission on Community Relations. In retrospect, she fondly recalled that the NCAI provided her "the first really heartfelt and deepseated pride and confidence that I ever had." Her resignation provided Burnette the opportunity that he needed to restructure the NCAI. In the end, the AICC proved to be the downfall of NCAI leadership that had boldly led NCAI through termination.[34]

With the sweeping changes of the 1960s, Wetzel and Burnette represented the new needs of reservation Indians. Wetzel had been past president of the Montana Inter-tribal Board and founding member of the Western Inter-Tribal Board. At a time when urban Indians were becoming more outspoken in their demands, the forty-three-year-old Wetzel stressed development of reservation resources.[35] At Lewiston, in September 1961, Wetzel appointed his recent Chicago ally, Burnette, as the new executive director. With the passing of one administration to the next, delegates at the Lewiston convention closed the conference by paying respects to the grave of founder Archie Phinney. With his earlier concerns about most reservation leaders' abilities to lead a national organization, however, Phinney might have shuddered at the new Montana/South Dakota coalition.

Born on the Rosebud, South Dakota, reservation in 1926, Burnette quickly became involved in reservation politics. After serving in the Marine Corps during the war years, he won election in 1952 to the Rosebud Tribal Council. Two years later, voters elected him tribal president. Elected three times, he served a total of eight years. During the late 1950s he helped organize intertribal councils in Arizona and California. Much as other young Indian leaders of his day had done, he demanded self-determination and an end to dictatorial government agents and corrupt tribal officials.

The thirty-five-year-old Burnette, whose Indian name is "Tokah Wasta," meaning "good leader," brought a different style of leadership to the NCAI.[36] Convinced that the organization had always operated from a defensive posture, he decided to "create the power to assume the offensive." Adopting a more combative stance, he did not hesitate to threaten and challenge leaders inside and outside the NCAI.[37] His approach made powerful enemies as well as friends.

Burnette particularly attacked D'Arcy McNickle, Peterson, Rainer, and Garry, whom he called the "old gang." He claimed that with little hard evidence the previous NCAI administration had used the organization for financial gain and power. More specifically, he maintained that Peterson and Garry had manipulated the substantial NCAI fund and private donations for their personal benefit. He also asserted that the outgoing administration had left behind large debts and unpaid taxes.[38] Always looking over his shoulder, he constantly worried that Peterson and Garry were trying to regain control over the organization. Burnette's aggressive manner also worsened the already poor relations between the NCAI and the Association of American Indian Affairs (AAIA), the rival reform organization of the NCAI. Oliver La Farge, president of the AAIA, complained that Burnette was "self-seeking, smooth, and unscrupulous."[39]

An outspoken critic of discrimination, Burnette persistently sought to enlist high-profile individuals and philanthropic organizations in the Indian struggle for justice. He made protection of Indian land and civil rights one of the dominant themes of his administration. Soon after his appointment as executive director, Burnette tried unsuccessfully to raise one-half million dollars to create an "American Indian Shrine Building" in Washington DC. He intended the building to serve not only as a monument to Indians but as a museum, an outlet for Indian crafts, and as new office space for the NCAI and the NCAI Fund.[40] In April 1963, hoping to bring visibility to the NCAI cause, Burnette invited British leader Winston Churchill, who was one-sixteenth Indian, to join the national Indian organization. Churchill, who had never attended any conventions, cheerfully accepted the invitation.[41] Burnette also solicited support from movie actor Marlon Brando in preventing South Dakota from exerting state jurisdiction over the Sioux reservations. Burnette, a strong supporter of the Kennedys, often wrote the president and attorney general about Indian affairs, especially civil rights violations in South Dakota. Burnette's persistent efforts to cultivate the Kennedys produced rewards. In September 1963, Attorney General Robert F. Kennedy agreed to address the twentieth annual convention at Bismarck, North Dakota. In his remarks Kennedy pledged to work toward making Indians full partners in American society.[42]

In March 1963, with Nash's help Burnette arranged a visit for NCAI leaders to the White House. Udall, Nash, and several western representatives and members of the subcommittees on Indian affairs joined the NCAI in their meeting with the president. On March 5, 1963, President Kennedy received the tribal representatives and other guests in the Rose Garden, and there they presented him with gifts as emblems of the favorable shift in Indian policy. Addressing the delegates, Kennedy remarked that "the American Indians hold a romantic grip on our imaginations, but I hope that they also hold a practical grip upon our efforts." The president assured his guests that the government had "responsibilities to some of our most distinguished and in a very real sense first citizens."[43]

Following an invitation from Jacqueline Kennedy, ten delegates returned to the White House the following day. After a tour of the president's home, the delegates, dressed in traditional clothing, performed Indian dances for Caroline, John Jr., and other children at the White House school. Without question, the White House visit deepened NCAI hopes for closer federal-Indian relations.[44] Thanking the president on September 22, 1963, for his personal interest in Indian affairs, Burnette hoped "that in the future God's hand shall guide you in your leadership of this country."[45]

Kennedy's "New Frontier," however, came to a sudden and violent end on November 22, 1963, when an assassin killed the president as he rode in a motorcade in Dallas, Texas. The shock of losing the young president who had become a symbol of hope and promise stunned the entire world. Many in the Indian community believed in the president's potential for greatness and spoke positively of what might have been had he lived.

Although historians disagree on the effectiveness of the Kennedy administration's Indian policy, it definitely marked a shift away from termination and reflected a greater respect for Indian culture. While many Seneca Indians today criticize him for failing to stop construction of the Kinzua Dam that flooded their lands in western New York, Kennedy successfully made Indian advances in economic development, educational reform, vocational training, and housing. His Area Redevelopment Act (ARA) of 1961 started an important new trend in Indian policy. It provided financial and technical assistance to depressed areas, including reservations, and opened new sources of funds for economic development. Tribal groups used ARA funds for a variety of projects, including new tribal headquarters and community centers. Similarly, tribal governments created tribal housing authorities to take advantage of Public Housing Administration

(PHA) programs. Likewise, Indians benefited from the Small Business Administration and the Public Works Program of 1962. Perhaps more importantly, Kennedy brought new hope to Indian nations. His altruistic rhetoric, Indian task force, appeals for economic assistance, respect and trust of others' cultures, and enunciation of federal cooperation with tribal groups energized hundreds, especially the young.

Much like John Collier nearly two decades earlier, President Kennedy's Indian commissioner, Philleo Nash, used both BIA funds and means outside the agency to finance new programs and make available new sources of credit. Targeting industrial and tribal enterprises, Nash also encouraged and attracted forty new manufacturing plants in Indian localities and created thirteen hundred new jobs for Indians. Moreover, Nash promoted a modernized version of Collier's "cultural pluralism." Combined, all of these accomplishments contributed to a raised national Indian conscience that increasingly moved toward greater self-determination.

In the aftermath of the Kennedy assassination, Robert Burnette and Walter Wetzel requested permission to dedicate the grave of a "close friend known to us as 'Chief High Eagle'". On January 20, 1964, the third anniversary of the inauguration of the late president, the NCAI paid tribute to the fallen leader in a graveside ceremony. Dressed in traditional clothing, the NCAI delegation stuck coup sticks on the grave and placed wreaths on the freshly dug earth in a show of respect.[46]

Honoring the memory of the fallen president, the NCAI pledged full support to the new Johnson administration. Responding to the backing of the NCAI, Johnson entertained the Indian organization in the East Room of the White House in January 1974. President Johnson promised the delegates that he would continue the Indian policies of the Kennedy administration. While the Kennedy administration had helped slow termination, promote self-determination, and block an heirship bill aimed at Indian land, he pledged he would go farther.[47]

Indian reservations during Johnson's "Great Society" received even more funds than during the Indian New Deal. Head Start, Job

Corps, Upward Bound, VISTA, and other initiatives attempted to improve reservation conditions. Johnson's Community Action Program also authorized tribal governments' and private organizations' direct access to grants from the Office of Economic Opportunity, independent of the BIA.[48] In Indian affairs, as with minority programs in general, Johnson passed several important economic and civil rights acts that had stymied his predecessor. While controversy over Vietnam would obscure the accomplishments of the Johnson presidency, it could not diminish the lasting legacy of the Great Society on American life. Federal aid to education, the enactment of Medicare and Medicaid, and, most importantly, the Civil Rights Acts of 1964 and 1965 irreversibly changed the nation.

Sudden turmoil among the leadership of the NCAI occurred almost simultaneously with changes on the national political scene. Concerned over persistent rumors that the NCAI had defaulted on debts from the 1963 Bismarck convention, Peterson, Garry, Rainer, and others had insisted on inspecting the financial records of the NCAI. When Burnette refused their request, the group hired the accounting firm of Leopold and Linowes and Attorney Albert J. Ahern to force an inspection of the records. After blocking many attempts to examine the accounts, Burnette finally submitted to an audit. Leopold and Linowes, however, reported that the records were so incomplete as to make a full audit impossible.[49] Peterson, still a powerful force within the NCAI, maintained that Burnette had removed most of the financial records from the previous six years and stowed them in the trunk of his car.[50]

Countering the charges, Burnette responded that the Peterson administration had left the NCAI bankrupt and deep in debt. He also complained that this was merely another attempt by the previous administration to discredit him and to regain control of the organization. He bitterly complained that if "Jesus Christ himself was the executive director of NCAI, the Peterson and Garry gang would find some way of spreading vicious rumors about him, too." Unfortunately, it is difficult to determine from the financial records which parties were correct in their allegations. The only certainty is that the feud ignited a factional war that lasted years and divided NCAI during one of the most critical social revolutions in American history, the 1960s.[51]

In one sense Burnette proved correct in his observations. Uncomfortable with Burnette's leadership, Peterson and her supporters had launched a full-scale campaign to force him out.[52] By early 1964, pressures began to mount on Burnette to resign. He complained that the American Indian Civil Liberties Trust (AICLT), whose board of trustees contained many Peterson supporters and whom the NCAI depended on for financial support, refused to provide him money to run the organization.[53] In late 1964, with the matter unresolved, his funds shut off, and his support slipping, Burnette resigned. Three years after the important Lewiston convention, Peterson and her allies achieved their long-awaited revenge. In late 1964, at the Sheridan, Wyoming, convention, Wetzel, with the support of Peterson and her associates, appointed Vine Deloria Jr. to replace Burnette.[54]

Burnette returned to the Rosebud Reservation in 1964 and continued his struggle for self-determination, sovereignty, and Indian civil rights. During the next two decades, he ran unsuccessfully for the tribal presidency several times. After serving as a mediator and nonviolent advocate in AIM events in the late 1960s and early 1970s, he regained the Rosebud presidency in 1974. Chronicling the Indians' difficult struggles, he published *The Tortured Americans* in 1971 and coauthored *The Road to Wounded Knee*. Charges of misconduct later forced him out of tribal office. A tribal court, however, later cleared him of the charges. Preparing to run for the tribal presidency in 1984, he died of a heart attack.[55]

The membership of NCAI called on Deloria, later a well-known author and Indian activist, to rebuild the organization. Deloria began his administration as a neutral bystander, caught in the middle of the internal feud between the Peterson and Burnette factions. The AICLT, which supported Deloria's appointment, withheld aid until the warring factions resolved the conflict.[56] Deloria, lacking adequate financial records and no funds to run the organization, had little choice but to sue Burnette to settle the matter. Burnette, however, countersued for back wages and expenses from the NCAI. On December 8, 1967, Burnette failed to prove his claims, and the U.S. District Court of Colorado dismissed the case.[57] Within months after taking office, Deloria complained that NCAI members unfairly judged his administration against the "memories of Helen Peterson" and her supporters. He also claimed that the Peterson administration had misappropriated funds of the NCAI. After offering his resignation, which NCAI leaders rejected, Deloria remained and brought new direction to the organization.[58]

Deloria had played an invaluable role in helping the NCAI through a difficult transition period. He helped restore both financial and managerial stability. Deloria, who inherited from the previous administration a debt of nearly ten thousand dollars, quickly made the NCAI solvent.[59] Deloria also led the NCAI at a time when black civil rights movements, student protests, and Indian activism shifted to more militant tactics. By the mid-1960s, twenty years after its founding, the NCAI had endured in spite of inadequate financial resources and internal differences.

During the 1960s, the NCAI, with its large reservation constituency, remained more moderate in approach than youth-oriented Indian urban movements such as the NIYC and AIM. Efforts to unite urban and reservation Indians into the NCAI failed. As the decade progressed, Indian militancy, modeled after many black protest movements, continued to rise. Concerns of the NCAI, however, often differed from the new Indian activism of the urban groups. The NCAI preferred to continue to fight its battles in the halls of Congress than to protest publically at targeted sites. While carrying on its role as legislative watchdog, the NCAI retained its interest in programs that affected reservations as a whole and placed less emphasis on urban Indians. Thus, the 1960s marked a period of transition for the NCAI. Termination no longer loomed on the immediate horizon to unite tribes in defense of a common legislative enemy. With the appearance of groups such as NIYC, AIM, WARN, and others, the NCAI went from the leading voice in Indian affairs to a more subscribed role. Indian history and the history of the NCAI had reached yet another significant turning point.

CONCLUSION

NCAI is our salvation—not our spiritual salvation, to be sure, but it is the salvation of our identity as a people, our heritage, the assets still in our possession.

JOSEPH GARRY, former president of NCAI, 1959

In 1993, alongside other surviving members of the NCAI, Helen Peterson comfortably sat at a large table in a classroom at the University of New Mexico in Albuquerque. Nearing the end of her Indian activism, yet still displaying the energy that marked her successful career, she reflected on the importance of NCAI to Indian people. "Every time I see that picture of the original founders of the NCAI," she contemplated, "a frog comes up in my throat again and I very, very seldom ever, ever, shed a tear, but I am today." With her voice soft and crackling with emotion and tears trickling down her face, she continued, "I just hope that we can somehow help the Indian people learn before it is too late that tribal survival, survival as a tribe can't happen unless we have a land base. . . . No matter how poorly our tribal officials do sometime," she told the gathering of people who listened intently, "still and all, they're the ones who keep the fires burning and we all refer to home no matter how far away or how long we are away from it. . . . Only NCAI, I think," she said forcefully, "will protect it."[1]

Placing tremendous faith in Indian communities' ability to cooperate intertribally, Peterson expressed continued high hopes and expectations for NCAI. Her beloved organization represented a milestone in Indian history as it marked the transition from tribal to supratribal mobilization. While NCAI has not always dictated major outcomes, it has helped shape events, and it remains an important vehicle for Indian political action.

During its founding years, for example, it scored important victories in the fight to create the Indian Claims Commission, to ensure voting and social security rights for native peoples, and in the struggle over termination. Many of the battles were waged inside the halls of Congress, where the specific battlegrounds were the Subcommittees on Indian Affairs and the weapons were lobbying tactics. More importantly, the limited success of the NCAI helped open a broader political arena within which more contemporary Indian activists and agendas have engaged.

The road from earliest recorded Indian history to the present has been built on remnants of the past. While many current leaders are more sophisticated and articulate in dealing with outside influences, today's Indian concerns remain surprisingly similar to those faced by earlier Indian leaders. Both past and present Indian leadership recognize that Indian treaty rights, tribal land bases, and federal trust responsibilities are essential to Indian survival.

As World War II ended, the process of political mobilization, which started even before Columbus entered the Americas, entered a new stage of progression. Throughout most of American history, Indians often attempted to ally themselves into larger political networks. Years of often one-sided federal-Indian interactions led to the development of an Indian presence in American pressure politics. Increasingly during the twentieth century, a general Indian identity, as distinct from tribal identity, became an important basis of reform action. In the aftermath of the Indian New Deal and wartime opportunities, Indian leaders unlocked new political doors. Astute Indian leaders—D'Arcy McNickle, Archie Phinney, Charles Heacock, and others—successfully bridged the gap between tribal and supratribal concerns. Anxious to secure full civil rights, these and other Indian leaders learned to establish their own agendas and interests in the larger national political arena. In 1944 these Indians took control of their own destinies through the establishment of the NCAI.

Changes in federal policy in the 1930s and the outbreak of World War II helped produce the NCAI. John Collier's Indian New Deal gave Indians a tribal alternative to assimilation. Collier's Indian Reorganization Act (IRA) of 1934 encouraged cultural pluralism, ethnic identity, and tribal self-government. The IRA tribal councils introduced a new generation of Indian leaders to white political systems. While the IRA governments were important at the tribal level, they were too limited in scope to be fully effective. As the IRA governments sputtered, several BIA employees and other Indian leaders sought a national Indian organization to promote common interests. When NCAI founders created a national and intertribal organization, they moved beyond IRA governments and placed Indians and their affairs on a much larger playing field.

World War II also contributed significantly to the creation of the NCAI. For many Indians, the conflict created greater economic opportunities and greater political awareness. Wartime employment needs kindled widespread Indian migration to urban war industries. National unity and war needs also thrust thousands of Indians into military service. Indian participation in the war effort, both as soldiers and as laborers, propelled many Indians from isolation into mainstream society. Greater exposure to a higher standard of living and respect brought to consciousness by the war motivated Indian leaders to demand rights both as U.S. citizens and as members of sovereign nations. Thus, the Indian New Deal and participation of Native Americans in World War II laid the foundation for post–World War II Indian ethnic mobilization.

After the war, however, strong conservative forces threatened to undo the gains of the New Deal and of World War II. The drive to stop communism during the Cold War dominated the American agenda. The anticommunist spirit of postwar America emphasized conformity that tended to discourage the preservation of Indian identity and Indians' communal lifestyle. Even the emerging Civil Rights Movement with its challenges to existing social and political institutions was at its base oriented toward assimilation. In the Cold War struggle against the Soviet Union, reservations smacked of communism, socialism, and dependency. Postwar conservatives favored the assimilation of Indians, a reduced federal role in Indian affairs, and decreased government spending. During the termination years, key individuals were more influential in deciding Indian affairs than federal legislation. Instead of destroying the NCAI, the Cold War atmosphere had the opposite effect. It served as a stimulus to help justify the role of the NCAI as a guardian of Indian rights.

In the mid-twentieth century the United States government launched an ill-fated attempt to terminate the federal trust status of Indian reservations. Rejecting the policy and the obvious threat to Indian legal and cultural liberties, the NCAI asserted the right of Indian communities to control their own destiny. Following a momentous 1954 emergency conference, the NCAI aggressively and successfully launched a drive to stop, or at least to slow, the termination movement. In many respects, termination represented an important turning point in the short history of the NCAI. The NCAI remarkably defeated many termination bills, which would have resulted in destroying the special rights and land base of Indians, and Indian tribal hopes for survival. Opposition to and success against termination fostered a high degree of unity and increased support for the NCAI. In other words, terminationist efforts to reduce or destroy Indian culture and ethnicity, ironically, became the means by which the NCAI renewed and regenerated ethnicity. The success against termination also taught that unity, political activism, and voter education were powerful weapons in the wars for ethnic preservation.

John F. Kennedy's election in 1960 marked a new direction in federal Indian policy. Rejecting the coercive termination policies of the previous administrations, Kennedy declared a war on Indian poverty and increased Indian self-determination. His short-lived administration failed to live up to all its promises and expectations. President Lyndon Johnson passed many civil rights bills that had evaded his predecessor. Johnson's War on Poverty and community development programs infused non-BIA federal resources into both Indian urban and reservation communities. Increased levels of federal Indian spending in the mid-1960s through early 1970s benefited the emerging Red Power activism. The growth of reservation and urban funds created a dramatic rise in Indian cultural, social, economic, and political programs. Indian access to federal funding facilitated an explosion of supratribal and pan-Indian growth in both the cities and on reservations. New sources of money from non-BIA agencies for reservation programs lessened tribal dependency on the BIA and contributed to demands for self-determination and increased activism. Most importantly, expanded federal spending encouraged activism by providing incentives for ethnic identification.

Although Native Americans shifted toward self-determination after 1960, they frequently found themselves caught in a conflicting trap. On the one hand they asserted that the federal government should maintain its trust responsibilities promised by treaties and statues; on the other, they insisted that tribes be treated as sovereign nations. Federal trust and Indian self-determination often are not always compatible, and the inharmonious goals produced much confusion and tension for both Indians and non-Indians. Total tribal autonomy remained illusive.

The road from the early days of the NCAI to the Red Power Movement and beyond has been a road from relative powerlessness to one of modest power. The efforts by founding members brought not only an Indian voice to national affairs but also new Indian movements as well. Beginning in the 1960s, the Red Power movement emerged to challenge the representation of all Indians by NCAI. The aftermath of the American Indian Chicago Conference marked an important transition in the NCAI and Indian politics. After the conference, NCAI no longer stood as the lone Indian voice in Indian affairs. New Indian activist groups used the energy of NCAI as a springboard to forge new Indian movements that included direct confrontation and civil disobedience. The bitterness over termination and relocation and the lessons and experiences of the 1950s contributed to the Indian youth movements and agitations of the 1960s. Native Americans on and off the reservations during the 1960s and 1970s became more militant, outspoken, and sophisticated about tribal sovereignty, civil and legal rights, and jurisdiction. Indian lobbying, following the example of the NCAI, produced important legislation on health care, education, religious freedom, civil rights, and self-determination. Through favorable congressional and court decisions, Indians achieved a greater voice in solving their own problems.

Native American protest tactics copied from civil rights and anti-war movements produced dramatic confrontations, such as the seizure of Alcatraz, fish-ins in the Pacific Northwest, the occupation of the BIA building, Wounded Knee II, and many smaller protests. Indian militancy and activism such as the organization of the American Indian Movement (AIM) and the National Indian Youth Council (NIYC) arose from the intertribal example of, and sometimes opposition to, the more moderate NCAI. Not linked to tribal governments of the BIA as was the NCAI, the NIYC and AIM moved Indian political action outside the institutional political arena. In particular, unlike NCAI and NIYC, which viewed tribal communities as essential for the preservation of Indian culture, AIM embraced a movement that subordinated tribalism for supratribalism. Building on the success of NCAI, the new Indian groups in the 1960s and 1970s transformed the world of Indian politics.

Differences in philosophy and tactics between the NCAI and the new nationalist Indian groups came to a head during the late 1960s and early 1970s. When the NCAI refused to participate in the Poor Peoples' March in 1968 because it felt the organizers lacked a clear objective, it distanced itself from Indian militants. During the AIM occupation of Wounded Knee in 1973, NCAI defended Pine Ridge tribal chairman Richard Wilson and his elected tribal council. Arguing that AIM violated tribal sovereignty by interfering in elected tribal government, NCAI further separated itself from Indian groups that viewed Wilson as a BIA-supported tyrant. Regardless of Wilson's misdeeds, the NCAI recognized the importance of the IRA governments. Ironically, NCAI benefited from its moderate stand and the more militant position of AIM. Government officials elected to cooperate with NCAI as a means of weakening the militants. Knowing this, the NCAI refused attempts by AIM to unite the two organizations into a single national coalition. Since the Wounded Knee occupation, NCAI has struggled to represent all Indians. During Jimmy Carter's presidency, the National Tribal Chairmen's Association (NTCA), vigorously opposed plans of NCAI to extend federal recognition to nonrecognized tribes. In particular, debates between the NCAI and the NTCA over extending recognition to smaller eastern tribes divided the one-time allies. The influence of NCAI also diminished slightly in the 1980s and the 1990s as Indian activism shifted from the legislative arena to the courts.

While NCAI has not won all its battles, it deserves recognition for the important role it has played in the shaping of federal policy and Indian action. Before its formation in 1944, the NCAI had no counterparts in the twentieth-century world of Indian politics. Its emphasis on treaty rights, tribal sovereignty, and identity had no equals in earlier intertribal movements such as the National Council of American Indians, the SAI, or the AIF. Unlike previous twentieth-century Indian groups' efforts, the NCAI had less preoccupation with the benefits of Indian assimilation than with distinct Indian rights and interests within tribal communities. In practice, it offered tribes legal aid and information, and it lobbied for Indian interests before courts, Congress, and the BIA. Its leaders used the conventional weapons of politics to promote the interests of Indian peoples. Not strictly confined to the national issues, it had fought campaigns on the local and regional level. While the NCAI has helped make Indian needs better known, it has not sacrificed a distinctive Indian style and focus. While not separated from the tribal world, it nonetheless acts on a level far different from daily reservation matters.

In structure and actions, the NCAI resembles other national reform organizations. The NCAI occupies a position similar to the National Association for the Advancement of Colored People (NAACP), the Chinese Benevolent Association (CBA), the Japanese American Citizens' League (JACL), the League of United Latin American Citizens (LULAC), and the Congress of Racial Equality (CORE). Through its Washington DC base it seeks improvement in the federal administration of Indian affairs by day-to-day monitoring. It holds annual conventions, publishes a newsletter and special publications, and lobbies Congress, federal departments, and state governments on behalf of Indian people. Like other pressure groups, the NCAI holds a breakfast at the end of every congressional session to express appreciation to members and staff of Interior Committees for their work on Indian legislation. Through its individual members and the tribal membership, the NCAI serves as a clearinghouse through which leaders distribute information and ideas, devise strategies, and establish common goals. Its purpose then is to synthesize the views and opinions of its members' tribes into a common voice.

The NCAI depends heavily upon the media to foster public awareness and sympathy for Indian concerns, and it often receives its most favorable publicity during its annual conventions. It often relies on press coverage to translate the speeches, resolutions, and actions of the conventions into public support. Through carefully orchestrated public relations campaigns, the executive director makes sure that media representatives quote the most knowledgeable, articulate, and succinct Indian leaders.

Ethnic movements such as the NCAI both generate and mirror the culture that produced them. Native American culture shaped the NCAI by providing the identities, strategies, grievances, and rhetoric necessary for activism. Identification of common problems reaffirmed Indians' shared history, values, and culture and provided an organizational base to recruit participants, appeal to members, and launch protest activities. Like other organizations concerned with racial or ethnic identities, the NCAI invoked key cultural symbols to sustain the movement and to mobilize its membership. Shared cultural experiences served as the magnet that attracted and bonded participants. In that sense, the NCAI used cultural construction and reconstruction as powerful tools to encourage ethnic identity, organization, and ethnic renewal.

The annual conventions usually were the staging ground where organizers used recognizable symbols to help overcome tribal differences among the participants. Frequently, these major emblems reflected the organization's main source of strength, the Plains Indians. Many Indians and non-Indians had come to consider these significant cultural markers as representative of Indians and an emerging

Indian identity. At the annual conventions the planners often placed tepees in the lobbies, displayed Indian arts and crafts, held Indian dances, and recognized the reigning Miss American Indian. Displaying their unity and a common Indian past, the delegates signed a Treaty of Peace and Friendship that organizers brought to every conference. Through conference skits, the leadership often parodied themselves and the BIA. Pageantry and ceremony also played an important role at the early conventions. Often the host tribe made colorful signs containing the name of every tribe. On the first evening of each convention, the delegates, often dressed in traditional clothing, marched in Olympic fashion carrying the signs. Color guards then escorted the president to the podium to open the conference. Through pageantry, members captured media attention and then used the spotlight to air their grievances.

In at least one instance an attempt by the NCAI to promote a shared Indian past backfired. In December 1959 organizers scheduled a mock buffalo hunt to open the fifteenth annual convention in Phoenix, Arizona. Six members of the Ute tribe from Fort Duchesne, Utah, planned to demonstrate a Plains Indian buffalo hunt on horseback, using blunted arrows. The demonstration was to take place at the Salt River Pima Reservation rodeo grounds just outside Phoenix. After the mock hunt, organizers planned to kill the two government-donated buffaloes from Oklahoma at a local slaughterhouse and barbecue them. Building the corral to hold the buffaloes, the Salt River Pimas promised the pens would be strong enough to hold the animals. When handlers unloaded the buffaloes, however, one animal immediately broke through the corral and afterward tore up fences and ran through cottonfields, yards, and clotheslines. When the buffalo was finally recaptured after a three-hour chase, handlers had to destroy it. Fortunately, the mock hunt with the remaining buffalo went off the next day without incident.[2]

The primary obstacles of the NCAI have been factionalism, inadequate funds and resources, and a tendency of tribes to provide indifferent support when not faced with pressing concerns. In the early years the strength of the organization rested in the Great Plains and the Northwest. The Navajos, the largest tribe in the United States, and eastern tribes played only minor roles. Largely tribally oriented, the NCAI has also generally failed to meet the needs of the urban Indians who now represent more than one-half of the Indian population. Often, the concerns of the membership have been local or regional, and giving these concerns immediate attention has detracted from achieving more important reform goals.

Financial resources played an important part in the ability, and in some cases inability, of the NCAI to mobilize its members. During its early founding years, the NCAI did not have access to the increased federal funding of the new Indian programs of the 1960s and 1970s. While the NCAI received some support from member tribes, it had relied heavily on the Robert Marshall Trust for financial support in the early years. Donations from individuals also helped make ends meet. During the mid-1950s, Elizabeth B. Morgan, granddaughter of J. P. Morgan, donated five thousand to eight thousand dollars annually to the NCAI. Throughout the Garry administration, tribes in the Northwest conducted bingo games and donated the proceeds to the NCAI. On two occasions in 1959, however, the NCAI lost money in fund-raising efforts featuring noted Indian jazz artist Russell "Big Chief" Moore and renowned Indian ballerinas Rosella Hightower and sisters Maria and Marjorie Tallchief.[3]

During the early years the NCAI relied on other reform organizations for support; in particular, the Indian Rights Association, the American Friends Service Committee, the Association on American Indian Affairs, the Friends Committee on National Legislation, the General Federation of Women's Clubs, and the Daughters of the American Revolution. Apart from other minorities, however, the special legal status of Indians has made it less desirable and productive for the NCAI to join forces in recent years with other ethnic reform groups. Unlike other minorities, the NCAI has sought to preserve not only civil rights, but those rights associated with treaties, tribal sovereignty, and the distinctive Indian relationship with the BIA.

When D'Arcy McNickle related his analogy about the "lowly fly" who overthrew the king to the audience at the annual convention in

1959, he correctly recognized the accomplishments of the founding fathers of the NCAI. In its first twenty years the NCAI battled to protect the rights of Alaska Natives, to end voting discrimination in Arizona and New Mexico, to create the Indian Claims Commission, to promote unrestricted legal counsel, to stop termination, and to push for Indian self-determination. By passing broad resolutions, the founders mapped a political strategy that would appeal to many Indians. Through steering a moderate course, the NCAI leadership has decreased the risk of distancing the reservation Indians from the urban, the more assimilated from the less, older Indians from the younger, and individuals from tribal groups. The broad appeal of the NCAI had successfully included a variety of interests and viewpoints. When the constitutional convention concluded in 1944, Native Americans had successfully created a new political voice that would reverberate throughout the nation's capital and beyond. Had the NCAI not succeeded in 1944 in trying to establish a national intertribal organization, it would have raised some interesting questions for the present. How would termination have operated in its absence? Would Indians have eventually developed an intertribal identity? Would the Red Power movement still have arisen? If it had, how would it have operated? While it is difficult to speculate on the answers to these counterfactual questions, it does become clear that without the NCAI the Indian world today would operate far differently than it does. Although the NCAI has had many crises, no other Indian organization has succeeded in the way that it has.

On the fiftieth anniversary of its founding (1994), NCAI leaders met with President Bill Clinton and a number of tribal groups on the south lawn of the White House. The meeting was reminiscent of NCAI historic White House visits during the Kennedy and Johnson years. Clinton reiterated the hope that the meeting with tribal leaders would produce "true peace, true friendship, and true progress." Grateful for the opportunity to discuss with the president of the United States the most pressing issues confronting Indian peoples, gaiashkibos, the chairman of the Lac Courte Oreilles and the NCAI president, nonetheless warned President Clinton "that we will not retreat." Please be assured, he told President Clinton, "that NCAI will continue to be on the forefront of the major issues facing Indian Country today. . . . We will continue to serve as the advocate for our nations and people," he stated, "just as the founding delegates of this great organization envisioned."[4] Indeed, fifty years after its founding, the shared blanket of the NCAI has endured, and the NCAI remains a leading source of Indian input into policymaking at the federal level. After years of Indian efforts at ethnic mobilization, the NCAI successfully fostered a national Indian identity. Today the river of Indian experience continues to ebb and flow. It is this vitality more than anything else that compels anthropologist Robert K. Thomas to conclude, "Pan-Indianism remains a vital social movement that is forever changing and growing."[5]

Notes

Introduction

1. National Anthropological Archives, Smithsonian Institution, Washington DC (hereafter cited as NAA), NCAI Records, Box 134, "Transcripts of Proceedings (Part II) 1959," 277–78.

2. Laurence Hauptman uses the phrase "warriors with attaché cases" as the title of chapter nine in his *Tribes and Tribulations* (Albuquerque: University of New Mexico Press, 1995).

3. Donald L. Parman, "Indians of the Modern West," in *The Twentieth Century West: Historical Interpretations,* ed. Gerald D. Nash and Richard W. Etulain (Albuquerque: University of New Mexico Press, 1989), 165–66; Francis Paul Prucha, "American Indian Policy in the Twentieth Century," *Western Historical Quarterly* 15 (Jan. 1984), 13; Robert F. Berkhofer Jr., "The Political Context of a New Indian History," *Pacific Historical Review* 40 (Aug. 1971), 357–82. Numerous others point to the need for increased attention to Indian affairs in the twentieth century. See, for example, Vine Deloria Jr., "The Twentieth Century," in *Red Men and Hat-Wearers: Viewpoints in Indian History,* ed. Daniel Tyler (Boulder CO: Pruett, 1976), and R. David Edmunds, "Coming of Age: Some Thoughts upon American Indian History," *Indiana Magazine of History* 85 (Dec. 1989), 312–21.

4. Francis Paul Prucha, *The Great Father: The United States Government and the American Indians,* abridged ed. (Lincoln: University of Nebraska Press, 1988).

5. Francis Paul Prucha, *The Great Father: The United States Government and the American Indian,* 2 vols. (Lincoln: University of Nebraska Press, 1984); Larry W. Burt, *Tribalism in Crisis: Federal Indian Policy, 1953–1961* (Albuquerque: University of New Mexico Press, 1982); Donald L. Fixico, *Ter-*

mination and Relocation: Federal Indian Policy, 1945–1960 (Albuquerque: University of New Mexico Press, 1986); Larry J. Hasse, "Termination and Assimilation: Federal Indian Policy, 1943–1961" (Ph.D. diss., Washington State University, 1974).

6. Hazel Hertzberg, *The Search for an American Indian Identity: Modern Pan-Indian Movements* (Syracuse NY: Syracuse University Press, 1971).

7. See Loretta Fowler, *Arapaho Politics, 1851–1978: Symbols in Crises of Authority* (Lincoln: University of Nebraska Press, 1982) and *Shared Symbols, Contested Meanings; Gros Ventre Culture and History, 1778–1984* (Ithaca NY: Cornell University Press, 1987).

8. Talcott Parsons, "Some Theoretical Considerations on the Nature and Trends of Ethnicity," in *Ethnicity*, ed. Nathan Glazer and Daniel Moynihan (Cambridge: Harvard University Press, 1975), 53.

9. Frederick Barth, ed., *Ethnic Groups and Boundaries: The Social Organization of Culture Difference* (London: Allen and Unwin, 1969), 32–35.

10. See, for example, Leo Despres, ed., *Ethnicity and Resource Competition in Plural Society* (The Hague: Mouton Publishers, 1975).

11. Charles Tilly, *From Mobilization to Revolution* (Reading MA: Addison-Wesley, 1978), 7.

12. George De Vos, "Ethnic Pluralism: Conflict and Accommodation," in *Ethnic Identity: Cultural Continuities and Change,* ed. George De Vos and Lola Romanucci-Ross (Palo Alto CA: Mayfield, 1975), 9; Anya Peterson Royce, *Ethnic Identity: Strategies of Diversity* (Bloomington: Indiana University Press, 1982), 18.

13. Barth, *Ethnic Groups and Boundaries,* 38.

14. Despres, *Ethnicity and Resource Competition,* 196.

15. Maurilio Vigil, "The Ethnic Organization as an Instrument of Political and Social Change: Maldef, A Case Study," *The Journal of Ethnic Studies* 18 (spring 1990): 15.

16. See, for example, Barth, *Ethnic Groups and Boundaries,* and G. Carter Bently, "Ethnicity and Practice," *Comparative Studies in History and Society* 29 (1987): 24–55.

17. Barth, *Ethnic Groups and Boundaries,* 15–16.

18. Abner Cohen, ed., *Urban Ethnicity* (London: Tavistock, 1974).

19. See Eric Wolf, *Peasants* (Englewood Cliffs NJ: Prentice Hall, 1966), and Julian H. Steward, *The People of Puerto Rico: A Study of Anthropology* (Urbana: University of Illinois Press, 1956).

20. For examples of discussions of pan-Indianism as a cultural phenomenon see James H. Howard, "Pan-Indian Culture," *The Scientific Monthly* 69 (1955): 215–20; Evon Z. Vogt, "The Acculturation of American Indians," *Annals of the American Academy of Political and Social Science* 311 (May 1957): 145–46; Ernest Schusky, "Pan-Indianism in the United States," *Anthropology Tomorrow* 6 (Dec. 1957): 116–23.

21. See Bernard J. James, "Social-Psychological Dimensions of Ojibwa Acculturation," *American Anthropologist* 63 (Aug. 1961): 744; Robert K. Thomas, "Pan-Indianism," in *The American Indian Today,* ed. Stuart Levine and Nancy O. Lurie (Deland FL: Everett Edwards, 1968).

22. Joan Ablon, "Relocated American Indians in the San Francisco Bay Area: Social Interaction and Indian Identity," *Human Organization* 23 (winter 1964): 303; Hertzberg, *Search for an American Indian Identity.*

23. Nancy O. Lurie, "An American Indian Renascence?" in *The American Indian Today,* 309, 315–16; Stephen Cornell, *The Return of the Native: American Indian Political Resurgence* (New York: Oxford University Press, 1988).

24. David Lopez and Yen Espiritu, "Panethnicity in the United States: A Theoretical Framework," *Ethnic and Racial Studies* 13 (Apr. 1990): 198–224.

1 River of Experience

1. James A. Clifton, "Alternative Identities and Cultural Frontiers," in *Being and Becoming Indian: Biographical Studies: of North America* (Chicago: Dorsey, 1989), 25–26.

2. Ronald Trosper, "American Indian Nationalism and Frontier Expansion," in *Ethnic Change,* ed. C. F. Keyes (Seattle: University of Washington Press, 1981), 247.

3. Francis Paul Prucha, *American Indian Policy in Crisis* (Norman: University of Oklahoma Press, 1976), esp. chap. 5.

4. See Thomas W. Cowger, "Dr. Thomas A. Bland, Critic of Forced Assimilation," *American Indian Culture and Research Journal* 16 (Dec. 1992): 77–97.

5. *United States Statutes at Large* 24 (1830): 388–91. Only the Five Civilized Tribes, the Osage, and several small bands in the Indian Territory were ex-

empted from the provisions of the Dawes Act. For more information on the Burke Act see Prucha, *The Great Father,* 2:875–76.

6. Donald J. Berthrong, "Legacies of the Dawes Act: Bureaucrats and Land Thieves at the Cheyenne-Arapaho Agencies of Oklahoma," *Arizona and the West* 21 (winter 1979): 335–54; Frederick E. Hoxie, *A Final Promise: The Campaign to Assimilate the Indians, 1880–1920* (Lincoln: University of Nebraska Press, 1984); *Land: The Dawes Act and the Decline of Indian Farming* (Westport CT: Greenwood Press, 1981).

7. Prucha, *The Great Father,* 2:677–715.

8. Hertzberg, *Search for an American Indian Identity,* 15–20; Cornell, *Return of the Native,* 114–15. For an example of the boarding school experience see Robert A. Trennert Jr., *The Phoenix Indian School: Assimilation in Arizona, 1891–1935* (Norman: University of Oklahoma Press, 1988).

9. Cornell, *Return of the Native,* 66.

10. Prucha, *The Great Father,* 2:785–89. For more information on the Peyote religion see Western La Barre, *The Peyote Cult,* 5th ed. (Norman: University of Oklahoma Press, 1989); Omer C. Stewart, *Peyote Religion* (Norman: University of Oklahoma Press, 1987); Edward F. Anderson, *Peyote: The Divine Cactus* (Tucson: University of Arizona Press, 1980); J. S. Slotkin, *The Peyote Religion: A Study in Indian-White Relations* (Glencoe IL: Free Press, 1956); for individual tribal case studies of peyote, see Paul B. Steinmetz, *Pipe, Bible, and Peyote among the Oglala Lakota: A Study in Religious Identity* (Knoxville: University of Tennessee Press, 1990), and David F. Aberle, *The Peyote Religion among the Navajo* (Chicago: University of Chicago Press, 1986).

11. Hertzberg, *Search for an American Indian Identity,* 239–57.

12. William K. Powers, *War Dance: Plains Indian Musical Performance* (Tucson: University of Arizona Press, 1990).

13. Hertzberg, *Search for an American Indian Identity,* 59–209; Cornell, *Return of the Native,* 115–18; Wilcomb E. Washburn, "The Society of American Indians," *The Indian Historian* 3 (winter 1970): 21–23.

14. Hertzberg, *Search for an American Indian Identity,* 213–36.

15. Hertzberg, *Search for an American Indian Identity,* 138–40, 170–72, 174–76, 180–82, 207–8; William Willard, "Zitkala Ša: A Woman Who Would be Heard!" *Wacozo Ša Review* 1 (spring 1985): 11–16.

16. Lewis Meriam et al., *The Problem of Indian Administration* (Baltimore:

Johns Hopkins University Press, 1928). See also Donald L. Parman, ed., "Lewis Meriam's Letters during the Survey of Indian Affairs, 1926–27," parts 1 and 2, *Arizona and the West* 24 (fall 1982): 253–80; (winter 1982): 341–70.

17. For works that deal with Collier's philosophy, see Kenneth R. Philp, *John Collier's Crusade for Indian Reform, 1920–54* (Tucson: University of Arizona Press, 1977); Lawrence C. Kelly, *The Assault on Assimilation: John Collier and the Origins of Indian Policy Reform* (Albuquerque: University of New Mexico Press, 1983); and Stephen J. Kunitz, "The Social Philosophy of John Collier," *Ethnohistory* 18 (summer 1971): 213–19.

18. Collier introduced the original bill in Feb. 1944. After several rounds of preliminary hearings, Congress modified and shortened the measure. Amendments deleted provisions for a system of special Indian courts and excluded the Indians of Oklahoma from coming under most of the bill's provisions. The final measure also made land consolidation voluntary. Philp, *John Collier's Crusade,* 140–59; Graham D. Taylor, *The New Deal and American Indian Tribalism: The Administration of the Indian Reorganization Act, 1934–45* (Lincoln: University of Nebraska Press, 1980): 20–25; Prucha, *The Great Father,* 2:957–63.

19. *United States Statutes at Large* 48 (1934): 984–88. Prucha, *The Great Father,* 2:254–63, traces the legislative history of the bill.

20. Lawrence C. Kelly, "The Indian Reorganization Act: The Dream and the Reality," *Pacific Historical Review* 44 (Aug. 1975): 291–312.

21. Taylor, *The New Deal and American Indian Tribalism,* critically examines why some tribes failed to adopt the tribal councils.

22. Taylor, *The New Deal and American Indian Tribalism,* 39–62.

23. For a thorough study of the AIF see Laurence M. Hauptman, "The American Indian Federation and the Indian New Deal: A Reinterpretation," *Pacific Historical Review* 52 (Nov. 1983): 378–402. See also, Philp, *John Collier's Crusade,* 170–73, 200–202.

24. On the IRS, see Kelly, "The Indian Reorganization Act," and William H. Kelly, ed., *Indian Affairs and the Indian Reorganization Act: The Twenty Year Record* (Tucson: University of Arizona, 1954).

25. See Donald L. Parman, *The Navajos and the New Deal* (New Haven: Yale University Press, 1976); Laurence M. Hauptman, *The Iroquois and the New Deal* (Syracuse NY: Syracuse University Press, 1981); and Robert F. Schrader,

The Indian Arts and Crafts Board: An Aspect of New Deal Indian Policy (Albuquerque: University of New Mexico Press, 1983).

26. Cornell, *Return of the Native*, 92.

27. *United States Statutes at Large* 48 (1934): 984–88; Prucha, *The Great Father*, 2:954–63; Alison R. Bernstein, *American Indians and World War II: Toward a New Era in Indian Affairs* (Norman: University of Oklahoma Press, 1991), 120.

28. Dorothy R. Parker, *Singing an Indian Song: A Biography of D'Arcy McNickle* (Lincoln: University of Nebraska Press, 1992), 93; Donald Smith, "Now We Talk—You Listen," *Rotunda* 23 (fall 1990): 48–52.

29. Proposed Circular to Foundations, Organizations and Individuals, Undated, NCAI Records, Unprocessed Papers, NAA, Smithsonian Institution; Albuquerque Conference, sponsored by the Smithsonian Institution, May 20–21, 1993, includes written transcripts, tape recordings, and photographs from the two-day conference deposited at the National Anthropological Archives (NAA), Smithsonian Institution, Washington DC, hereafter abbreviated as AC.

30. Parker, *Singing an Indian Song*, 105.

31. Russell Thornton, *American Indian Holocaust and Survival: A Population History since 1942* (Norman: University of Oklahoma Press, 1987), 162–63.

32. Richard Lowitt, *The New Deal and the West* (Bloomington: Indiana University Press, 1984).

33. James T. Patterson, "The New Deal in the West," *Pacific Historical Review* 38 (Aug. 1969): 317–27.

34. Gerald D. Nash, *The American West Transformed: The Impact of the Second World War* (Bloomington: Indiana University Press, 1985).

35. Richard White, *It's Your Misfortune and None of My Own: A History of the American West* (Norman: University of Oklahoma Press, 1991), 496–531.

36. Prucha, *The Great Father*, 2:1007.

37. Bernstein, *American Indians and World War II*; Nash, *The American West Transformed*, 128–47; and Tom Holm, "Fighting a White Man's War: The Extent and Legacy of Indian Participation in World War II," *Journal of Ethnic Studies* 9 (summer 1981): 69–81.

38. Bernstein, *American Indians and World War II*, 89–111.

2 The Constitutional Convention

1. Helen Peterson and Erma Hicks Walz, AC, May 20, 1993.

2. Bernstein, *American Indians and World War II*, 112–13.

3. Erma Hicks Walz, AC, May 20, 1993.

4. Arthur Phinney to John Collier, Sept. 1, 1943, *John Collier Papers*, Reel 16, Microform Collection, Purdue University, West Lafayette, Indiana.

5. John Rainer, Helen Peterson, and Erma Hicks Walz, AC, May 20, 1993.

6. Memorandum for the Press, Archie Phinney Papers (hereafter APP), Northern Idaho Agency, Records of the Bureau of Indian Affairs, RG 75, National Archives–Pacific NW Region, hereafter abbreviated NA–PNWR.

7. Archie Phinney to Arthur C. Parker, Aug. 28, 1942; Parker to Phinney, Sept. 1, 1942, both in APP, Northern Idaho Agency, Conferences–NCAI, Box 10, Society of American Indians, 1942, 1944, RG 75, NA–PNWR.

8. Phinney to Lois E. Harlan, Sept. 19, 1944, APP Northern Idaho Agency, Conferences–NCAI, Box 10, NCAI Correspondence Aug.–Sept. 1944, RG 75, NA–PNWR.

9. Notes on talk given by Archie Phinney, Feb. 9, 1944, APP, Northern Idaho Agency, Conferences–NCAI, Box 10, NCAI Correspondence Jan.–Dec. 1944, RG 75, NA–PNWR.

10. Heacock to Phinney, Dec. 27, 1943, APP, Northern Idaho Agency, Conferences–NCAI, Box 10, NCAI Correspondence 1943, RG 75, NA–PNWR.

11. Archie Phinney, "Indian Participation," [1942], and Phinney to McNickle, Aug. 15, 1944, both in APP, Northern Idaho Agency, Conferences–NCAI, Box 10, NCAI Correspondence Aug.–Sept. 1944, RG 75, NA–PNWR.

12. McNickle to Phinney, Sept. 30, 1944, APP, Northern Idaho Agency, Conferences–NCAI, Box 10, NCAI Correspondence Aug.–Sept. 1944, RG 75, NA–PNWR.

13. McNickle to Phinney, Feb. 1, 1944, APP, Northern Idaho Agency, Conferences–NCAI, Box 10, NCAI Correspondence Jan.–Dec. 1944, RG 75, NA–PNWR.

14. McNickle to Phinney, Oct. 16, 1944, Heacock to Phinney, Jan. 18, 1944; Phinney to Heacock, Oct. 7, 1944; Heacock to Phinney, Oct. 13, 1944; Phinney to Heacock, Oct. 14, 1944, all from APP, Northern Idaho Agency, Conferences–NCAI, Box 10, NCAI Correspondence Jan.–Dec. 1944, RG 75, NA–PNWR.

15. Charles E. J. Heacock to Phinney, Sept. 1, 1942, APP, Northern Idaho Agency, Conferences–NCAI, Box 10, NCAI Correspondence 1942, Comments on Indian Participation, RG 75, NA–PNWR.

16. Heacock to McNickle, Nov. 23, 1943, APP, Northern Idaho Agency, Conferences–NCAI, Box 10, NCAI Correspondence 1943, RG 75, NA–PNWR.

17. "Indian Participation" [1942], APP, Northern Idaho Agency, RG 75, NA–PNWR.

18. Ernest E. Maes to Phinney, Dec. 22, 1943, APP, Northern Idaho Agency, Conferences–NCAI, Box 10, NCAI Correspondence 1943, RG 75, NA–PNWR.

19. Phinney to McNickle, Dec. 15, 1943, and McNickle to Phinney, Dec. 22, 1943, APP, Northern Idaho Agency, Conferences–NCAI, Box 10, NCAI Correspondence 1943, RG 75, NA–PNWR.

20. McNickle to Phinney, Feb. 7, 1942, and June 11, 1943, APP, Northern Idaho Agency, Conferences–NCAI, Box 10, NCAI Correspondence 1942, Comments on Indian Participation, RG 75, NA–PNWR.

21. Heacock to Phinney, Jan. 18, 1944, APP, Northern Idaho Agency, Conferences–NCAI, Box 10, NCAI Correspondence Jan.–Dec. 1944, RG 75, NA–PNWR.

22. Others on the board included: George LaMotte, Kent Fitzgerald, Ben Dwight, Arthur Parker, Mark Burns, and John Joseph Matthews. "Memo to" Roy E. Gourd, Feb. 11, 1994, APP, Northern Idaho Agency, Conferences–NCAI, Box 10, NCAI Correspondence Jan.–Dec. 1944, RG 75, NA–PNWR.

23. McNickle to Phinney, Mar. 6, 1944; McNickle to Phinney, Mar. 20, 1944, APP, Northern Idaho Agency, Conferences–NCAI, Box 10, NCAI Correspondence Jan.–Dec. 1944, RG 75, NA–PNWR.

24. D'Arcy McNickle to Helen Maynor, Aug. 13, 1959, NCAI Records, NAA, Box 19, McNickle, D'Arcy, 1955–60.

25. McNickle to Mrs. John Rogers Jr., Apr. 28, 1944; McNickle to Heacock, May 1, 1944, APP, Northern Idaho Agency, Conferences–NCAI, Box 10, NCAI Correspondence Jan.–Dec. 1944, RG 75, NA–PNWR.

26. McNickle to Heacock, Mar. 23, 1944, APP, Northern Idaho Agency, Conferences–NCAI, Box 10, NCAI Correspondence Jan.–Dec. 1944, RG 75, NA–PNWR.

27. See Robert A. Hecht, *Oliver La Farge an the American Indian: A Biography* (Metuchen NJ: Scarecrow Press, 1991); D'Arcy McNickle, *Indian Man: A Life of Oliver LaFarge* (Bloomington: Indiana University Press, 1971).

28. Meeting with Dr. Eduard Lindeman, Treasurer-Controller, Executive Committee, American Association of Indian Affairs, NCAI Records, Unprocessed Papers, NAA.

29. Phinney to Heacock, May 8, 1944; Heacock to Phinney, APP, Northern Idaho Agency, Conferences–NCAI, Box 10, NCAI Correspondence Jan.–Dec. 1944, RG 75, NA–PNWR.

30. Meeting with Dr. Eduard Lindeman, Treasurer-Controller, Executive Committee, American Association of Indian Affairs, NCAI Records, Unprocessed Papers, NAA; Charles E. J. Heacock to Hiram N. Clark, June 17, 1944, Unprocessed Papers, NCAI Records, NAA.

31. Summary of the Proceedings of the Working Committee on National Indian Organization held in Chicago on May 25, 26, 27, 1944, NCAI Records, Unprocessed Papers, NAA.

32. McNickle to Maynor, Aug. 13, 1959.

33. John Rainer, AC, May 20, 1993.

34. Summary of the Proceedings of the Working Committee on National Indian Organization held in Chicago May 25, 26, and 27, 1944.

35. Constitution of Federal Employees Union No. 780, Box 1, Policies and Procedures, NCAI Records, NAA.

36. Constitution and By-Laws of the National Council of American Indians, NCAI Records, Unprocessed Papers, NAA.

37. Constitution and By-Laws of the National Council of American Indians, NCAI Records, Unprocessed Papers, NAA.

38. Erma Hicks Walz, AC, May 20, 1993.

39. Memo from Mark Burns to Tribal Councils, Oct. 16, 1944, NCAI Records, Unprocessed Papers, NAA.

40. Roy E. Gourd to Area Leaders, Committee Members and Other Interested Friends, Aug. 1944, NCAI Records, Unprocessed Papers, NAA.

41. Memo to the NCAI Executive Committee, Nov. 2, 1944, NCAI Records, Unprocessed Papers, NAA.

42. Official Transcript of the Constitutional Convention of the National Conference of American Indians, James Curry Papers, NAA, Box 122, Alpha-File, Ind. Affs., 1944, 6–7; hereafter cited as the Official Transcript of the NCAI Constitutional Convention.

43. Phinney to Charles E. J. Heacock, Oct. 7, 1944, APP, Northern Idaho Agency, RG 75, NA–PNWR.

44. McNickle to Phinney, Oct. 16, 1944, APP, Northern Idaho Agency, RG 75, NA–PNWR.

45. McNickle to Maynor, Aug. 13, 1959.

46. The most useful biographical information came from a packet of short biographical sketches that Helen Peterson and her staff collected in preparation for a fifteenth anniversary edition of the founding of the NCAI (Dec. 7–11, 1959). See NCAI Records, Unprocessed Papers, NAA. See also a clipping from the Browning, Montana, newspaper entitled "Little Sketches of Convention Folk," NCAI Records, Box 3, Correspondence 1945; and Charter Members of the National Congress of American Indians Nov. 1944, NCAI Records, Unprocessed Papers, NAA.

47. Highlights from the Official Transcript of the NCAI Constitutional Convention, 2; McNickle to Maynor, Aug. 13, 1959, quoted in Parker, *Singing an Indian Song*, 106.

48. Official Transcript of the NCAI Constitutional Convention, 10–11.

49. Highlights from the Official Transcript of the NCAI Constitutional Convention, 3.

50. The debate over the proposal can be found in the Official Transcript of the NCAI Constitutional Convention, 30–34.

51. Parker, *Singing an Indian Song*, 108.

52. Bernstein, *American Indians and World War II*, 120–21.

53. Official Transcript of the NCAI Constitutional Convention, 22–23; Erma Hicks Walz, AC, May 20, 1993.

54. Constitution and By-Laws of the National Congress of American Indians, NCAI Records, Box 1, Policies and Procedures, NAA.

55. Official Transcript of the NCAI Constitutional Convention, 42–43.

56. Official Transcript of NCAI Constitutional Convention, 42–43; Bernstein, *American Indians and World War II*, 119–20.

57. Official Transcript of the NCAI Constitutional Convention, 46–54.

58. Highlights from the Official Transcript of the NCAI Constitutional Convention, 11–12.

59. McNickle to Heacock, May 27, 1945; James E. Sanford to N. B. Johnson, May 24, 1945; McNickle to Johnson, May 26, 1945; Heacock to McNickle, undated letter in 1945, APP, Northern Idaho Agency, Conferences–NCAI, Box 10, NCAI Correspondence May 1945.

60. Heacock to Phinney, May 20, 1945, APP, Northern Idaho Agency, Conferences–NCAI, Box 10, NCAI Correspondence May 1945, RG 75, NA–PNWR.

61. Heacock to McNickle, July 16, 1945; Heacock to Phinney, Sept. 17, 1945; Heacock to Phinney, May 20, 1945, APP, Northern Idaho Agency, Conferences–NCAI, Box 10, NCAI Correspondence May, July–Dec. 1945, RG 75, NA–PNWR.

62. Biographical sketch of Heacock, NAA, NCAI Records, material found in a noncataloged box of NCAI material in the NCAI photo collection.

63. Alec Barbrook and Christine Bolt, *Power and Protest in American Life* (New York: St. Martin's Press, 1980), 126–59.

3 Prisoners in the Homeland

1. *Rocky Mountain News,* Dec. 14, 1948, in NAA, NCAI Records, Box 3, General Material, 1948.

2. Convention Call, Nov. 6–9, 1946, NAA, NCAI Records, Box 3, General Material, 1946.

3. N. B. Johnson, "The National Congress of American Indians," *The American Indian* 3 (summer 1946), 4.

4. House Committee on Indian Affairs, *Investigate Indian Affairs,* 78th Cong., 2d sess., 1944, 345.

5. On Truman's record on social issues, see Donald R. McCoy, *The Presidency of Harry S. Truman* (Lawrence: University Press of Kansas, 1984); Gary W. Reichard, *Politics as Usual: The Age of Truman and Eisenhower* (Arlington Heights IL: Harlan Davidson, 1988); Alonzo L. Hamby, *Beyond the New Deal: Harry S. Truman and American Liberalism* (New York: Columbia University Press, 1973).

6. Bernstein, *American Indians and World War II,* 122.

7. S. Lyman Tyler, "William A. Brophy, 1945–48," in *The Commissioners of Indian Affairs, 1824–1977,* ed. Robert M. Kvasnicka and Herman J. Viola (Lincoln: University of Nebraska Press, 1977), 284.

8. Hasse, "Termination and Assimilation," 74.

9. Hasse, "Termination and Assimilation," 92–96.

10. Hasse, "Termination and Assimilation," 81–86.

11. Clayton R. Koppes, "From New Deal to Termination: Liberalism and Indian Policy, 1933–1953," *Pacific Historical Review* 46 (Nov. 1977): 543–66.

12. Bernstein, *American Indians and World War II*, 124.

13. Ruth M. Bronson to John Gates, Oct. 19, 1948, NCAI Records, Box 48, Folder: Sioux (Standing Rock—SD), 1948–55, 1948 NCAI Convention Proceedings, NCAI Records, Box 3, Proceedings, 1948.

14. Johnson, "The National Congress of American Indians," 3; Convention Call, Nov. 6–9, 1946, 3.

15. John Rainer and Helen Peterson, AC, May 20, 1993.

16. Johnson, "The National Congress of American Indians," 3.

17. Ruth M. Bronson to N. B. Johnson, Apr. 17, 1947, NAA, James Curry Papers, Box 122, Alpha-File, Indian Affairs, 1947.

18. Bernstein, *American Indians and World War II*, 122–23, and Randolph Downes, "Indian Claims Commission Bill," *The American Indian* 2 (spring 1946): 3–5; Convention Call, Nov. 6–9, 1946, 3; Bernstein, *American Indians and World War II*, 123.

19. Harvey Daniel Rosenthal, "Their Day in Court: A History of the Indian Claims Commission" (Ph.D. diss., Kent State University, 1976), 10–25.

20. Convention Call, Nov. 6–9, 1946, 3; Johnson, "The National Congress of American Indians," 3; House Committee on Indian Affairs, "Creation of Indian Claims Commission," *Hearings on H.R. 1198 and H.R. 1341*, 79th Cong., 1st sess., Oct. 25, 1945, 1–2.

21. Rosenthal, "Their Day in Court," 115–39.

22. "Creation of Indian Claims Commission," 15–17, 25–28.

23. Convention Call, Nov. 6–9, 1946, 3.

24. *U.S. Statues at Large* 60, 1049.

25. Memo from N. B. Johnson to NCAI membership, Aug. 13, 1946, NCAI Records, Box 18, Johnson, N. B. (Pres. NCAI), 1946–51.

26. Convention Call, Nov. 6–9, 1946, 4.

27. Warren R. Metcalf, "Lambs of Sacrifice: Termination, the Mixed-Blood Utes, and the Problem of Indian Identity," *Utah Historical Quarterly* 64 (fall 1996): 323–43.

28. Ruth M. Bronson to Harry S. Truman, Undated Letter, Library of Congress, Harold L. Ickes Papers, Container 61, General Correspondence 1946–52, and Indians, 1949 July–Dec.; Ruth M. Bronson, "Shall We Repeat Indian History in Alaska?" *Indian Truth* 24 (Jan.–Apr. 1947), 7.

29. Oscar Chapman to Solicitor, June 14, 1946, Truman Library, Independence MO, Oscar Chapman Papers, Box 103; Ernest Gruening to Oscar Chapman, July 3, 1947, Truman Library, Oscar Chapman Papers, Box 20; Juneau Chamber of Commerce to Matthew J. Connelly, Dec. 8, 1947, Truman Library, General File Indian-Indiana, A–H, Box 1172, Indian; E. L. Bartlett to James E. Curry, May 29, 1947, Harry S. Truman Library, Warner Gardner Papers, Box 3, Alaska-Timber Bill, 1947; Warner Gardner to Solicitor White and Assistant Secretary Warne, June 27, 1947, Harry S. Truman Library, Warner Gardner Papers, Box 3, Alaska Native Land Claims.

30. NCAI *Washington Bulletin* (May 1950), 1, 3; Speech of John Rainer at Eighth Annual Convention, NCAI Records, Box 4, General Material, 1951.

31. Bronson, "Shall We Repeat Indian History in Alaska?" 7.

32. NCAI Convention Proceedings of 1947, NCAI Records, Box 3, Proceedings, 1947, 48–52; Ruth M. Bronson, "Our National Honor and the Indians of Alaska," *The American Indian* 4 (2, 1947), 15, 18; compare with Bronson, "Shall We Repeat Indian History in Alaska?"; NCAI Press Release, May 20, 1947, NCAI Records, Box 67, Releases 1947–52, 1955, 1959, 1963, and 1966; NCAI *Washington Bulletin* (June–July 1947), 4; Alaska Pulp Timber Bill, Report of Alaskan Native Witnesses on Their Visit to Washington During June and July 1947, James Curry Papers, Box 61.

33. NCAI *Washington Bulletin* (Feb. 1947): 3–4, and (June–July, 1947): 1. On the Tongass Timber Act, see Stephen W. Haycox, "Economic Development and Indian Land Rights in Modern Alaska: The 1947 Tongass Timber Act," *Western Historical Quarterly* 21 (Feb. 1990): 21–46.

34. Draft Copy of the NCAI *Washington Bulletin* (June–July 1947), NCAI Records, Box 67, Washington Bulletin (Selected Copies) 1947–61, 21.

35. *The* NCAI *News Letter* (Oct. 1947), NCAI Records, Box 67, NCAI Newsletter 1947, 1, 4.

36. William Brophy to William Warne, Sept. 22, 1947, Truman Library, Brophy Papers, Box 8.

37. Ruth M. Bronson to Harold L. Ickes, May 29, 1949, Library of Congress, Harold L. Ickes Papers, Container 61, General Correspondence Indians, 1946–52.

38. NCAI *Washington Bulletin* (Jan.–Feb. 1948), 1, 4; John Rainer, AC, May 20, 1993; Report of James E. Curry to the NCAI 1948 Convention, NCAI Records, Box 55, Curry, James E., Attorney Correspondence 1947–50.

39. Memo of Mar. 4, 1949, Library of Congress, Julius A. Krug Papers, Box 68, Subject File, Office of Indian Affairs; BIA Release of Jan. 6, 1949, Relating to Advisory Committee on Indian Affairs, and Minutes of the Fourth Meeting of the Advisory Committee, NA, RG 48, CCF 1937–53, Files 5–11, Administrative General, Box 3527, File Advisory Committee.

40. NCAI *Washington Bulletin* (Jan.–Feb. 1948), 1; Ruth Bronson to Harry S. Truman; James E. Curry to Powell Charles, Dec. 1, 1949, Library of Congress, Harold L. Ickes Papers, Container 61, General Correspondence 1946–52, Indians 1949–July–Dec.

41. NCAI *Washington Bulletin* (Jan. 1950), 1.

42. Prucha, *The Great Father,* 2:1132.

43. Report of James E. Curry, General Counsel of the National Congress of American Indians, to the Convention at the Congress at Denver on Dec. 12, 1948, NCAI Records, Box 55, Curry, James E., Attorney Correspondence 1947–50, 1.

44. Michael L. Lawson, *Dammed Indians: The Pick-Sloan Plan and the Missouri River Sioux* (Norman: University of Oklahoma Press, 1982), 12–13, 15–16, 17.

45. NCAI *Washington Bulletin* (Apr.–May 1949), 1–5.

46. NCAI *Washington Bulletin* (Feb. 1947): 2, and (June–July 1947), 11, 12.

47. Lawson, *Dammed Indians,* 29–30.

48. Author interview with Francis Horn, Sept. 8, 1992, Washington DC.

49. Daniel McCoy, "Indian Voting," in *American Indian Policy in the Twentieth Century,* ed. Vine Deloria Jr. (Norman: University of Oklahoma Press, 1985); Henry Christman, "Southwestern Indians Win the Vote," *American Indian* 4 (Sept.–Oct. 1948): 6–10.

50. Christman, "Southwestern Indians Win the Vote," 8–10; 1948 NCAI Proceedings, NCAI Records, NAA, Box 3, 26–28; Report of James E. Curry to Fifth Convention in "The NCAI: What It Does and What It Stands For," James Curry Papers, Box 122, Alpha-File, Indian Affairs, 1948.

51. NCAI *Washington Bulletin* (Mar.–Apr. 1948), NCAI Records, Box 67, Washington Bulletin (Selected Copies), 1947–61.

52. Quoted in Christman, "Southwestern Indians Win the Vote," 10.

53. Richard White, *The Roots of Dependency: Subsistence, Environment, and Social Change Among the Choctaws, Pawnees, and Navajos* (Lincoln: University of Nebraska Press, 1983), 250–314.

54. Department of Interior Memo, Oct. 21, 1947, NCAI Records, Box 41, Navajo Tribe (AZ), 1946–47.

55. *The NCAI News Letter* (Apr. 1947), NCAI Records, Box 67, NCAI Newsletter 1947, 4.

56. Philip Johnston to Ruth M. Bronson, Apr. 14, 1947, NCAI Records, Box 41, Navajo Tribe (AZ) 1946–47.

57. *The Gallup Independent* (Albuquerque NM), Dec. 6, 1947, NCAI Records, Box 3, General Material, 1946.

58. *The Gallup Independent* (Albuquerque NM), N. B. Johnson to Sam Ahkeah, Jan. 1, 1948; Proceedings of the Fourth Convention, NCAI Records, Box 2.

59. NCAI *Washington Bulletin* (June–July, 1949), 3.

60. 1948 NCAI Proceedings, NCAI Records, Box 3, 43–49.

61. "Test Case on Arizona Indian Social Security Rights," NCAI Records, Box 55, Curry, James E., Attorney Correspondence 1952–57; Curry Report in "The NCAI: What It Does and What It Stands For"; *Washington Bulletin* (Oct.–Nov. 1947), 1 and (Apr.–May 1949), 1; Ruth Bronson to Katherine Harrelly, Aug. 24, 1948, NCAI Records, Box 41, Navajo tribe (AZ) 1948; Oscar L. Chapman to Harry S. Truman, July 8, 1948, Truman Library, OF 1945, OF 121A, Box 535, Unemployment Insurance, Social Insurance (May 1948–Feb. 1949); 1949 NCAI Proceedings, NCAI Records, Box 3, Proceedings, 1949.

62. NCAI *Washington Bulletin* (June–July 1949), 3; William D. Hassett to Ruth M. Bronson, Oct. 19, 1949, NCAI Records, Box 41, Navajo Tribe (AZ) 1949; Roger N. Baldwin to Ruth M. Bronson, Oct. 5, 1949, NCAI Records, Navajo Tribe (AZ) 1949.

63. John Collier, "Hour of Crisis for American Indians," *New York Herald Tribune*, Oct. 4, 1949, clipping in NCAI Records; John Collier Memo of Aug. 1, 1949, NCAI Records, Navajo Tribe (AZ) 1949.

64. William D. Hassett to Ruth M. Bronson, Oct. 19, 1949, NCAI Records, Box 41, Navajo Tribe (AZ), 1949.

65. Memo Release from the President to the Senate, Oct. 17, 1949, NCAI Records, Box 41, Navajo Tribe (AZ), 1949.

66. Peter Iverson, *The Navajo Nation* (Westport CT: Greenwood Press, 1981), 56–82; Garrick Bailey and Roberta Glenn Bailey, *A History of the Navajos: The Reservation Years* (Santa Fe: School of American Research Press, 1986), 234.

67. Vine Deloria Jr., ed., *The Red Man in the New World Drama* (New York: Macmillan, 1971), 372–73.

68. NCAI *Washington Bulletin* (Feb. 1950): 1, 4.

69. John Rainer, AC, May 20, 1993.

70. William J. Vanden Heuvel, "ARROW, Inc., and the National Congress of American Indians: An Appraisal of Their Relationship," NCAI Records, Box 74, ARROW, Inc., 1956–65; By-Laws for ARROW Inc.; NCAI Records, Box 74, AR-ROW, Inc., 1956–57.

71. Ruth Bronson to John Rainer, Aug. 30, 1949, NCAI Records, Box 20, John Rainer, 1947–51.

72. Vanden Heuvel, "ARROW and the NCAI," 3; John C. Rainer to Clarence Wesley, 1956, NCAI Records, Box 20; John Rainer, AC, May 20, 1993.

73. James Curry Memo to NCAI, Oct. 9, 1951; James Curry to N. B. Johnson, Oct. 1, 1951, NCAI Records, Box 55, Curry, James E., Attorney Correspondence 1951.

74. Dillon S. Myer, *An Autobiography of Dillon S. Myer* (Berkeley: University of California Oral History Office, 1970), 185. I found one of the few remaining copies of this title in the Truman Library.

75. Hasse, "Termination and Assimilation," 127–29.

76. N. B. Johnson to Oscar Chapman, Undated, NCAI Records, Myer, Dillon: Press Releases, Memoranda, Correspondence 1948–52; "Address of Hon. Dillon S. Myer, Commissioner of Indian Affairs," Resolutions, Box 4, Proceedings, 1950.

77. Bronson to Myer, Sept. 20, 1950, NCAI Records, Box 4, Correspondence.

78. Report on the Findings of Special Committee to Investigate the Status of Tribal Self-Government at the Mescalero Apache Reservation, Mescalero, New Mexico, NCAI Records, Box 40, Mescalero (Apache–New Mexico) 1946–62. The incident touched off a flurry of correspondence. See Box 40 for numerous documents concerning the issue.

79. N. B. Johnson to Governors of New Mexico Pueblos, Feb. 25, 1948, NCAI Records, Box 18, Johnson, N. B. (Pres. NCAI), 1946–51; 1947 Proceedings, 36–40.

80. For examples of this type of symbolism, see Eva J. Nichols to Ruth M. Bronson, Jan. 21, 1949, NCAI Records, Box 3, General Correspondence 1949.

81. Address by McNickle to the Eighth Convention of the NCAI, 1951, NCAI Records, Box 5, Speeches, 1951.

82. Ruth M. Bronson to John R. Nichols, Undated Letter in 1948, NCAI Records, Box 72, Nichols, John R., Correspondence 1948–49.

4 Attorney Contracts

1. *New York Times,* Jan. 4, 1952, clipping in NAA, NCAI Records, Box 54, Attorney Contracts: Indians' Right to Counsel (hereafter referred to as Attorney Contracts), 1952.

2. See Charles F. Wilkinson, *American Indians, Time, and the Law* (New Haven: Yale University Press, 1987).

3. *United States Statutes at Large* 48 (1934): 984–88.

4. NCAI *Washington Bulletin* (June–July 1950), NAA, NCAI Records, Box 67, Washington Bulletin (Selected Copies) 1947–61, 3.

5. NCAI *Washington Bulletin* (June–July 1950), 3; N. B. Johnson to Ed Rogers, Aug. 6, 1952, NAA, James Curry Papers, Box 25, 1952 (May–Aug.)

6. Author interview with Frances L. Horn, Sept. 8, 1992, Washington DC; NCAI *News Letter* (Oct. 1947), NAA, NCAI Records, Box 67, NCAI Newsletter, 1947, 1.

7. James E. Curry to Felix Cohen, Jan. 21, 1948, NAA, James Curry Papers, Box 122, Alpha-File, Ind. Affs., 1948; Memo from Curry to Bronson and Ben Dwight, Dec. 8, 1948, NAA, NCAI Records, Box 3, General Material, 1948; Curry to Bronson, July 5, 1951, and Memo from Curry to Rainer, James Curry Papers, Box 123, Alpha-File, Ind. Affs., Aug. 1950; Curry to Charles de Y. Elkus, Feb. 8, 1951, NAA, NCAI Records, Box 55, Curry, James E., Attorney Corre-

spondence 1951; John Rainer to Clarence Wesley, Apr. 27, 1951, NAA, NCAI Records, Box 46, San Carlos Apache (AZ), 1947–55.

8. John Rainer, AC, May 20, 1993; and author interview with Francis L. Horn, Sept. 8, 1992, Washington DC; author interview with Helen L. Peterson, Oct. 16, 19–21, 1992, Washington DC.

9. Martha C. Knack and Omer C. Stewart, *As Long As the River Shall Run: An Ethnohistory of Pyramid Lake Indian Reservation* (Berkeley: University of California Press, 1984), 90–93, 123–238.

10. Summary of Argument of National Congress of American Indians Against S. 17, NAA, NCAI Records, Box 44, Paiute Pyramid Lake (NV) 1936, 1947–49; Oliver La Farge to Ruth M. Bronson, May 19, 1950, NAA, NCAI Records, Box 45, Paiute Pyramid Lake (NV) 1950; Telegram from Avery Winnemucca to N. B. Johnson, Jan. 26, 1949, NAA, NCAI Records, Box 44, Paiute Pyramid Lake (NV) 1936, 1947–49; James E. Curry to Avery Winnemucca, June 5, 1950, NAA, NCAI Records, Box 45, Paiute Pyramid Lake (NV) 1950; Pat McCarran to Dillon Myer, Aug. 29, 1950, and H. Rex Lee to Pat McCarran, Sept. 8, 1950, both in NAA, NCAI Records, Box 45, Paiute Pyramid Lake (NV) 1950; NCAI Press Release of Oct. 15–16, 1950, NAA, NCAI Records, Box 67, Releases 1947–52, 1955, 1959, and 1966; *Nevada State Labor News*, Sept. 28, 1951, clipping in NAA, NCAI Records, Box 54, Attorney Contracts, 1952. Box 54 in the NCAI Records contains a great deal of material on the attorney controversy. Curry's version of events is in James E. Curry, "Condemned to Poverty," in NAA, NCAI Records, Box 45, Paiute Pyramid Lake (NV) 1951–61.

11. Dillon Myer to Oscar Chapman, Oct. 1, 1951, Harry S. Truman Library, Independence, Missouri, Dale E. Doty Papers, Box 9, Department of Interior Subject File–Indian Affairs Correspondence; John C. Rainer to Avery Winnemucca, Sept. 28, 1950; Ruth M. Bronson to Oliver La Farge, Sept. 30, 1950; John C. Rainer to Oliver La Farge, Oct. 6, 1950; Telegram from E. Reeseman Fryer to John Rainer, Sept. 29, 1950; Telegram from John C. Rainer to Harry S. Truman, Oct. 10, 1950; NCAI Press Release "Pyramid Lake Indian Superintendent Fryer 'Acquiesces' in His Transfer by Indian Commissioner Dillon S. Myer," undated, all in NAA, NCAI Records, Box 45, Paiute Pyramid Lake (NV), 1950.

12. Confidential Memorandum to the Board of Directors of AAIA, Harry S. Truman Library, Philleo Nash Papers, Box 23, Fryer Incident; NCAI News Release, Oct. 16, 1950, NAA, NCAI Records, Box 45. Ickes and Collier published several articles in papers such as the *Washington Post*.

13. E. Reeseman Fryer to John Rainer, Dec. 7, 1950, NAA, NCAI Records, Box 45, Paiute Pyramid Lake (NV), 1950; see also John Collier Press Release of Dec. 20, 1950, in the same file.

14. Ruth M. Bronson to E. Reeseman Fryer, Oct. 14, 1950; E. Reeseman Fryer to John C. Rainer, Nov. 7, 1950; Ruth M. Bronson to E. Reeseman Fryer, Nov. 14, 1950; E. Reeseman Fryer to John Rainer, Dec. 7, 1950, all in NAA, NCAI Records, Box 45, Paiute Pyramid Lake (NV), 1950; Memo from Ruth M. Bronson to James E. Curry, Dec. 11, 1950, Library of Congress, Harold L. Ickes Papers, General Correspondence 1948–52 and Nov.–Dec. 1950.

15. Statement by Commissioner Dillon S. Myer before a Subcommittee of the Senate Committee on Interior and Insular Affairs, Jan. 21, 1952, Box 2, Myer Papers, Truman Library, Independence MO.

16. Memo from Dillon Myer to Bureau Officials and Tribal Officials, Nov. 9, 1950, Harry S. Truman Library, Philleo Nash Files, Box 22, Attorney Contracts. Myer's in-depth defense of his position in Dillon Myer to Charles De Y. Elkus, Feb. 6, 1951, NAA, NCAI Records, Box 54, Attorney Contracts, Jan. 1951–July 1951.

17. James E. Curry to Harold L. Ickes, Sept. 7, 1950; compare with clipping from *Reno Evening Gazette*, Oct. 25, 1950, both in NAA, NCAI Records, Box 5, Attorney Contracts, 1950.

18. Memo from Dillon Myer to Oscar Chapman, Oct. 2, 1950, Truman Library, Dale E. Doty Papers, Department of Interior, Subject File (G–I), Box 8, Department of Interior Files, Subject Attorney Contracts; Memo from Dillon Myer to Oscar Chapman, Oct. 18, 1950, NAA, NCAI Records, Box 54, Attorney Contracts, 1950.

19. Dale E. Doty to Oscar Chapman, Nov. 7, 1950, Truman Library, Dale E. Doty Papers, Box 8; Doty's memory of the contract controversy is in Jerry S. Hess Oral History Interview with Dale E. Doty, conducted in Washington DC, Aug. 24, 1972, 13–18, Harry S. Truman Library.

20. Memorandum on the Right of Indian Tribes to Counsel—An Answer to the Memorandum of Dec. 14, 1950, Issued by the "Joint Efforts" Law Firm and Others, Mar. 16, 1951, NAA, NCAI Records, Attorney Contracts, Jan. 1951–July 1951; Memorandum on American Bar Association Report on Commissioner Myer's Proposed Attorney Regulations, NAA, NCAI Records, Box 54, Attorney Contracts, Aug. 1951–Dec. 1951.

21. Statement by Commissioner of Indian Affairs, D. S. Myer, on Proposed

Attorney Contract Regulations, NAA, NCAI Records, Box 54, Attorney Contracts, 1952.

22. NCAI Press Release, Oct. 24, 1950, NAA, NCAI Records, Box 54, Attorney Contracts, 1950; Report by John Rainer, NCAI Eighth Annual Convention, St. Paul MN, NAA, NCAI Records, Box 4, General Material.

23. Ruth M. Bronson to Harold L. Ickes, Sept. 16, 1950, Library of Congress, Harold L. Ickes Papers, General Correspondence 1946–52, 1950– Apr.–Oct.; NCAI Memo "Concerning Employment of Tribal Attorneys," NAA, NCAI Records, Box 54, Attorney Contracts, 1950; Memo is also in Harry S. Truman Library, Papers of Dale E. Doty, Box 8, Department of Interior Files, Subject File—Indians.

24. Memo from NCAI to Tribal Officials, Bureau Officials, and Tribal Attorneys, Nov. 22, 1950; Memo from James E. Curry to NCAI, Dec. 5, 1950; Memo for Mrs. Houghton from Elizabeth Roe, Dec. 10, 1950; Memo from John Rainer to Tribal Officials, Dec. 1950; "Brief Analysis of Policy Statement of Commissioner Myer, dated Nov. 9, 1950, on Contracts between Attorneys and Indian Tribes," Telegram from John Rainer to Oscar L. Chapman, Nov. 2, 1950; Memo from NCAI to Tribal Chairman, Councilmen, and Leaders, Oct. 15, 1950, all in NAA, NCAI Records, Box 54, Attorney Contracts, 1950.

25. Draft of NCAI Letter to President Truman, Dec. 5, 1950, NAA, NCAI Records, Box 54, Attorney Contracts, 1950.

26. Ruth M. Bronson to Harold L. Ickes, Sept. 16, 1950, Library of Congress, Harold L. Ickes Papers, General Correspondence 1946–52, 1950 Apr.–Oct.

27. Harold L. Ickes to John Collier, Dec. 6, 1950, Library of Congress, Harold L. Ickes Papers, General Correspondence 1946–52, 1950– Nov.–Dec.; Harold L. Ickes, "'Justice' in a Deep Freeze," *New Republic* 124 (May 21, 1951): 17; Doty Oral History interview, 15.

28. Harold L. Ickes to John Collier, Sept. 14, 1950, Library of Congress, Harold L. Ickes Papers, General Correspondence 1946–52, 1950 Apr.–Oct.; Harold L. Ickes to John Collier, Dec. 6, 1950, Library of Congress, Harold L. Ickes Papers, General Correspondence 1946–52, 1950 Nov.–Dec.

29. Press Release, John Collier of the Institute of Ethnic Affairs, Jan. 3, 1951, NAA, NCAI Records, Box 54, Attorney Contracts, Jan. 1951–July 1951; compare with Collier Press Release of Nov. 28, 1950, NAA, NCAI Records, Box 54, Attorney Contracts, 1950.

30. Dillon S. Myer, *An Autobiography of Dillon S. Myer* (Berkeley: University of California Oral History Office, 1970), 255 (copy found in Truman Library); Memo from Dillon Myer to William Flanery, Jan. 25, 1951, Truman Library, Dale E. Doty Papers, Box 8, Department of Interior Files, Subject File—Indian Affairs, Attorney Contracts.

31. Special Committee on Appeals of James E. Curry to Secretary, Feb. 28, 1951, Truman Library, Dale E. Doty Papers, Box 8, Department of Interior Files, Subject File—Indian Affairs, Attorney Contracts. The report is also in NAA, NCAI Records, Box 54, Attorney Contracts, Jan. 1951–July 1951.

32. Telegram from Avery Winnemucca to John Rainer, Feb. 14, 1951; telegram from John Rainer to Harry S. Truman, Feb. 20, 1951; Telegram from John Rainer to Oscar Chapman, Feb. 14, 1951, all in NAA, NCAI Records, Box 45, Paiute Pyramid Lake (NV), 1951–61.

33. Bronson to Hiram B. Runnels, July 17, 1951; Runnels to Bronson July 27, 1951; Marguerite M. Lentz to Bronson, Aug. 24, 1951; Runnels to Bronson, Aug. 20, 1951, NAA, NCAI Records, Box 33, Colville Tribe (WA), 1948–54; Curry to N. B. Johnson, Oct. 1, 1951; "Curry Memo to NCAI Officers and Committeemen," Oct. 9, 1951, NAA, NCAI Records, Box 55, Curry, James E., Attorney Correspondence 1951.

34. H. Rex Lee to Clee Fitzgerald, Oct. 29, 1951, NAA, NCAI Records, Box 45, Paiute Pyramid Lake (NV), 1951–61; Memo from the Solicitor to the Secretary of Interior, July 2, 1951, Harry S. Truman Library, Philleo Nash Papers, Box 23, Pyramid Lake Paiute Indians. The memo is also contained in NAA, NCAI Records, Box 45, Paiute Pyramid Lake (NV), 1951–61.

35. Charles L. Black Jr., "Counsel of Their Own Choosing," *American Indian* 6 (fall 1951): 3–17; Harold L. Ickes, "Go East, Young Indian!" *New Republic* 125 (Sept. 3, 1951): 17; Ickes, "The Indian Loses Again," *New Republic* 125 (Sept. 24, 1951): 16.

36. Harold Ickes to Oscar Chapman, Aug. 30, 1951, Harry S. Truman Library, Oscar Chapman Papers, Box 47; Ickes to Chapman, Sept. 14, 1951, Harry S. Truman Library, Dale E. Doty Papers, Box 6; Ickes to Chapman, Aug. 22, 1951, NAA, NCAI Records, Attorney Contracts, Aug. 1951–Dec. 1951.

37. Drew Pearson, "Justice Comes High for the Indians," *Washington Post*, Aug. 14, 1952; Curry's rebuttal to the attack appeared in the *Post* on Aug. 30, 1952. Both of the *Washington Post* articles as well as the numerous editorials

attacking the BIA policy can be found in the NAA, NCAI Records, Box 54, Attorney Contracts, 1952.

38. Ruth Bronson to Alexander Lesser, Sept. 3, 1951, and Statement of Thurgood Marshall in support of the Petition of the Pyramid Lake Paiute Tribe for the Right to Counsel of Their Own Choosing, Jan. 3, 1952, NAA, NCAI Records, Box 54, Attorneys Contracts, Aug. 1951–Dec. 1951, 1952.

39. Address by Dillon S. Myer, Commissioner of Indian Affairs, at the Eighth Annual Convention of the NCAI, St. Paul, Minnesota, July 25, 1951, NAA, NCAI Records, Box 72, Myer, Dillon; Press Releases, Memoranda, Correspondence 1948–52.

40. Eighth Annual Resolutions, NCAI Records, Box 4, Proceedings, 1951.

41. Hearings Set for Indian Attorney Regulations, NAA, NCAI Records, Box 54, Attorney Contracts, 1952.

42. Ruth M. Bronson to N. B. Johnson, Dec. 3, 1951, NAA, NCAI Records, Box 54, Attorney Contracts, 1952; Hearing on Proposed Regulations to Govern Indian Tribal Attorney Contracts, Jan. 3–4, 1952, National Archives, Washington DC, Box 3517, Secretary of the Interior Files, RG 48, 16–25, 295–325.

43. Memo from Office of the Secretary, Jan. 24, 1952, NAA, NCAI Records, Attorney Contracts, 1952. Opposition at the hearings is covered in *The American Indian* 6 (spring 1952): 24–31.

44. Telegram from N. B. Johnson and Ruth Bronson to Oscar L. Chapman, Undated, NAA, NCAI Records, Box 54, Attorney Contracts, Aug. 1951–Dec. 1951.

45. *New York Times*, Friday, Jan. 4, 1952, NAA, NCAI Records, Box 54, Attorney Contracts, 1952.

46. Frank George to Oscar L. Chapman, June 14, 1952, Harry S. Truman Library, Philleo Nash Papers, Box 22, Attorney Contracts.

47. Attorney Contracts with Indian Tribes, Partial Report of Jan. 16, 1953, Senate Report No. 8, 83d Cong., 1st sess., 1–15. The full transcript of the hearing contains nearly twenty-six hundred pages of testimony.

48. Attorney Contracts with Indian Tribes, Partial Report of Jan. 16, 1953, 6.

49. Attorney Contracts with Indian Tribes, Partial Report of Jan. 16, 1953, 7; Ruth M. Bronson to Clinton P. Anderson, June 20, 1952, NAA, NCAI Records, Box 54, Attorney Contracts, 1952; Ben Dwight in Detail Disc. 88A, Mar. 18, 1952, NAA, James Curry Papers, Box 125, 1952 (Jan.–Apr.)

50. Ben Dwight to N. B. Johnson, Mar. 20, 1952, NAA, NCAI Records, Box 18, Johnson, N. B. (Pres. NCAI, 1952–60); telegram from Ben Dwight to N. B. Johnson, Nov. 12, 1952, NAA, NCAI Records, Box 1, NCAI Constitution and By-Laws 1, 1944–55.

51. Edward L. Rogers to N. B. Johnson, Aug. 13, 1952, NAA, James E. Curry Papers, Box 125, 1952 (May–Aug.); Ben Dwight to N. B. Johnson, Oct. 2, 1952, NAA, NCAI Records, Box 18, Johnson, N. B. (Pres. NCAI, 1952–1960).

52. Curry Draft of Letter to NCAI Leaders about Resignation, June 16, 1952, NAA, James E. Curry Papers, Box 125, 1952 (May–Aug.).

53. Excerpt from *Congressional Record*, June 25, 1952, and Memo from James E. Curry, June 28, 1952, both in NAA, James E. Curry Papers, Box 125, 1952 (May–Aug.); News Release by James E. Curry, June 27, 1952, Truman Library, Philleo Nash Papers, Box 22, Attorney Contracts.

54. James E. Curry to Robert Marshall Civil Liberties Trust, Sept. 28, 1952; James E. Curry to John Finerty, Sept. 15, 1952, both in NAA, NCAI Records, Box 54, Attorney Contracts, 1952.

55. James E. Curry to John Finerty, Sept. 15, 1952; James Curry to the Trustees of the Robert Marshall Civil Liberties Trust, Sept. 28, 1952, both in NAA, NCAI Records, Box 54, Attorney Contracts, 1952.

56. Radio addresses of Oct. 26, 1952, Nov. 2, 1952, Nov. 9, 1952, all in NAA, NCAI Records, Box 54, Attorney Contracts, 1952; James E. Curry to the Trustees of the Robert Marshall Civil Liberties Trust, Sept. 28, 1952, NAA, NCAI Records, Box 54, Attorney Contracts, 1952.

57. James E. Curry to D'Arcy McNickle, Sept. 30, 1952, NAA, James Curry Papers, Box 125, 1952 (Sept.–Dec.); N. B. Johnson to James E. Curry, Oct. 6, 1952, NAA, James E. Curry Papers, Box 125, 1952 (Sept.–Dec.); *The Washington Post*, Oct. 30, 1952, clipping in Harry S. Truman Library, Joel D. Wolfsohn Papers, Subject File A–CH, Box 27, BIA–Legal Representation.

58. The *Washington Post*, Oct. 30, 1952, 24–27, clipping in Harry S. Truman Library, Joel D. Wolfsohn Papers.

59. James E. Curry to Helen L. Peterson, Apr. 30, 1955, NAA, NCAI Records, Box 55, Curry, James E., Attorney Correspondence 1952–57.

60. Robert Bennett, AC, May 21, 1993.

5 Termination or Self-Determination

1. Author interview with Helen Peterson, Oct. 16, 1992, Washington DC.

2. Prucha, *The Great Father*, 2:1058–59.

3. See Fixico, *Termination and Relocation;* Burt, *Tribalism in Crisis;* and Hasse, "Termination and Assimilation."

4. Address of William Zimmermann Jr. to the NCAI, Omaha, Nebraska, Nov. 19, 1954, NCAI Records, Box 7, Speeches, 1954.

5. While some writers associate the term "withdrawal" with Myer's administration and the term "termination" with Eisenhower's administration, I am using the two terms interchangeably.

6. Kenneth R. Philp, "Termination: A Legacy of the Indian New Deal," *Western Historical Quarterly* 14 (Apr. 1983): 165–80.

7. Koppes, "From New Deal to Termination," 543–66; O.K. Armstrong, "Set the American Indian Free!" *Readers Digest* 47 (Aug. 1945): 47–52; Hasse, "Termination and Assimilation," 73–74, 77–79, 96–97; and Donald L. Parman, *Indians and the American West in the Twentieth Century* (Bloomington: Indiana University Press, 1994), 124.

8. Lurie, "The Contemporary American Indian Scene," *The American Indian Today,* 456.

9. Delegates at the 1953 convention accepted the inevitable goal of assimilation. 1953 Proceedings, Resolution 4, NCAI Records, Box 5, Resolutions Adopted, 1953: 4.

10. Address by N. B. Johnson, 1948 Proceedings, NCAI Records, Proceedings, 1948, Box 3, 12, and Address by Johnson, 1950 Proceedings, NCAI Records, Box 4, Proceedings, 1950, 48; see the address of Robert Yellowtail, NCAI Proceedings of 1948; U.S. Congress, Joint Committees on Interior and Insular Affairs, *Termination of Federal Supervision over Certain Tribes of Indians, Joint Hearings before the Subcommittees of the Committees on Interior and Insular Affairs,* 83d Cong., 2d sess., parts 1–12, 76, 78.

11. NCAI Proceeding of 1949, NCAI Records, Box 3, Proceedings, 1949, 53–55; NCAI Proceedings of 1948, 45–46.

12. NCAI Proceedings of 1948, 12; NCAI Proceedings of 1948, 16, 17.

13. Release of Apr. 3, 1948, NCAI Records, Box 67, Releases 1947–52, 1955, 1959,

and 1960; NCAI Records, Box 68, Bronson, Ruth M., "Outreach," 4, and NCAI Proceedings of 1948, 18, 75.

14. NCAI Proceedings of 1948, Resolution 21, 76; NCAI Proceedings of 1949, Resolution 20, 77; Bronson, "Outreach," 3–4.

15. Opposition regarding the area offices can be found in NCAI Records, Box 72, Memoranda and Correspondence Concerning Area Office Organization, 1948–51.

16. NCAI Proceedings of 1948, 16; Frank George to Sam Ahkeah, May 12, 1953, Box 41, Navajo Tribe, 1951–53. For resolutions opposing any "Emancipation" bills, see, for example, Resolution No. 20, NCAI Proceedings of 1949, NCAI Records, Box 3; Resolution No. 18, NCAI Proceedings of 1950, NCAI Records, Box 4, Resolutions, 1950.

17. Parman, *Indians and the American West*, 133–34; author interview with Peterson, Oct. 18, 1992, Washington DC.

18. Kenneth R. Philp, "Stride Toward Freedom: The Relocation of Indians to the Cities, 1952–1960," *Western Historical Quarterly* 16 (Apr. 1985), 175–90.

19. Hasse, "Termination and Assimilation," 108–64, and Richard Drinnon, *Keeper of Concentration Camps* (Berkeley: University of California Press, 1987), 167–71; Account of Helen L. Peterson and Robert L. Bennett, AC, May 21, 1993.

20. Eleanora W. Schoenbaum, ed., *Political Profile: The Eisenhower Years* (New York: Facts on File, 1977), 633–35; "Oral history interview with O. Hatfield Chilson," by Thomas F. Scopes, Mar. 1, 1976, Eisenhower Library, Abilene KS.

21. "Oral history interview with O. Hatfield Chilson"; Account of Robert L. Bennett, AC, May 21, 1993. *Book of Mormon* is full of references to the relationship between the Lamanites and Nephites. Joseph Smith's prophecies concerning the Lamanites can be found in the *Doctrine and Covenants*, particularly sections 49 and 57 (Salt Lake City UT: The Church of Jesus Christ of Latter-Day Saints, 1989), 88, 90, 102–3. See also Edward L. Kimball, ed., *The Teachings of Spencer W. Kimball* (Salt Lake City UT: Bookcraft, 1982): 595–620.

22. Arthur V. Watkins, "Termination of Federal Supervision: The Removal of Restrictions over Indian Property and Person," *Annuals of the American Academy of Political and Social Science* 311 (May 1957): 42–47.

23. U.S. Congress, Joint Committees on Interior and Insular Affairs, *Termination of Federal Supervision over Certain Tribes*, 83d Cong., 2d sess., 1954, pt. 1–12, p. 52.

24. Bennett, AC, May 21, 1993.

25. NCAI Proceedings of 1948, 60–66; NCAI Proceedings of 1948, 57–58.

26. Oscar L. Chapman to N. B. Johnson, Jan. 20, 1950, National Archives, Washington DC, RG 48, CCF 1937–1953, File No. 5–11, General 5–11, Indian Chartered Corp Gen (Pt. 4), Box 3529; Oliver La Farge to Helen L. Peterson, Dec. 4, 1953, NCAI Records, Box 5, General Correspondence 1953.

27. Address by D'Arcy McNickle to the NCAI, July 24–27, 1951, NCAI Records, Box 5, Speeches, 1951; undated newspaper clipping in NCAI Records, Box 5, Newspaper Clippings.

28. Account of Peterson, AC, May 21, 1993; Copy of the Draft Substitute of the Constitution and By-laws of the NCAI Presented by Paschal Sherman to the Members of the Executive Council, Oct. 30, 1952, NAA, James Curry Papers, Box 125, 1952 (Sept.–Dec.); Memo for N. B. Johnson from James E. Curry, Aug. 28, 1952, Curry Papers, Box 125, 1952 (May–Aug.); John W. Cragun to Peterson, May 24, 1954, NCAI Records, Box 1, NCAI Constitution and By-Laws, 1.

29. Peterson, AC, May 21, 1993; author interview with Peterson in Washington DC, Oct. 16, 19, 20, 21, 1992; W. W. Short to Peterson, Oct. 20, 1953, NCAI Records, Box 5, General Correspondence 1953.

30. W. W. Short to Ramon Roubideaux, Sept. 8, 1953; Short to Ruth Bronson, Nov. 3, 1953; Bronson to Short, Sept. 17, 1953; Peterson to Short, all in NCAI Records, Box 21, Short, W. W.; and Short to Bronson, Nov. 3, 1953; Short to Peterson, Oct. 10, 1953; Short to Peterson, Oct. 15, 1953; all in NCAI Records, Box 5, General Correspondence 1953.

31. Author interview with Peterson; *News Bulletin of the NCAI* (Nov. 1953), NCAI Records, Box 67, Washington Bulletin (Selected Copies) 1947–61: 2; NCAI Press Release of Aug. 18, 1955, NCAI Records, Box 27, Miscellaneous Mail, 1968–49.

32. Account of Peterson, AC, May 21, 1993; NCAI *Bulletin* (Nov.–Feb. 1953), NCAI Records, Box 67, Washington Bulletin (Selected Copies 1947–61), 1, 3.

33. Account of Peterson, AC, May 21, 1993; Biographical Sketch of Joseph Garry, July 25, 1959, in NCAI Records, Box 75, "Pendleton Round-Up" (Indian Encampment).

34. *United States Statutes at Large* 67 (1953): B132; NCAI Records, Emergency Conference, Box 56, Conference Call (Feb. 1954), 2.

35. *United States Statutes at Large* 67 (1953): 588–90.

36. Keynote Address by Clarence Wesley to the NCAI, Dec. 7, 1953, NCAI Records, Box 5, Speeches, 1953; *The Phoenix Gazette*, Dec. 4, 1953, and Dec. 7, 1953, clippings in NCAI Records, Box 5, Newspaper Clippings.

37. Statement by Commissioner of Indian Affairs Glenn L. Emmons to Be Read on His Behalf at the Annual Conference of the NCAI, Dec. 7, 1953, NCAI Records, Box 5, Speeches, 1953; Resolutions Adopted by the NCAI at Its Tenth Annual Convention, 4–7, and Statement by Glen A. Wilkinson, July 8, 1954, NCAI Records, Box 28, Correspondence and Memoranda, 1954–55; D'Arcy McNickle, "A Battle Yet to Wage," Paper Presented to the Institute on American Indian Assimilation, May 8, 9, 10, 1952, NCAI Records, Box 19, McNickle, D'Arcy (1943–54).

38. John B. Hart to Orme Lewis, Jan. 11, 1954, NCAI Records, Box 32, Turtle Mountain ND, 1953–54; Steven C. Schulte, "Removing the Yoke of Government: E. Y. Berry and the Origins of the Termination Policy," *South Dakota History* 14 (spring 1984): 48–55.

39. For transcripts of the hearings, see U.S. Congress, *Joint Committees on Interior and Insular Affairs, Termination of Federal Supervision over Certain Tribes*, 83d Cong., 2d sess., 1954, parts 1–12.

40. Bronson and Peterson to Jay Nash, Feb. 12, 1954, Box 54, Emergency Conference: General Correspondence.

41. Report on the Emergency Conference of American Indians, Feb. 25–28, NCAI Memo, Feb. 12, 1954, NCAI Records, Box 56, Emergency Conference; NCAI Press Release, Feb. 21, 1954, included in Report of the Emergency Conference of American Indians on Legislation, NCAI Records, Box 56, Emergency Conference; Bronson and Peterson to Nash, Feb. 12, 1954, Peterson to Joseph Garry, Nov. 6, 1954, NCAI Records, Box 6, General Correspondence (Outgoing), 1954; Peterson to Theodore Haas, Apr. 8, 1954, NCAI Records, Box 54, Emergency Conference; and Annabelle Price to Peterson, Mar. 14, 1954, NCAI Records, Box 56, Emergency Conference: General Correspondence.

42. Jim Hayes to Lawrence Lindley, Mar. 29, 1954, Box 54, NCAI Records, Emergency Conference; M. Muller-Fricklen to the NCAI, Dec. 12, 1957, NCAI Records, Box 71, Subversive Organizations: Attorney General List 1957, 1958.

43. Proceedings of the Emergency Conference of American Indians on Leg-

islation, NCAI Records, Box 56, Emergency Conference Bulletin, 1954; W. H.
H. Pilcher to Lorena M. Burgess, Mar. 20, 1954, NCAI Records, Box 6, General
Correspondence (Incoming), 1954.

44. Joseph R. Garry to President Dwight D. Eisenhower, Mar. 10, 1954, with
attached Declaration of Indian Rights, NCAI Records, Box 28, Correspondence 1954–59; Peterson to Arthur LeBlanc, Nov. 5, 1954, NCAI Records, Box
30, Bay Mills Community (MI) 1949–55.

45. *The Washington Star,* Feb. 28, 1954, clipping in NCAI Records, Box 54,
Emergency Conference, General Material; Resolutions of the NCAI, NCAI
Records, Box 7, Resolutions and Policy Statements, 1954.

46. Statement of Joseph Garry Regarding the Competency Bill, May 3, 1953,
NCAI Records, Box 58; Competency Bill, 1953–54, NCAI Records, Box 66, Legislative Reports 22–23; Resolutions of 1953, Resolutions 4, 10–11; and Statement of Helen Peterson, NCAI Records, Box 6, "Dictabelt" Transcripts of
Proceedings, Nov. 1954, 10–F: 3–6; Peterson to Susan H. LaMotte, Aug. 7,
1954, NCAI Records, Box 19, Susan LaMotte.

47. Statement of Peterson, NCAI Records, Box 6, "Dictabelt" Transcripts of
Proceedings, Nov. 18–2, 1954, 10–F: 2; Peterson to LaMotte, Aug. 7, 1954.

48. McNickle had originally proposed a "Ten-Point Plan." Congress by 1953,
however, had fulfilled one of the suggestions, so the NCAI submitted a "Nine-
Point Program." Point Four Program, NCAI Records, Box 58, Point Four Program (83d–85th Cong.), 1954–57; Hatfield Chilson to James E. Murray, July 1,
1957, Truman Library, Papers of Sidney R. Yates, Correspondence Files
(1958), Box 13, Indians-American (1958).

49. Peterson to LaMotte, Aug. 7, 1954; Peterson to Jonathan M. Steere, Apr. 6,
1954, NCAI Records, Box 56, Emergency Conference: Hayes Correspondence
1954; Peterson to Jonathan M. Steele, Apr. 6, 1954; Peterson Testimony, "Dict-
ablet," Transcripts of Proceedings 1954, 9–F: 4–5 and 10–F: 1.

50. Account of Rainer and Peterson, AC, May 20, 1993.

51. Helen L. Peterson, "American Indian Political Participation," *The Annals
of the American Academy of Political and Social Science* 311 (May 1957):
116–26; John G. Cornelius to Peterson, Apr. 4, 1957, and John G. Cornelius to
Peterson, Aug. 21, 1957, both in NCAI Records, Box 76, American Heritage
Foundation, 1956–61; Vine Deloria Jr. and Clifford Lytle, *The Nations Within:
The Past and Future of American Indian Sovereignty* (New York: Pantheon,
1984), 195.

52. Radio Broadcast of Fred A. Seaton, Secretary of Interior, at Window Rock, Arizona, Sept. 13, 1958, NCAI Records, Box 72, Seaton, Fred: Statement, Radio Broadcast, Correspondence 1956, 1958, 1959; NCAI *Bulletin,* Nov. 1, 1958, NCAI Records, Box 67, Washington Bulletins (Selected Copies 1947-61), 1.

53. *United States Statutes at Large 67* (1953): B132.

54. L. D. Arnold to William Zimmerman, Aug. 14, 1947, and Oscar L. Chapman to Wade Crawford, Aug. 1, 1947, both letters in National Archives, RG 75, Office Records of Assistant Commissioner Wm. Zimmerman, Memoranda 1944–50, D–M, Memo to Washington 1946, Entry 190; Keith Mobley, "The Klamath Indians: Federal Trusteeship, 1864–1954" (unpublished paper presented to the University of Oregon School of Law, Portland), 18–19, included in the unprocessed papers of the NCAI; Ruth M. Bronson to N. B. Johnson, Aug. 8, 1947, NCAI Records, Klamath Tribe (OR) 1948–56.

55. Ruth M. Bronson to N. B. Johnson, Aug. 8, 1947, NCAI Records, Klamath Tribe (OR) 1948–56; NCAI Resolutions of 1956, NCAI Records, Box 16, Convention Resolutions, 1956; Helen L. Peterson to Kenneth B. Pomeroy, Dec. 11, 1957, Box 38, Klamath Tribe (OR), 1957; Glenn A. Wilkinson to Delford Lang, June 4, 1957, NCAI Records, Box 38, Klamath Tribe (OR), 1957.

56. Susan Hood, "Termination of the Klamath Indian Tribe of Oregon," *Ethnohistory* 19 (fall 1972): 384–85; *United States Statutes at Large* 71 (1957): 348, and *United States Statutes at Large* 72 (1952): 846.

57. Hasse, "Termination and Assimilation," 293–94; William T. Trulove, "Economics of Paternalism: Federal Termination of the Klamath Indians" (Ph.D. diss., University of Oregon, Portland, 1973), 172, 180.

58. La Verne Madigan, *The American Indian Relocation Program* (New York: Association on American Indian Affairs, 1956).

59. Joseph R. Garry and Helen L. Peterson to Henry Grady, Jan. 2, 1959, NCAI Records, Box 57, Kaleidoscope Television Program: "The American Stranger," 1958–59.

60. Robert Hecht, *Oliver La Farge and the American Indian: A Biography* (Metuchen NJ: Scarecrow Press, 1991), 251–59; Memo to Oliver La Farge and Joseph R. Garry, May 2, 1957, NCAI Records, Box 10, Records of the Legal Workshop, 1957; Statement to Accompany Chart of Proposed Coordination of Main Activities of National Indian Interest Organization. On the reorganization, see NCAI Records, Box 12, Inquiries and Replies Concerning Reorganization Proposal, 1959.

61. Rainer and Peterson, AC, May 21, 1993; author interview with Peterson. Allen C. Queton, a Kiowa, coined the term "Operation Moccasin" in *Drumbeats* 1 (May 1958), in NCAI Records, Box 78, Puerto Rico Study Trip.

62. House Committee on Interior and Insular Affairs, *Operation Bootstrap for the American Indian: Hearings before the Subcommittee on Indian Affairs, H.R. 7701, 8803, and 8590*, 86th Cong., 2d sess., 1960.

63. Parker, *Singing an Indian Song*, 132–68, 181–87; Paul Chaat Smith and Robert Allen Warrior, *Like a Hurricane: The Indian Movement from Alcatraz to Wounded Knee* (New York: New Press, 1996), 40; John Rainer, AC, May 21, 1993; Rosalie H. Wax, "A Brief History and Analysis of the Workshops on American Indian Affairs Conducted for American Indian College Students, 1956–1960, Together with a Study of Current Attitudes and Activities of Those Students," Oct. 1961, in NCAI Records, Box 74, American Indian Development: Workshops on Indian Affairs.

64. Figures quoted in Prucha, *The Great Father*, 2:1058–59; Fixico, *Termination and Relocation*, 184.

6 The New Indian Trail

1. John Rainer, AC, May 21, 1993.

2. John Rainer and Helen L. Peterson, AC, May 21, 1993; author interview with Helen L. Peterson, Oct. 16, 19, 20, 21, 1992, Washington DC; Memo from NCAI on Parade Order, Undated, NCAI Records, Box 24, "Chronological Correspondence Jan.–Mar. 1961"; *NCAI Bulletin* (May 1961), NCAI Records, Box 67, "Washington Bulletin, Selected Copies 1947–61," 6.

3. *Arizona Republic*, Dec. 14, 1959, and Dec. 16, 1959, and *Great Falls Tribune*, Dec. 16, 1959, clippings in Convention Report, NAA, NCAI Records, Box 13, "Miscellaneous Convention Material 1960." For details on the controversial vote count, see Helen L. Peterson to Illiff McKay, Jan. 11, 1960, NCAI Records, Box 30, "Blackfeet (Mont.) 1956–1961."

4. Marceline Kevis to Clarence Wesley, Jan. 29, 1960, NCAI Records, Box 19, "Kevis Complaint 1960"; see, for example, clippings from the *Albuquerque Journal*, Jan. 31, 1960, *Baltimore Sun*, Jan. 28, 1960, and *New York Herald Tribune*, Jan. 29, 1960, all of which can be found in NCAI Records, Box 19, "Kevis, Marceline"; Peterson to Allen Slickpoo, Feb. 9, 1960, NCAI Records, Box 21, "Slickpoo, Allen Paul."

5. Allen P. Slickpoo to Peterson, Feb. 2, 1960; Edward L. Whiteman to Clarence Wesley, Feb. 1, 1960; Wilkinson, Cragun, and Barker to Clarence Wesley, Feb. 19, 1960; Marceline Kevis to Helen L. Peterson, Feb. 15, 1960, all in NCAI Records, Box 19, "Kevis Complaint 1960."

6. Platform planks on Indian Affairs of John F. Kennedy and Richard M. Nixon, NCAI Records, Box 23, "Chronological Correspondence Nov.–Dec. 1960."

7. Statement of Frank George, Chairman, American Indian Section, Nationalities Division, Democratic National Committee, at Hyannis Port MA, Aug. 6, 1960, and Press Release from Sen. John F. Kennedy, Aug. 6, 1960, both in NCAI Records, Box 23, "Chronological Correspondence July–Aug., 1960"; Peterson to Officers of the NCAI, Oct. 26, 1960, NCAI Records, Box 79, "Voter Education 1959–60." See also Statement of Frank George before the Democratic Platform Committee, May 27, 1960, at the Denver-Hilton Hotel, Denver CO, NCAI Records, Box 23, "Chronological Correspondence July–Aug. 1960," and Statement of Clarence Wesley before the National Conference on Constitutional Rights and American Freedoms, Park Shearton Hotel, New York City, Oct. 12, 1960. A side-by-side comparison of the 1960 Democratic Platform on American Indians and the plank suggested by the NCAI can be found in NCAI Records, Box 13, "Miscellaneous Convention Material 1960."

8. Peterson to Officers of the NCAI, Oct. 26, 1960; Information Letter No. 1 to NCAI Executive Council, Individual Tribes, Oct. 24, 1960, NCAI Records, Oct. 24, 1960, Box 67, "Information Letters Selected 1955–58, 1960."

9. Telegram from Kennedy to Clarence Wesley, Nov. 16, 1960, NCAI Records, Box 13, "Miscellaneous Convention Material 1960"; Address by Clarence Wesley to the Seventeenth Annual Convention, Nov. 14–18, 1960, NCAI Records, Box 14, "Speeches 1960."

10. Address by Clarence Wesley to the Seventeenth Annual Convention and Keynote Address by Francis McKinley, NCAI Records, Box 14, "Speeches 1960"; "Statement of Clarence Wesley before the National Conference on Constitutional Rights and American Freedom, Oct. 12, 1960," NCAI Records, Box 23, Chronological Correspondence (Sept.–Oct. 1960).

11. Address of Stewart L. Udall to the NCAI, NCAI Records, Box 13, "Transcripts of Proceedings 1959," and Address of Udall to the NCAI, Denver CO, Oct. 17, 1960, NCAI Records, Box 14, "Speeches 1960"; Address of Stewart L. Udall to the NCAI.

12. *A Program for Indian Citizens: A Summary Report* (Albuquerque: Commission on the Rights, Liberties, and Responsibilities of the American Indian, 1961). The full report was later published as William A. Brophy and Sophie D. Aberle, *The American Indian, America's Unfinished Business: Report of the Commission on the Rights, Liberties, and Responsibilities of the American Indian* (Norman: University of Oklahoma Press, 1966).

13. *Report to the Secretary of Interior by the Task Force on Indian Affairs,* July 10, 1961, NCAI Records, Box 60, "Task Force Report: Development of Human and Natural Resources 87th Cong. 1961"; Press Release from Secretary Udall, July 12, 1961, NCAI Records, Box 28, "Correspondence and Memoranda 1956–61." The questionnaire prepared by the NCAI for use by the task force is in NCAI Records, Box 72, "Questionnaires and Memoranda Relating to the Task Force Report 1961."

14. Margaret Connell Szasz, "Philleo Nash, 1961–66," in *The Commissioners of Indian Affairs, 1824–1977,* ed. Robert M. Kvasnicka and Herman J. Viola (Lincoln: University of Nebraska Press, 1979), 311–13; Rainer, Bennett, and Peterson, AC, May 21, 1993; Address of Philleo Nash, Commissioner Designate to the NCAI, Lewiston, Idaho, Sept. 21, 1961, NCAI Records, Box 14, "Speeches 1961."

15. Sol Tax Diary, Entries of June 12–16, 1960, NAA, Sol Tax Papers, Box 1, "Diary Record Apr.–Dec. 1960."

16. Tax Diary, Nov. 14–16, 1960; Peterson and Wesley, Oct. 14, 1960, NCAI Records, Box 14, "Notes and Correspondence Concerning College Session 1 1960"; Peterson to Tax, Nov. 4, 1960, NAA, Sol Tax Papers, Box 9, "Helen Peterson"; Memo from Walter Taylor to Friends of the American Friends Service Committee, Jan. 1961, Sol Tax Papers, Box 1, "Press Release—AFSC; Resolutions Adopted by the Seventeenth Annual Convention, Nov. 14–18, 1960"; NCAI Records, Box 14, "Resolutions 1960."

17. Others attending the meeting were Georgeann Robinson, recording secretary of the NCAI, Martha Burch Evenson, Gallup area vice-president of the NCAI, and Alvin Warren, Indian Education, BIA. Wesley to Tax, Dec. 1, 1960, Sol Tax Papers, Box 1, "Historical Beginning of the AICC."

18. Wesley to Tax, Dec. 1, 1960, and Peterson to Nancy O. Lurie, Undated Letter, Sol Tax Papers, NAA, Box 9, "Helen L. Peterson"; Rainer and Peterson, AC, May 21, 1993.

19. Wesley to Tribal Leaders, Dec. 1, 1960, NAA, Helen L. Peterson Papers, Box

10, "(AICC) Correspondence, Notes, Nov. 1960–Jan. 1961." The file contains a copy of the statement along with notes in the margin by Tax.

20. Tax to Wesley, Dec. 7, 1960, Sol Tax Papers, Box 9, "NCAI."

21. Lurie to John C. Ewers, May 22, 1961, Sol Tax Papers, Box 6, "E–General." In March 1961, Tax worried "that we are too much NCAI." See Tax to Lurie, Mar. 1961, Sol Tax Papers, Box 8, "N. O. Lurie Mar. 1961." For other examples of the split between eastern/western tribes and acculturated/traditional, see Lurie to Robert Merrill, Mar. 22, 1961, Sol Tax Papers, Box 8, "Me–Mz"; Joan Ablon to R. A. Schermerhorn, Aug. 8, 1961, Sol Tax Papers, Box 10, "S–General"; Red Thunder Cloud to Lurie, Mar. 24, 1961, Sol Tax Papers, Box 10, "R–General"; Freddy DeLaguna to Tax, Apr. 11, 1961, Sol Tax Papers, "N. O. Lurie Apr.–May 1961."

22. William Rickard to Tax, Feb. 16, 1961; Tax to Rickard, Feb. 22, 1961, both in Sol Tax papers, Box 8, "N. O. Lurie Jan.–Feb. 1961"; Rickard to Tax, Mar. 8, 1961; Rickard to Tax, Mar. 6, 1961; Rickard to Tax, Undated; "Meeting of Indian Leaders, University of Chicago, Chicago, Illinois," by William Rickard, all in Sol Tax papers, Box 10, "William Rickard."

23. "Report of American Indian Chicago Conference, University of Chicago, Chicago, Illinois, June 13–20, 1961," by William Rickard, Sol Tax Papers, Box 10, "William Rickard."

24. Lurie to Tax, Jan. 28, 1961, Box 8, "N. O. Lurie Jan.–Feb. 1961"; Lurie to Woodrow Wilson, Sol Tax Papers, Box 9, "Helen Peterson"; Frederica de Laguna to Tax, Apr. 16, 1961, Sol Tax Papers, Box 8, "N. O. Lurie Apr.–May 1961"; Tax to General Holdridge, Jan. 23, 1961, Sol Tax Papers, Box 8, "N. O. Lurie Jan.–Feb. 1961"; Dr. B. Frank Belvin to Peterson, Feb. 7, 1961, NAA, Helen L. Peterson Papers, Box 10, "(AICC) Correspondence, Notes, Feb. 1961-Aug. 1961, Undated."

25. Burnette to Tax, July 6, 1961, Sol Tax Papers, Box 6, "Delegate to the White House"; Ethel Nurge to Tax, Apr. 14, 1961, Sol Tax Papers, Box 9, "N–General"; Robert Burnette, *The Road to Wounded Knee* (New York: Bantam, 1974), 160.

26. Tax to McNickle, Jan. 17, 1961, Sol Tax Papers, Box 8, "N. O. Lurie"; Tax to Lawrence B. Moore, Feb. 15, 1961, Sol Tax Papers, "F–Fra"; AICC Press Release, Feb. 15, 1961, Sol Tax Papers, Box 6, "Delegates to the White House"; AICC Meeting of Indian Advisory Committee, Feb. 10–14, 1961, Chicago, Illinois, Sol Tax Papers, Box 8, "N. O. Lurie Jan.–Feb. 1961."

27. American Indian Chicago Conference Committee Meeting, Apr. 26–30, 1961, University of Chicago, Sol Tax Papers, Box 8, "N. O. Lurie Apr.–May 1961"; NCAI *Bulletin* (May 1961), NCAI Records, Box 67, "Washington Bulletin, Selected Copies 1947–61," 3.

28. McNickle to Tax, May 5, 1961, Sol Tax Papers, Box 9, "D'Arcy McNickle"; Wesley to Walter S. Wetzel and Others, May 26, 1961, NCAI Records, Box 52, "Montana Inter-Tribal Council 1956–61"; Wetzel to McNickle, June 4, 1961, Sol Tax Papers, Box 9, "D'Arcy McNickle"; William L. Paul Sr. to the NCAI, Sept. 16, 1961, Sol Tax Papers, Box 9, "P–General"; "Statements on Walter Wetzel's Report on the Chicago Conference" by William L. Paul Sr., Undated, Sol Tax papers, Box 9, "P–General"; Wetzel to McNickle, May 31, 1961, Sol Tax Papers, Box 11, "We . . ."; Peterson to Tax, Oct. 19, 1961, July 3, 1961, Sol Tax Papers, Box 9, "Helen Peterson"; McNickle to Sister Providencia, May 31, 1961, Sol Tax Papers, Box 9, "D'Arcy McNickle"; Wesley to Wetzel and Others, May 26, 1961, NCAI Records, Box 52, "Montana Inter-Tribal Council 1956–61."

29. "Declaration of Indian Purpose" (Chicago: American Indian Chicago Conference, 1961). Copy of the document is in the John F. Kennedy Library, Boston, Massachusetts (hereafter cited as Kennedy Library). See also Nancy O. Lurie, "The Voice of the American Indian: Report on the American Indian Chicago Conference," *Current Anthropology* 2 (Dec. 1961): 478–500.

30. Press Release of Aug. 15, 1962, Kennedy Library, President's Office File (POF), Speech Files, June 11–Sept. 12, 1962, Box 39, Folder Aug. 15, 1962; Rainer and Bennett, AC, May 21, 1993.

31. Clyde Warrior, "We Are Not Free," in *Red Power: The American Indians' Fight for Freedom,* ed. Alvin M. Josephy Jr. (New York: McGraw-Hill, 1971), 72.

32. Robert Burnette's Notice of Meeting, July 20, 1961; Resolutions from the Meeting of Aug. 5, 1961; and Helen Peterson's "Memorandum for the File," Sept. 17, 1961, all in NCAI Records, Box 1, Policy and Procedure Papers 1944–65, "Burnette's Proposal to Reorganize"; Frank Beaver to Peterson, July 27, 1961, and Peterson to Frank Beaver, July 28, 1961, both in NCAI Records, Box 51, "Winnebago (Neb.) 1949–51, 1956–61."

33. Peterson to the Executive Council of the NCAI, Sept. 23, 1961, Box 14, "Executive Council Meeting 1961"; Peterson to Patrick Gourneau, Jan. 4, 1960, NCAI Records, Box 23, "Chronological Correspondence Jan. 1960."

34. Author interview with Peterson, Oct. 19, 1992, Washington DC; Peterson, AC, May 21, 1993.

35. Biographical Sketch of Walter S. Wetzel, Aug. 10, 1957, and Campaign Platform of Walter Wetzel, both in NCAI Records, Box 21, "Wetzel, Walter (Pres. of NCAI)"; Report of the President of the NCAI to Nineteenth Annual Convention, Cherokee NC, Sept. 6, 1962, NCAI Records, Box 15, "Convention Material 1962."

36. The *Washington Daily News* on Oct. 28–30, 1963, ran a three-part article on Robert Burnette. The clippings are in Helen L. Peterson Papers, Box 4, "Oct. 9–10, 1964."

37. See, for example, Burnette to Frank George, Dec. 14, 1962, NCAI Records, Box 17, "Burnette, Robert"; Burnette to Rainer, Dec. 13, 1962, NCAI Records, Box 17, "Burnette, Robert." Burnette to John Shaw, Dec. 17, 1962, NCAI Records, Box 25, "Chronological Correspondence Jan. 1963."

38. Burnette to John Shaw, NCAI Records, Box 17, "Burnette, Robert"; Burnette to Robert Yellowtail, Feb. 21, 1962, NCAI Records, Box 24, "Chronological Correspondence Jan.–Feb. 1962"; Burnette to Susan LaMotte, May 29, 1962, NCAI Records, Box 24, "General Correspondence Jan.–Aug. 1962"; Burnette to Letitia Shankle, Feb. 20, 1964, NCAI Records, Box 26, "Chronological Correspondence Feb. 1964."

39. Burnette to Letitia Shankle, Feb. 5, 1963, NCAI Records, Box 25, "Chronological Correspondence Feb. 1963"; Letitia Shankle to Burnette, Sept. 20, 1963; Burnette to E. B. Mayberry, Sept. 30, 1963; Burnette to Earl Boyd Pierce, Sept. 18, 1963; and Burnette to Roger Baldwin, Sept. 22, 1963, all in NCAI Records, Box 25, "Chronological Correspondence Sept. 1963"; La Farge to Tax, Aug. 24, 1962, Sol Tax Papers, Box 7, "LA . . . ."

40. Burnette to Freedman Foundation, Mar. 13, 1962, NCAI Records, Box 24, "Chronological Correspondence Mar.–Apr., 1962."

41. Burnette to Churchill, Apr. 11, 1963; Churchill to Burnette, Mar. 23, 1963, both in NCAI Records, Box 25, "Chronological Correspondence Apr. 1963"; Burnette to Churchill, May 4, 1963, NCAI Records, Box 25, "Chronological Correspondence May 1963." A copy of Churchill's pedigree is in NCAI Records, Box 15, "Convention Material, 1963."

42. Burnette to Brando, Dec. 30, 1963, NCAI Records, Box 26, "Chronological Correspondence Dec. 1963"; Third Oral History Interview with Philleo Nash, by William W. Moss, Kennedy Library: 5–6; Remarks by Attorney General Kennedy to the NCAI, Sept. 13, 1963, Bismarck ND, NCAI Records, Box 15, "Convention Material, 1963."

43. Burnette to Kennedy, Feb. 13, 1963, and Lee C. White to John O. Crow, Jan. 22, 1963, both in Kennedy Library, White House Central Files, Box 38, file "IN 12–1–62"; White House Press Release of Mar. 5, 1963, Kennedy Library, POF, Speech Files Feb. 25–Apr.30, 1963, Box 613, Folder marked March 5, 1963.

44. *NCAI Sentinel* (Feb.–Mar. 1963), NCAI Records, Box 67, "*NCAI Sentinel* 1963, 1966," and Burnette to Kennedy, Mar. 20, 1963, Kennedy Library, White House Central Office Files, Box 380, "IN 12-1-62." The NCAI photo collection at the NAA contains photos of the White House visit. When Burnette became the executive director, he changed the name of the *NCAI Bulletin* to the *NCAI Sentinel*.

45. Burnette to Kennedy, Sept. 22, 1963, NCAI Records, Box 25, "Chronological Correspondence Sept. 1963."

46. Wetzel to Burnette, Dec. 11, 1963, and Burnette to Representative Julie Butler Hansen, Dec. 26, 1963, both in NCAI Records, Box 26, "Chronological Correspondence Dec. 1963." Photos of the grave dedication are in NCAI Photo Collection in NAA.

47. Burnette to Wetzel, Dec. 11, 1963; Burnette to Representative Julie Butler Hansen, Dec. 26, 1963; Burnette to Udall, Dec. 24, 1964; and Burnette to Johnson, Dec. 31, 1963, all in NCAI Records, Box 26, "Chronological Correspondence Dec. 1963"; Sister Providencia to Mansfield, Jan. 23, 1964, and Burnette to William A. Wall, Feb. 17, 1964, both in NCAI Records, Box 26, "Chronological Correspondence Feb. 1964"; Robert Burnette, *The Tortured American* (Englewood Cliffs NJ: Prentice-Hall, 1971), 82.

48. D'Arcy McNickle, *Native American Tribalism: Indian Survivals and Renewals* (New York: Oxford University Press, 1973), 118–19.

49. Miles Brandon to Burnette, Nov. 15, 1963; Burnette to Miles Brandon, Nov. 19, 1963; and Memo from Miles Brandon, Jan. 24, 1964, all in NCAI Records, Box 2, "Memoranda to Treasurer." Peterson to W. W. Keeler et al., Dec. 13, 1964, NAA, Helen L. Peterson Papers, Box 10, "Correspondence 1964"; Author interview with Peterson, Oct. 16, 19, 20, 21, 1992.

50. Peterson to W. W. Keeler et al., Dec. 13, 1964, NAA, Helen L. Peterson Papers, Box 10, "Correspondence 1964"; Vine Deloria Jr. to Eugene Johnson, Feb. 8, 1965, NCAI Records, Box 27, "General Correspondence Feb. 1965"; author interview with Peterson, Oct. 20, 1992, Washington DC.

51. Burnette to Letitia Shankle, Feb. 20, 1964, NCAI Records, Box 26, "Chronological Correspondence Feb. 1964"; Burnette to Wetzel, Mar. 6, 1964, NCAI Records, Box 2, "Memoranda to Treasurer"; Burnette to John B. Tiger, Feb.

25, 1965, NCAI Records, Box 26, "Chronological Correspondence Feb. 1965"; Burnette to Susan H. LaMotte, Feb. 18, 1964, NCAI Records, Box 26, "Chronological Correspondence 1964."

52. Peterson to W. W. Keeler et al., Dec. 13, 1964, and Peterson to Rainer et al., both in Helen L. Peterson Papers, Box 10, "Correspondence 1964."

53. The AICLT was founded by the Robert Marshall Civil Liberties Trust on which the NCAI had depended for support almost from its inception.

54. Peterson to W. W. Keeler et al., Dec. 13, 1964, Helen Peterson Papers, Box 10, "Correspondence 1964."

55. Alvin M. Josephy in *Encyclopedia of North American Indians,* ed. Frederick E. Hoxie (New York: Houghton Mifflin, 1996), 89–90.

56. Paschal Sherman to Vine Deloria Jr., Nov. 13, 1965, NCAI Records, Box 27, "Chronological Correspondence Nov. 1965"; Paschal Sherman to Peterson, Sept. 22, 1964, NCAI Records, Box 27, "Chronological Correspondence, Sept. 1964."

57. The legal documents for the court case are contained in NCAI Records, Box 17, "Burnette Case."

58. Deloria to Peterson, July 23, 1965, Helen Peterson Papers, Box 10, "Correspondence 1965"; Deloria Jr. to Paschal Sherman, June 13, 1965, and Deloria to Sherman, June 17, 1965, both in NCAI Records, Box 27, "Chronological Correspondence June 1965"; Deloria to Peterson, July 23, 1965, Helen L. Peterson Papers, Box 10, "Correspondence 1965."

59. Deloria to Paschal Sherman, Mar. 17, 1965, NCAI Records, Box 27, "General Correspondence Mar. 1965."

Conclusion

1. Helen Peterson, AC, May 21, 1993.

2. Helen L. Peterson, AC, May 21, 1993; author interview with Helen L. Peterson, Oct. 16, 19, 20, 21, 1992.

3. Helen L. Peterson, AC, May 20, 1993; Peterson to W. W. Keeler and Paul Pitts, May 22, 1959; Peterson to Allen Quetone, May 2, 1959, both in NCAI Records, Box 2, file "General Correspondence Nov. 1958–Dec. 1959."

4. NCAI *Sentinel,* Commemorative Issue, June 1994, 1–2.

5. Thomas, "Pan-Indianism."

Bibliographical Essay

Several manuscript collections at the National Anthropological Archives (NAA), Smithsonian Institution, Washington DC, are invaluable sources for further research on the NCAI, Indian policy, or tribal affairs during the period. For this book, the most important of these collections was the records of the NCAI, which include correspondence, memoranda, newspaper clippings, news releases, convention programs and reports, speeches, resolutions, photographs, financial records, and other documents. Helen Peterson's papers have also been deposited at the NAA, and they contain a significant number of documents relating to Peterson's stint as the executive director of the NCAI. While much of the Peterson collection duplicates material found elsewhere in the records of the NCAI, it also includes a number of supplemental materials relating to a wide range of Indian interests and activities. Specifically useful in relation to the NCAI are her miscellaneous administrative documents and correspondence files. The papers of NCAI and tribal attorney James Curry are also deposited at NAA. Material in this collection includes correspondence, published government documents, notes, newspaper clippings, and other printed items relating to his legal work in Indian affairs.

Anthropologist Sol Tax and the University of Chicago donated to NAA the records from the American Indian Chicago Conference of 1961. Included in the collection are materials from the conference's inception to its conclusion. Insights into the activities of the NCAI and into Indian affairs during the period can also be garnered from an oral history project featuring founding members of the NCAI (John Rainer, Helen Peterson, and Erma Hicks Walz). The Smithsonian Institution sponsored the project, which was held in Albuquerque, New Mexico, May 20–21, 1993. Written transcripts, tape recordings, and photographs from the two-day conference are stored at NAA.

Several other repositories house important manuscript materials relating to NCAI founders or federal policymakers. The papers of D'Arcy McNickle are at the McNickle Center, Newberry Library in Chicago, Illinois. Those of founder Archie Phinney are housed at the National Archives Pacific NW Regional Branch in Seattle, Washington. The Harry S. Truman Library in Independence, Missouri; the Dwight D. Eisenhower Library in Abilene, Kansas; the John Fitzgerald Kennedy Library in Boston, Massachusetts; and the National Archives in Washington DC contain manuscript materials, printed government documents, and oral interviews with official policymakers that present the government perspective on Indian affairs during the period.

Studies of pan-Indian, supratribal, or intertribal activity or of Indian political organization are few and far between. That is not to say, however, that there are not some fine studies. Among these are Hazel W. Hertzberg, *The Search for an American Indian Identity: Modern Pan-Indian Movements* (Syracuse University Press, 1971); Stephen Cornell, *The Return of the Native: American Indian Political Resurgence* (Oxford University Press, 1988); Joanne Nagel, *American Indian Ethnic Renewal: Red Power and the Resurgence of Identity and Culture* (Oxford University Press, 1996); Robert K. Thomas, "Pan-Indianism," and Shirley H. Witt, "Nationalistic Trends among Indians," both in *The American Indian Today,* ed. Stuart Levine and Nancy Lurie (Everett Edwards, 1968).

N. B. Johnson, "The National Congress of American Indians," *Chronicles of Oklahoma* 30 (summer, 1952): 140–48, and Alison R. Bernstein, *American Indians and World War: Toward a New Era in Indian Affairs* (University of Oklahoma Press, 1991), both provide nice introductions to the creation of the NCAI. Dorothy R. Parker ably chronicles the life of NCAI founder D'Arcy McNickle in *Singing an Indian Song: A Biography of D'Arcy McNickle* (University of Nebraska Press, 1992).

Termination policy and its origins are aptly detailed in several standard works. These include: Donald L. Fixico, *Termination and Relocation: Federal Indian Policy, 1953–1961* (University of New Mexico Press, 1986); Larry W. Burt, *Tribalism, Federal Indian Policy, 1953–1961* (University of New Mexico Press, 1982); Larry J. Hasse, "Termination and Assimilation: Federal Indian Policy, 1948–1961" (Ph.D. diss., Washington State University, 1974); Kenneth R. Philp, "Termination: A Legacy of the Indian New Deal," *Western Historical Quarterly* 14 (April 1983): 165–80; Clayton R. Koppes, "From New Deal to Termination: Liberalism and Indian Policy, 1933–1953," *Pacific Historical Review* 46 (November 1977): 543–66; and Charles F. Wilkinson and Eric R. Biggs, "The Evolution of the Termination Policy," *American Indian Law Re-*

view 5, no. 1 (1977): 139–84. Several insightful case studies of the termination policy in application have been written in recent years. These include Nicholas C. Peroff, *Menominee Drums: Tribal Termination and Restoration, 1954–1974* (University of Oklahoma Press, 1982); Laurence M. Hauptman, *The Iroquois Struggle for Survival: World War II to Red Power* (Syracuse University Press, 1986); and Warren R. Metcalf, "Arthur V. Watkins and the Indians of Utah: A Study of Federal Termination Policy" (Ph.D. diss., Arizona State University, 1995).

Twentieth-century Indian affairs have been the study of several recent scholars. The best general treatments include Donald L. Parman, *Indians and the American West in the Twentieth Century* (Indiana University Press, 1994); Peter Iverson, *"We Are Still Here": American Indians in the Twentieth Century* (Harlan Davidson, 1988); and James S. Olson and Raymond Wilson, *Native Americans in the Twentieth Century* (Brigham Young University Press, 1983). James J. Rawls, *Chief Red Fox Is Dead: A History of Native Americans since 1945* (Harcourt Brace, 1996), and Fergus M. Bordewich, *Reinventing the White Man's Indian* (Doubleday, 1996), provide a general overview of Indian affairs from the post–World War II era to the present.

One of the most readable introductions to Indian law is Charles F. Wilkinson's *American Indians, Time, and the Law: Native Societies in a Modern Constitutional Democracy* (Yale University Press, 1987). Other useful starting points for information on Indian legal rights include Vine Deloria and Clifford M. Lytle, *American Indians, American Justice* (University of Texas Press, 1983), and John R. Wunder, *Retained by the People: A History of American Indians and the Bill of Rights* (Oxford University Press, 1994).

Index